THE
CLASSIC FAIRY
TALES

IONA and PETER OPIE

THE
CLASSIC
FAIRY TALES

'It is grown people who make the nursery
stories; all children do, is jealously to preserve
the text.'

ROBERT LOUIS STEVENSON

LONDON
OXFORD UNIVERSITY PRESS
NEW YORK TORONTO

Oxford University Press, Ely House, London w1
Glasgow New York Toronto Melbourne
Wellington Cape Town Salisbury Ibadan
Nairobi Dar es Salaam Lusaka Addis Ababa
Bombay Calcutta Madras Karachi Lahore
Dacca Kuala Lumpur Singapore Hong Kong Tokyo

This book was designed and produced by
George Rainbird Ltd,
Marble Arch House, 44 Edgware Road, London w2

House Editor: Sue Unstead
Designer: George Sharp

ISBN: 0 19 211559 6
Library of Congress Catalog Card Number 73–90332

The book was printed by
Ebenezer Baylis & Son Ltd, Leicester and London
and bound by Dorstel Press Ltd, Harlow.

PRINTED IN ENGLAND

Other Books by Iona and Peter Opie
published by Oxford:
The Oxford Dictionary of Nursery Rhymes
The Oxford Nursery Rhyme Book
The Lore and Language of Schoolchildren
Children's Games in Street & Playground
The Oxford Book of Children's Verse
Three Centuries of Nursery Rhymes and
Poetry for Children (A Catalogue)

Frontispiece: 'Pamela tells a nursery tale.'
Detail of the painting by Joseph Highmore,
which was executed shortly after the
publication of Richardson's novel *Pamela, or
Virtue Rewarded,* 1741

PREFACE

In 1832 when Walter Scott contemplated a work on fairy tales there were still people who regarded nursery literature as being beneath the notice of a great man of letters, and he was concerned whether he could make it 'a neat thing' that would be 'obnoxious to ridicule'. No such scruple has troubled subsequent scholars. Fairy tales are now considered a reputable subject for research; doctoral theses are footnoted on them, standard identification numbers accorded them, and conferences convened to discuss them. The literature existing today on fairy tales is voluminous. If all the collections and studies that have been made of fairy tales were placed on top of each other only a modest conjuration would be necessary to make the pile rival the beanstalk Jack climbed to reach the sky. Yet no volume has been produced, as far as we are aware, that brings together the texts of the best-known tales as they were first published in English; and no work, as far as we are aware, has looked at the texts from the point of view of their entry into the English language.

The reason such a work has not been attempted before is not immediately apparent. It may be that folklorists today are so preoccupied with orally communicated texts that literary research has become unpalatable. Certainly a great gulf has opened up since the days of Andrew Lang, between the collector of *Märchen* and the student of popular literature. The folklorist today commonly eschews texts that have come under literary influence, even when these texts are the sources of the most-loved stories of a nation; and the fact that an amount of material of literary origin continues to be found in folklore collections is due, as Dr Linda Dégh has observed, 'solely to the ignorance of the researchers concerning the field of cheap literature'. Again, the reason why a collection such as this has not hitherto been undertaken may be due to the fiendish rarity of the early texts, so that a work of this nature has seemed impracticable. (Indeed, half the tales in the present volume come from editions so rare they are known only by single copies.) Or it may well be that such a collection has not been assembled for the most simple of reasons: that tales like 'Cinderella', 'Puss in Boots', 'Beauty and the Beast', and 'Jack the Giant Killer', are so well known it has been taken for granted a work must already exist in which the early versions have been brought together, and their histories discussed.

In the present volume we give the texts of twenty-four of the best-known fairy tales as they were first printed in English, or in their earliest surviving or prepotent text, believing these texts to be worth reading for their own sakes, to be fascinating for the social sidelights they contain, and to be remarkable in the annals of literature as records of the most popular fictions in the language.

Each text is given here as it appeared in the original work. There has been no modernizing of the texts, the original spelling and punctuation has been retained even where faulty, and the only alterations (a minute number) have been the correcting of obvious printers' errors in the original publications.

For making this work possible we are indebted to the Pierpont Morgan Library, New York, for microfilms of their unique copy of *The History of Tom Thumbe*, 1621; to Harvard College Library, who had already deposited photostats of their unique copy of Perrault's *Histories, or Tales of past Times*, 1729, in the British Museum; to Mr Richard Abel of Richard Abel & Co., Beaverton, Oregon, for the use of his privately-issued facsimile of Mr Lawton Kennedy's apparently unique edition of *The History of Jack and the Giants* in two parts; and to the Trustees of the British Museum for allowing photocopies to be made of the Addey edition of *Household Stories collected by the Brothers Grimm*, and of *The History of Four Kings*, which is dated '1750?' in the catalogue, but which was probably issued some twenty years later. The remaining texts are from our own library, three of the eight sources being editions apparently unrecorded.

In addition we have attempted to summarize the history and points of interest in each tale, particularly from the textual point of view; and to show by our selection of illustrations how the tale has been depicted at different periods. The way a tale has been illustrated can be significant in its history. Illustrations almost invariably determine the setting of a tale and the nature or appearance of the leading characters; and can even, over a course of years, have an influence on a tale's popularity.

In the preparation of this work, we are grateful for the use we have been able to make of the libraries of the British Museum, the Victoria and Albert Museum, the London Library, and the Folklore Society; and we are indebted, as always, to our family, and to friends and correspondents, amongst whom we would particularly like to mention Mr Roland Knaster, Professor Mary Ann Nelson and Professor T. S. Dorsch. Most especially we are indebted to Miss F. Doreen Gullen, to whom, happily, some fairy godmother gave all the accomplishments that would prove the most valuable to us.

I.O. & P.O.

West Liss in Hampshire
1974

CONTENTS

'The recollection of such reading as had delighted him in his infancy, made him always persist in fancying that it was the only reading which could please an infant . . . "Babies do not want (said he) to hear about babies; they like to be told of giants and castles, and of somewhat which can stretch and stimulate their little minds".'

Mrs. Thrale, *Anecdotes of Samuel Johnson*, 1786

'Think what you would have been now, if instead of being fed with tales and old wives' fables in childhood, you had been crammed with geography and natural history!'

Charles Lamb to Samuel Coleridge, 23 October 1802

'Independently of the curious circumstance that such tales should be found existing in very different countries and languages, which augurs a greater poverty of human invention than we would have expected, there is also a sort of wild fairy interest in them, which makes me think them fully better adapted to awaken the imagination and soften the heart of childhood than the good-boy stories which have been in later years composed for them.'

Walter Scott to Edgar Taylor, 16 January 1823

'I foresee that the Andersen and Fairy Tale fashion will not last; none of these things away from general nature do.'

Mary Russell Mitford to Charles Boner, 28 January 1848

'Some persons, indeed, consider our once popular nursery fictions calculated to make children idle, and indisposed for the acquirement of knowledge; but, if such be their effects, we would respectfully ask how it happens that the present generation is so superlatively sensible, seeing that it was, in infancy, a greedy devourer of the dainties of Mothers Bunch and Goose?'

Advertisement for Rosewarne's fairy tale booklets, *c.* 1850

'Let him know his fairy tale accurately, and have perfect joy or awe in the conception of it as if it were real; thus he will always be exercising his power of grasping realities: but a confused, careless, and discrediting tenure of the fiction will lead to as confused and careless reading of fact. Let the circumstances of both be strictly perceived, and long dwelt upon, and let the child's own mind develop fruit of thought from both. It is of the greatest importance early to secure this habit of contemplation, and therefore it is a grave error, either to multiply unnecessarily, or to illustrate with extravagant richness, the incidents presented to the imagination.'

John Ruskin, introduction to *German Popular Stories*, 1868

'Never, in all my early childhood, did any one address to me the affecting preamble, "Once upon a time!" I was told about missionaries, but never about pirates; I was familiar with humming-birds, but I had never heard of fairies. Jack the Giant Killer, Rumpelstiltskin and Robin Hood were not of my acquaintance, and though I understood about wolves, Little Red Ridinghood was a stranger even by name. So far as my "dedication" was concerned, I can but think that my parents were in error thus to exclude the imaginary from my outlook upon facts. They desired to make me truthful; the tendency was to make me positive and sceptical. Had they wrapped me in the soft folds of supernatural fancy, my mind might have been longer content to follow their traditions in an unquestioning spirit.'

Edmund Gosse, *Father and Son*, 1907

'If you really read the fairy-tales, you will observe that one idea runs from one end of them to the other–the idea that peace and happiness can only exist on some condition. This idea, which is the core of ethics, is the core of the nursery-tales.'

G. K. Chesterton, *All Things Considered*, 1908

Cinderella and the Fairy Godmother.
Reversible head drawn by Rex Whistler
to amuse a child

When the wonderful happens, when a holiday abroad is a splendid success or an unlikely romance ends happily, we commonly exclaim it was 'just like a fairy tale', overlooking that most events in fairy tales are remarkable for their unpleasantness, and that in some of the tales there is no happy ending, not even the hero or heroine escaping with their life. Very possibly the story we have in mind is the story of Cinderella, as we imagine it to be, or have seen it in a prettified abridgement: the story of a poor, hard-working drudge – who we are certain represents ourselves – who is transformed by magic into a beauty, a social success, the belle of the ball, the charmer who brings a king's heir-apparent literally to her feet.

We forget that in the story Perrault told, which is the basis of virtually all subsequent retellings in English, Cinderella is not any ordinary girl being scrubbed clean, dressed sumptuously, and endowed with virtues before being conveyed to a gathering of her social superiors. Her story is not one of rags to riches, or of dreams come true, but of reality made evident. Despite Cinderella's menial position in the opening scene – a position she accepts with dignity and good humour – Cinderella is in fact her father's heir, she has been stated already to be 'of unparalleled goodness', she has as much right by position and birth to be at the ball as have others who have been invited, and no fairy godmother was required to make her beautiful. Her clothes only, not her features, are transformed by the magic wand; her feet do not become large after midnight; and the courtier who comes from the palace searching for the unidentified guest recognizes her beauty despite the shabbiness of her attire, and urges she should be allowed to try on the glass slipper.

In the most-loved fairy tales, it will be noticed, noble personages may be brought low by fairy enchantment or by human beastliness, but the lowly are seldom made noble. The established order is not stood on its head. Snow White and Sleeping Beauty are girls of royal birth. Cinderella was tested, and found worthy of her prince. The magic in the tales (if magic is what it is) lies in people and creatures being shown to be what they really are. The beggar woman at the well is really a fairy, the beast in 'Beauty and the Beast' is really a monarch, the frog is a handsome prince, the corpse of Snow White a living princess. Fairy tales are unlike popular romances in that they are seldom the enactments of dream-wishes. We would ourselves be unwilling to face the hazards the heroes have to face, even if we were certain, as the heroes are not, of final reward. Indeed, in fairy tales wishes are rarely granted; and when they are the wisher may be made to look as foolish as King Midas. He finds he has wished a sausage onto the end of his wife's nose, or that he himself has acquired an embarrassment of sexual organs. Stringent conditions may be laid down before a wish is granted: a mother must pledge her first born, a gay cavalier marry one who is repugnant to him. Even Cinderella's licence expires after a few hours. Enchantment, in practice, is the opposite to the golden dream. The wonderful happens, the lover is recognized, the spell of misfortune is broken, when the situation that already exists is utterly accepted, when additional tasks or disappointments are boldly faced, when poverty is seen to be of no consequence, when unfairness is borne without indignation, when the loathsome is loved. Perhaps, after all, fairy tales are to be numbered amongst the most philosophic tales that there are.

THE SPELL IN THE TALES

Further analysis may show the tales to be even less like the popular conception of them. Of the twenty-four classic stories in this collection, four are literary tales which have kept their literary form: 'The Yellow Dwarf', 'Thumbelina', 'The Swineherd', and 'The Tinder Box'. Of the remaining twenty, 'Little Red Ridinghood' and 'The Three Bears' have nothing magical about them other than that the animals behave to a greater or lesser degree like human beings, and are able to speak, an accomplishment which comes as no surprise to students of Aesop. The tale of Bluebeard contains a single magical incident (the reappearance of blood on the key to the forbidden chamber), an incident inessential to the story. Two further tales, 'The Three Wishes' and 'The Princess on the Pea', are definitely magical, but they are magical for a work-a-day purpose, they are fables rather than tales of romance. The long stories about Tom Thumb, Jack the Giant Killer, and Jack the Beanstalk Climber, the three best-known tales that are indigenous to Britain, although packed with fantastical happenings, are only incidentally romances. In essence they are simple adventure stories, as is the tale of that dressed-up cheat Puss in Boots. Two further adventure stories are 'Hansel and Gretel' and 'Hop o' my Thumb'. They concern peaceful characters of humble origin, who have no desire to battle with ogres, but who, when put to it, use native wit to outsmart the forces of evil. The stories of 'Rumpelstiltskin' and 'The Twelve Dancing Princesses' might almost be classed along with them, as describing two further skirmishes with the supernatural; but in the versions given by the Grimm brothers they are both stories in which the reader is singularly uninterested in the fate of the principal character. However, in the stories that are central to the fairy-tale tradition, the tales of royal romance and magical transformation – tales which are mostly of great age, and all of which are in one way or another related to each other – we find ourselves closely identifying with the principal characters. These characters are Cinderella, Snow White, Sleeping Beauty, the unnamed heroine of 'Diamonds and Toads', the King of Colchester's daughter in 'The Three Heads in the Well', Beauty in 'Beauty and the Beast', and the young princess in 'The Frog Prince'.

With Cinderella, whose story is at least one thousand years old, we have not only a girl who is worthy of becoming a princess, as has already been suggested, but a girl who is being supernaturally *prevented* from becoming a princess. When her situation is closely examined, particularly with the aid of parallels from different countries, she is seen to be under enchantment not when she is in her beauteous state, for that is her natural condition, but when she is in her *kitchen state*. Perrault's story, for all its wit and compassion, is a worldly and somewhat sentimentalized version of older, darker stories, which have many strange undertones. For instance, in a number of the variants it is apparent that the magical assistance the heroine receives comes to her from the spirit of her dead mother. Indeed, there are analogous tales in which the mother is also the indirect cause of the girl's distressed condition. In these stories the girl, who is often already a princess, has been obliged to leave her royal home and take kitchen employment elsewhere, due to a terrifying circumstance. Her mother, on her deathbed, has commanded her father not to marry again until he finds a woman who is as lovely as herself, or who possesses a finger so delicate it will fit her ring. After much searching the father, a king, realizes there is only one person as beautiful as was his wife, or with the ability to wear the ring, and this is his own daughter, whom he determines to marry. Hence the girl's flight.

In the story of Snow White, who also suffers because of her beauty, the fact of her being under a spell during her formative years (from the age of seven to, probably, fifteen) is more obvious than in Cinderella's case. During these years she is laid out in a coffin apparently dead. Release from the enchantment can be effected, it is evident, only through the seemingly unlikely event of someone (necessarily of royal birth?) falling in love with her lifeless body. The explanation that she comes to life through the piece of poisoned apple falling from her lips when her body is moved, poetic though the notion may be, is a mere rationalization; as can be seen by comparing her history with that of Sleeping Beauty, who we are explicitly told is under a spell, and whose sleeping body must necessarily be discovered by a king's son, or, in an earlier text, be raped by a king, if she is to be freed from the enchantment that has kept her in a coma for a hundred years.

In 'Diamonds and Toads', and more especially in 'The Three Heads in the Well' – surely the weirdest of the tales – we are at the heart of fairy-tale morality, where girls in a distressed state yet possess the charity to care for the condition of others. In 'The Three Heads in the Well' a princess willingly picks up one dismembered head after another, washing it, and combing its hair, and laying it down gently, actions requiring the courage, and the tranquil acceptance of a surprising situation, which it is well known many women do possess in an emergency. Thus, when the compassion of the King of Colchester's daughter is appreciated, her relationship to Beauty in 'Beauty and the Beast' becomes clear, as also to the heroine of the more explicit tale of 'The Frog Prince', in which the girl has to let the frog have intercourse with her before the creature can be revealed to be a prince. These two tales are, then, the counterparts of Snow White and Sleeping Beauty, the roles of the sexes being reversed.

In these deeply-penetrating tales, fairy godmothers do not suddenly materialize, waving wands that make everything come right. The power of the godmothers is limited. Sometimes all they are able to offer is advice. They are never able, it seems, to change a worldly situation, or alter a wicked heart. What they can do, on occasion, is assist in the breaking of a spell or in the alleviation of its ill effect. In the story of Cinderella, the most interesting of the tales since the spell is the least apparent, we are repeatedly told, in variants, firstly of the girl's essential goodness; and, secondly, not only of the poor and even ridiculous clothes she wears, the rags, the grey bedgown, the garment made of rushes, but of her dirtiness – a condition we would not expect of the kind of person we know her to be, no matter how humble her employment, were she not, as she is, under a spell to appear sluttish. Nobody outside her family, it is apparent, must know she is other than a menial until a prince, who has only a sign to go by, finds her, as if guided by a star, and offers himself to her while she is still in her unattractive state. Further, she herself must behave as if she was a menial. The reason she returns home before midnight is to ensure that not even members of her family shall associate her with the vision of virtue and loveliness they have been admiring at the ball. The prince's admiration of her in her party dress is worthless. It is essential he plights himself to her while she is a kitchen maid, of the spell can never be broken; and in this a curious parallel to the Christ story is apparent. The man of perfect heart, living in the guise of a poor carpenter's son, has to be accepted in his lowly state. He could not reveal himself to be anyone but a simple though high-minded Nazarene, even when a purple robe was draped round his shoulders, a crown of thorns placed on his head, and he was mocked. Nor, if his mission was to be a success, could God the Father assist him with a direct sign. Had Christ been shown in his full glory, recognition of his virtues, whether by pauper or by prince, would have been valueless. On the face of it the message of the fairy tales is that transformation to a state of bliss is effected not by magic, but by the perfect love of one person for another. Yet clearly even this is not the whole story. The transformation is not an actual transformation but a disenchantment, the breaking of a spell. In each case we are aware that the person was always noble, that the magic has wrought no change in the person's soul, only in his or her outward form. In fairy tales there is no saving of the wicked in heart. Their fate is to have inflicted on them the evil they would inflict on others. The tub filled with toads and vipers shall become the murderous queen's final resting place.

THE NATURE OF THE TALES

Compared with the age of some of the tales the term 'fairy tale' is modern. It does not seem to have entered the language until the eighteenth century (the earliest *The Oxford English Dictionary* knows it is 1749), and almost certainly it came from France; not, as might be expected, from Perrault, who styled his tales *contes du temps passé* or *contes de ma mère l'Oye*, but from his contemporary, Madame d'Aulnoy, whose *Contes des fées* were published in 1698, and translated into English the following year as

Tales of the Fairys. During the next several decades the Countess's tales were multi-fariously reprinted, the term 'fairy tale' first appearing on one of her title-pages in 1752. By this time, however, the term was well established. It had appeared, for instance, in the introduction to a 1721 collection of her tales, when a friend of the Countess wished to 'lend her some Fairy Stories that would divert her very agreeably' ('They must be none of my own writing then,' replied she smartly); and it had appeared in Pluche's essay on 'The Exercises of Children' translated in *Nature Display'd*, vol. VI, 1748, where the author required an impenetrable barrier to be erected between the child and 'all Fairy-Tales, Stories of Thefts and Murders, of Imprisonments and Executions, and to all Pictures of Visions, Bull-beggars, and Hob-gobblings'. The kind of tale Pluche was here warning against, however, was not so much the fairy tale as we think of it today, as the fairy legend, the story about fairy-folk and their activities, that in the eighteenth century was half-believed to be true.

A characteristic of the fairy tale, as told today, is that it is unbelievable. Although a fairy tale is seldom a tale about fairy-folk, and does not necessarily even feature a fairy, it does contain an enchantment or other supernatural element that is clearly imaginary. Usually the tale is about one person, or one family, having to cope with a supernatural occurrence or supernatural protagonist during a period of stress. The hero is almost invariably a young person, usually the youngest member of a family, and if not deformed or already an orphan, is probably in the process of being disowned or abandoned.[1] The characters in the stories are, nevertheless, stock figures. They are either altogether good or altogether bad, and there is no evolution of character. They are referred to by generic or descriptive names, as 'Jack' (for lad), 'Beauty', 'Snow White', 'Silver Hair', 'Tom Thumb', 'Red Ridinghood', 'Cinder-girl'. Fairy tales are more concerned with situation than with character. They are the space fiction of the past. They describe events that took place when a different range of possibilities operated in the unidentified long ago; and this is part of their attraction. Children often remark that the tales they read first in a book are the ones beginning with the evocative formula 'Once upon a time'. They feel certain these tales will be the best. 'Once upon a time there was a king and a queen, as in many lands have been . . .' 'Once upon a time, and be sure 'twas a long time ago . . .' 'Once upon a time, and twice upon a time, and all times together as ever I heard of . . .' 'Once upon a time, and a very good time it was, though it was neither in your time nor my time, nor nobody else's time . . .'[2] The stories would, curiously, not be so believable if the period in which they took place was specified, or if the place where they occurred was named.

---

[1] A curious exception is the hero of 'The Twelve Dancing Princesses' who is an old soldier.

[2] The openings of the three British tales 'The History of Tom Thumbe', 'The History of Jack and the Giants' and 'The Three Heads in the Well' hark back to a mythical past. In their early texts they begin respectively: 'In the old time, when King Arthur ruled this land . . .' 'In the reign of King Arthur . . .' and 'Long before Arthur and the Knights of the Round Table . . .' This accords with the manner in which the Wife of Bath commenced her fairy tale:

> In th'olde dayes of the Kyng Arthour,
> Of which that Britons speken greet honour,
> Al was this land fulfild of fayerye.

In the history of 'Jack and the Giants' it comes as a jolt when an actual location is mentioned ('a Market-town in Wales'), the tale thereafter seems a foolish tale, the spell has been broken. Yet fairy tales are nothing if not realistic; and it is their cynicism that keeps them lively. Wonders may take place without remark; but a sharp eye is kept on practical details. In 'Diamonds and Toads' the prince shrewdly appreciates that a girl capable of producing diamonds when she speaks is marriageable without a dowry. In 'Sleeping Beauty' the point is made that the prince who has entered the enchanted castle is an eligible young man, since he is 'of another family from that of the sleeping princess'. In a Hungarian version of 'The Frog Prince', after the frog had spent the night with the girl and turned into a handsome youth, 'they hastened to celebrate the wedding, so that the christening might not follow it too soon'. It will be noticed that traditional stories are seldom soft, and never sentimental. A premium may be placed on beauty but not on virginity, on riches but not on learning, on worldly success but not on the means by which the success is achieved. The virtues which get rewarded are presence of mind, kindliness, willingness to take advice, and courage. The rewards sought after are wealth, comfortable living, and an ideal partner.

Indeed some details that appear to us romantic today may merely reflect social conditions when the tales were formulated. The prevalence of stepmothers is accounted for by the shortness of life in past times, by the consequent shortness of marriages, and by the practice of the surviving partner marrying again without unnecessary delay. When lives were short, too, girls of distinction married early. The princess in 'The Three Heads in the Well' who becomes a bride at fifteen, and Sleeping Beauty who welcomes her prince when 'fifteen or sixteen' (if the hundred years she has been asleep are not counted), were simply conforming to the practice of their time, a practice emphasised in Madame d'Aulnoy's story of 'The Yellow Dwarf', where the queen is deeply concerned her daughter will die an old maid the way she continues, at the age of fifteen, to disdain the kings who come to court her.[1] Likewise the prominent place that wells have in some tales will be understood by anyone who has lived, as we have, in a village where all water had to be fetched in a bucket. No meeting place so central to daily routine as a communal well exists in modern urban life unless, perhaps, it is the gate where the afternoon concourse gathers to fetch small children from school. Fairy tales are thus more realistic than they may appear at first sight; while the magic in them almost heightens the realism. The magic sets us wondering how we ourselves would react in similar circumstances. It encourages speculation. It gives a child licence to wonder. And this is the merit of the tales, that by going beyond possibility they enlarge our daily horizon. For a man not given to speculation might as well walk on four legs as on two. A child who does not feel wonder is but an inlet for apple pie.

[1]This becomes unsurprising if it is realized that when Madame d'Aulnoy herself was born, *c.* 1650, her mother was still only fifteen; and Madame d'Aulnoy in her turn, married when she was only fifteen or sixteen. It is recorded of Gilles de Rais—who some say was the original Bluebeard—that his actual circumstances were that he was betrothed when he was thirteen, and the girl dying, he was freshly betrothed at fourteen or fifteen, and that girl dying, he was betrothed a third time, and married when just sixteen. This was in Brittany at the beginning of the fifteenth century.

For the past century and a half, in fact ever since the publication in 1812 of the *Kinder-und Haus-Märchen* of Jacob and Wilhelm Grimm, fairy tales have received more attention and aroused more controversy than any other form of traditional literature. This is easily understandable, since even if the aesthetic qualities of the tales are ignored (which is difficult), the stories are a marvel to contemplate from the folkloristic point of view. To the inquiring mind the tales are of utmost interest as being stories possibly of ancient origin; as being stories that possibly have been continuously remembered since the days they were first told; and as being continuously living entities that have not only been preserved by past centuries, but nourished by them. The student of fairy tales wishes to know where they come from, why they have continued to be told, and what changes have taken place in them over the years.

He is aware, of course, if he is experienced, that however ancient the stories may be he must not think of them as if they were archaeological remains, as if they were the actual objects that existed in the past; nor must he regard them (as folklorists used to do) as antiques that have been so scarred by time they have become almost unrecognizable, for this presupposes that they were once whole and perfect, and have ever since been in a state of decay. He knows instead that since they are living things, not fossils, they are subject to mutation. They are as likely to have grown as they became older, as to have shrunk. They are as likely to have acquired significance, or to have acquired fresh significance, as they have passed through sophisticated communities, as to have lost it. Yet he finds himself faced by the astonishing fact that a body of the tales have been found to be not merely ancient but to be traditional in a variety of countries and cultures; and that versions of a story told in widely separated parts of the earth will sometimes not merely bear resemblance, but possess actual points of detail in common.

Nevertheless, if he is wise, he avoids any general theory to account for this phenomenon. He is conscious that the theories there have been in the past concerning the origin or meaning of the tales have tended to pour darkness on their subject rather than light. Certain scholars have taken it for granted, for instance, that the tales originated during the childhood of man, and that the traits found in them of cannibalism, metamorphism, and totemism, must be expressions of primitive thought. Others have sought to show that the tales are of Aryan stock, and have all made their way from India; or have postulated that each tale has arisen spontaneously in a number of separate places throughout the world wherever man was passing through a particular stage of development. Some have seen in the tales the debris of a mythology that accounted for the courses of the sun and other celestial bodies, or have believed that the tales stemmed from ritual celebrations of the seasons and initiation rites; or they have convinced themselves that the tales are dream sequences, the products of psychological difficulties, and particularly, need it be added, of complexes that are sexual.

Happily such all-embracing theories are now regarded with scepticism. It is no longer felt that any one theory is likely to account satisfactorily for the origin of even a majority of the tales. Their well-springs are almost certainly numerous, their ages likely to vary considerably, their meanings – if they ever had meanings – to be diverse. Each tale, it is now believed, should be studied separately. As many recordings should be gathered together as possible of the oral transmission of a particular story, and they should be plotted on a map to ascertain whether, through frequency of occurrence, a geographical centre can be located from which the tale may have spread; while the variants of the tale should be compared to see whether, in association with the geographical locations, an archetype can be identified or reconstructed.

In such work literary references and historical records of a tale are not to be ignored. The written record of a tale in a past century proves, at the very least, that a particular version was current at a particular place, or anyway known at a particular place, at an ascertainable point in time. The tale cannot be less old than the date when it was first referred to or recorded; and such recordings must effectively provide the framework upon which any hypothesis about the story's origin or meaning must eventually be fitted. Further, early recordings or references to a story are valuable as revealing the attitude to the tale prevailing at that time; and we notice here, without further turning of pages, that although in some early collections of the tales it was felt necessary to append morals, it is apparent that during the past thousand years no deep significance has been placed on them. In general there seems to have been no motive for telling them other than for wonder and for entertainment.

THE EARLY COLLECTIONS

The earliest collections of tales to be enriched with stories similar to our fairy tales were made in the East. The vast assemblage of Indian folk tales set down a thousand years ago by Somadeva, a Kashmir Brahmin, entitled *Katha Sarit Sāgara* (Ocean of Streams of Story), contained stories with elements that, happily, are still familiar to the young of today: helpful animals, invincible swords, shoes of swiftness, and vessels which continuously provide good things to eat no matter how much is taken from them. In particular the collection contained a splendid version of Hans Andersen's 'The Princess on the Pea', a story also to be found in the select anthology *Vetālapañchāviṁśati*. Even older is the *Panchatantra* (the Five Tantras or Books), the most famous of Hindu collections, which dates back to the third century A.D., and which has long been known to English readers as the *Fables of Bidpai* (or *Pilpay*). Amongst the tales is a forerunner to the story of 'The Three Wishes' in which a poor weaver, who has been given a single wish, ill-advisedly asks for two heads and four hands so that he can do twice as much work; and there is also, incidentally, a story of a cat which fared much less well than Puss in Boots when it determined to find its fortune in a king's palace.

Cinderella, Red Ridinghood, Bluebeard, and Hop o' my Thumb. Hand-coloured engravings from *Tabart's Popular Stories for the Nursery*, 1804, which was the first collection of fairy tales to have coloured illustrations. Amongst those who possessed an edition of this work were the Grimm brothers.

A fully developed version of 'The Three Wishes' appeared in *The Book of Sindibâd*, a book probably of Persian origin composed about the beginning of the ninth century. This is the book known in Europe as *The Book of the Seven Wise Masters*, *The Book of the Seven Sages*, or *The Seven Sages of Rome*. The frame story, which concerns a king's son who is under notice of death, somewhat resembles the framework of *The Arabian Nights' Entertainments*. To postpone the execution seven philosophers successively tell stories of female iniquity, while a woman strenuously defends her sex. *The Arabian Nights* which contains, of course, the stories of 'Sindbad the Sailor', 'Aladdin and his Wonderful Lamp', and 'Ali Baba and the Forty Thieves', is of interest here as giving an Eastern account of a locked room, such as Bluebeard's wife was forbidden to enter, and for the similarities between the tale of Aladdin and Andersen's 'The Tinder Box'.

The earliest European storybook to include fairy tales was Straparola's collection of tales and jests *Le piacevoli Notti* (The Delightful Nights), published in Venice in two parts, 1550–1553. Despite the popularity the stories enjoyed in sixteenth-century Italy, not much is known about Gianfrancesco Straparola (c.1480–c.1557), other than that he came from Caravaggio near Milan; and despite the fact that the tales were published in France as early as 1560 (second volume 1573), they have been little known in England. A certain crudeness in some of the jests, and the earthy manner in which they are told, has limited their publication to costly volumes for connoisseurs. Straparola, himself, was at pains to excuse his style, saying the tales were written down direct 'from the lips of ten young girls', a delightful excuse that unfortunately does not stand examination. Nevertheless a number of the tales were undoubtedly in oral circulation when the book was produced; and none of the seventy-four pieces, which include jests and tall stories that can still be heard in bar-parlours today, seem to be original. Further, amongst the longer tales is the story of 'Puss in Boots', virtually as Perrault was to tell it, together with a nightmare prototype of 'Beauty and the Beast', and a tale containing the central motif of 'Diamonds and Toads'.

The most important collection of fairy tales to appear before Perrault's *Contes*, and one of the most remarkable collections of all time, was also Italian; but with this difference, that it was written in the Neapolitan dialect. *Lo Cunto de li Cunti* (The Tale of Tales) was published in five volumes, volumes I–III being dated 1634; volume IV, 1634 and 1635; and volume V, 1636. The author, Giambattista Basile, a much-travelled poet, soldier, courtier, and administrator, was born in Naples about 1575, and died when Governor of the Giugliano district, near Naples, in 1632. His collection, now usually known as the *Pentamerone*, was thus published posthumously.[1] The fifty tales, which according to the frame-story were told by common townswomen, are almost all fairy tales; and there seems little doubt that the majority of them were tales that Basile himself had heard told in Naples and elsewhere, although his manner

---

[1] The work acquired the title *Il Pentamerone* in the 1674 edition, under the influence of the *Decamerone*. In our notes we adopt the common practice of referring to it as the *Pentamerone*, although the date accompanying the reference is, of course, that of the appropriate original volume.

of telling them is a mixture of the idiomatic and the baroque. Amongst these tales are portions or complete versions of the stories of 'Cinderella', 'Sleeping Beauty', 'Beauty and the Beast', 'Diamonds and Toads', 'Snow White', and 'Puss in Boots'; and most of Basile's versions add to our understanding of the tales as we know them today. Further, the quantity of the tales, and the loving detail with which they are told, give us positive evidence of the vitality of wonder tales in the early years of the seventeenth century; while the happy chance that Basile chose to publish the tales in a semi-archaic form of the Neapolitan dialect, ensured that their publication would have a minimal effect on the general stream of oral transmission. Indeed the tales were not translated even into Italian until 1747 (and thereafter not into German until 1846, nor into English until 1848), so that it seems improbable, on the face of it, that Perrault ever read the tales himself; while a comparison of Perrault's texts with Basile's virtually convinces that Perrault was uninfluenced by them. Thus we are in the fortunate position of being able to look at Perrault's tales, being aware of some of their antecedents of which he himself was almost certainly unaware.

CHARLES PERRAULT

At the end of the seventeenth century the lives of certain fairy tales were wholly transformed by their being set down in a manner so vivid that no retelling could improve them. They ceased to be stories whose survival depended on cottage memories, and became literature. The man who worked this magic was the retired civil servant and member of the *Académie française*, Charles Perrault (1628–1703); and the book they appeared in, *Histoires ou Contes du temps passé. Avec des Moralitez*, was published in Paris, January 1697. The eight tales in the volume, all but one of which are now world-renowned, were the following:

'La Belle au bois dormant' (Sleeping Beauty)
'Le petit chaperon rouge' (Little Red Ridinghood)
'La Barbe bleüe' (Bluebeard)
'Le Maistre Chat, ou le Chat Botté' (Puss in Boots)
'Les Fées' (Diamonds and Toads)
'Cendrillon, ou la petite pantoufle de verre' (Cinderella)
'Riquet à la Houppe' (the story of a deformed prince's romance with a princess who is lovely but witless)
'Le Petit Poucet' (Hop o' my Thumb)

Probably no other storybook has enjoyed such instant success and had such continuing popularity. But the reasons for the book's success have not always been recognized, for they are contradictory and seemingly incompatible. The literary skill employed in the telling of the tales is universally acknowledged; yet it also appears that the tales were set down very largely as the writer heard them told. The evidence for this lies not only in the simplicity of the tales, and in the use of words which at that time were described as 'populaire' and 'du bas peuple', but in the fact that, as in other tales that are genuinely traditional, there are passages that are vestigial, that are superfluous to the plot, and that do not illuminate the rest of the narrative: passages that certainly would not have been included – or not have been included in the way they have been – if the author had been attempting a work of art. Thus at the beginning of 'Sleeping Beauty' we are told Beauty's parents had great difficulty in having a child: 'They went to all the waters in the world, vows, pilgrimages, everything was tried and nothing came of it'. This circumstance is clearly a hangover from some earlier telling of the tale, since it is without relevance to the rest of the story as here narrated. Similarly in the tale of Bluebeard the key to the forbidden room is shown to be magical, though this is a tale that is otherwise innocent of supernatural trappings, and this single example of uncanniness adds nothing to the plot. Likewise in 'Puss in Boots', although the idea of a booted cat is splendid, the cat's insistence on being well shod as a condition to aiding his master, is nowhere explained, nor developed in the story, nor referred to again except in a single facetious aside. And again, in the story of 'Le petit Poucet', we are informed that the hero was – like the British Tom Thumb – 'no bigger when he was born than one's thumb'; but the fact of his extraordinary littleness, if indeed he *was* little, is thereafter disregarded, and Little Poucet is treated as if he were a child of normal growth.

Charles Perrault

Perrault's achievement was that he accepted the fairy tales at their own level. He recounted them without impatience, without mockery, and without feeling they required any aggrandisement, such as a frame-story, though he did end each tale with a rhymed *moralité*. If only it had occurred to him to state where he had obtained each tale, and when, and under what circumstances, he would today probably be revered as the father of folklore.

But another century was to pass before men realized that to give the source of a tale was to add to its interest; and Perrault seems to have been at pains to dissociate even his name from the tales, though whether this was from embarrassment, or out of good nature, will probably never be known.

The doubt about whether he was wholly responsible for setting down the stories arises from the fact that the book's dedication, which was to Elisabeth Charlotte d'Orléans, niece of Louis XIV, is signed 'P. Darmancour'. Darmancour was the name adopted by Perrault's third son, Pierre, who had been born in 1678; and the assumption has been that although the father, a prolific author in his retirement, may have given his son a hand in the production, the simple tales must have been set down by Pierre, then aged eighteen. Neither contemporary evidence nor a reassessment of the situation altogether supports this view.

Perrault senior is known to have long been interested in *contes de vieilles* or, as they were commonly termed at that time, *contes de ma mère l'oye*. In 1693, for instance, he had published a versified account of 'The Three Wishes' (*Les Souhaits Ridicules*), and in 1694 a traditional tale on the Cinderella theme (*Peau d'Ane*). Further, a manuscript exists of five of the prose tales dated 1695, when Pierre Perrault was only sixteen or seventeen, not a likely age for someone to have been writing down fairy tales, particularly someone who was to show no further literary inclinations and to become a soldier. Certainly several contemporaries spoke of the tales as being by Pierre; but there were others, who must have known who was responsible for them, who were strangely circumspect in their references. (The relevant quotations have been usefully assembled by Jacques Barchilon.) Thus when Pierre died in 1700, his obituary made no mention of his being connected with the tales; yet when his father died three years later the same paper alluded to his being responsible for 'La Belle au bois dormant' which the paper had published in 1696. Our own knowledge of such situations is that whereas children rarely let it be assumed that work which is theirs was produced by a parent (however much the parent assisted), fathers are commonly happy to attribute work of theirs to their children, no matter how little the offspring assisted in it. This is particularly so when, as in Charles Perrault's case, the father is deeply interested in his family, and is approaching the end of his life.

After the first edition of the *Contes du temps passé* had appeared, with its frontispiece depicting three young people listening to an old dame, beneath a placard inscribed 'CONTES DE MA MERE LOYE', unauthorized editions kept being printed in Amsterdam which attributed the tales to 'le Fils de Monsieur Perreault' (sic). Then, in 1721, the printer's widow issued a corrected edition in which the tales were no longer given as by Perrault's son but as 'Par M. Perrault' (correctly spelt), and with an additional tale 'L'Adroite Princesse' by Mlle l'Héritier, who had been a friend of the Perraults, and who, now that both father and son were dead, may have advised that Charles should be acknowledged as the author.

Whatever the circumstances, this edition, or its Parisian original, seems to have been

The arrival of Mother Goose in Britain. The placard on the wall, in this frontispiece to Robert Samber's translation of Perrault's tales, 1729, was the starting-point of the Mother Goose legend in English-speaking homes.

the one Robert Samber used when he translated the tales into English. *Histories, or Tales of Past Times, By M. Perrault*, appeared in a neat volume, printed in London 'for J. Pote, at Sir Isaac New-ton's Head, near Suffolk-street, Charing-cross; and R. Montagu, the Corner of Great Queen-street, near Drury-lane', in 1729. And it was this volume, advertised in June 1729 as being 'very entertaining and instructive for children', that introduced the tales that have become the most loved in the English language.[1]

MADAME D'AULNOY AND MADAME DE BEAUMONT

Perrault's tales were not however France's only contribution to the English nursery at this time. In 1699 some of Madame d'Aulnoy's *Contes des fées* had been translated, such as 'Gracioça and Percinet' and 'The Blue Bird'; and in 1707 a larger number appeared in the fourth part of her *Diverting Works*, which in fact preceded the magnificent and now rare collection of her later tales issued in three volumes, 1721–1722, entitled simply *A Collection of Novels and Tales, Written by that Celebrated Wit of France, The Countess D'Anois*. Here, for the first time in English, appeared the novelette, 'The White Cat', the tales of deep enchantment, 'The Royal Ram' and 'The Story of Finetta the Cinder-Girl' (in part equivalent to Cinderella), and Dickens's favourite, the still haunting story of 'The Yellow Dwarf', which probably best reveals the Countess's talent.

Marie Catherine Le Jumel de Barnville (c.1650–1705), wife of François de la Motte, Comte d'Aulnoy (or d'Anois, d'Aunois, Dunois, etc.), a lady of good family, good looks, good mind, sharp wit, and strange life (few women can have plotted to have their husband executed for high treason), was the foremost teller of fairy tales in her day, and indeed the innovator, it seems, of the fairy tale as a literary genre. Her tales, though sometimes based on old themes or embodying episodes from old stories, have little of the economy or rhythm of a traditional tale. They are wild, undisciplined, almost feverishly imaginative, saved only by the precision of her descriptions, a virtue in story-telling which unfortunately was seldom possessed by her imitators.

An exception was Madame Leprince de Beaumont (1711–1780), whose claim to be honoured by the young is perhaps greater even than Madame d'Aulnoy's, although admittedly her period was fifty years later when new ideas current in the real world were already beginning to affect the realm of fairyland. Born in Rouen, and like the Countess unhappily married, she emigrated to England about 1745 at the time when playbooks for children were first being issued, and when writers who were interested in education (Madame de Beaumont became a governess) were beginning to see that children could confidently be addressed as people who would remain children for some

---

[1]Until 1951 doubt was cast on whether Robert Samber was in fact the first to translate the tales into English. An edition was said to be in existence, and is, entitled *Histories or Tales of Past Times, told by Mother Goose, with Morals. Written in French by M. Perrault, and Englished by G. M. Gent*, bearing on the title-page the date M,DCC,XIX (1719). However in *The Oxford Dictionary of Nursery Rhymes* pp. 39–40, we were able to show this date was a misprint for M,DCC,XCIX (1799), and that Robert Samber was undoubtedly the original translator.

years, rather than as small adults who were only momentarily disguised as young people. Whereas Madame d'Aulnoy had written merely to amuse herself and her fashionable friends, Madame de Beaumont wrote out of deep involvement with the young, genuinely seeking to engage the minds of her pupils, and doing so intelligently and not too earnestly. Her *Magasin des enfans, ou dialogues entre une sage Gouvernante et plusieurs de ses Élèves*, printed in London in 1756, was translated as *The Young Misses Magazine* in 1761. Clearly inspired by Sarah Fielding's *The Governess; or, Little Female Academy*, which had appeared in 1749, her linked miscellany of tales and expositions, in which 'the useful' was 'blended throughout with the agreeable', was written in a plain colloquial style that had scarcely been used before when addressing 'young misses' of ten and twelve years old.

Whether good writers are people who recognize a good story when they see one, or whether they themselves make the story good, might provide a subject for a thesis. The happy chance that Perrault should have known the story of Cinderella, and that, for instance, Southey should have been the man who came across the story of 'The Three Bears', may be felt to be equalled by our good fortune that Marie Leprince de Beaumont should have been the person who realized that 'Beauty and the Beast' and 'The Three Wishes' were tales that would divert such young misses as 'Miss Molly' and 'Lady Mary' and 'Lady Charlotte'.

The Grimm Brothers and Hans Andersen

Despite the popularity of Perrault and Madame d'Aulnoy, or perhaps because of it, as the eighteenth century grew older fairy tales were looked upon with increasing disfavour. They were felt to be an affront to the rational mind; to be the preserve merely of nursemaids, and of wayward children with their ninepenny illustrated collections attributed to 'Mother Goose' (mostly tales written by Perrault) and 'Mother Bunch' (in general tales by Madame d'Aulnoy). 'We do not allude to fairy tales,' commented the Edgeworths in 1798, 'for we apprehend these are not now much read.' But in Britain, as elsewhere, this attitude was to change. In 1823 fairy tales became, almost overnight, a respectable study for antiquarians, an inspiration for poets, and a permissible source of wonder for the young. The event that brought this about was the publication of *German Popular Stories*, translated by Edgar Taylor and his family from the *Kinder- und Haus-Märchen* of the brothers Grimm. This enterprising duodecimo volume was, firstly, a highly readable collection of stories for 'young minds'; secondly, an instantly acceptable gift, illustrated by the best illustrator of the day, George Cruikshank; and thirdly, a learnedly annotated revelation of the antiquity and diffusion of traditional tales. Seldom have young and old, the romantic and the scholarly, been so well provided for in a single volume.

The two studious brothers, Jacob Grimm (1785–1863) and Wilhelm Grimm (1786–1859), were natives of Hesse-Cassel, the orphan sons of a lawyer, who were educated largely through the generosity of an aunt. Their *Kinder- und Haus-Märchen*, which

Jacob and Wilhelm Grimm. Drawing by their younger brother Ludwig Emil Grimm

had been published in Berlin in 1812 (vol. II, 1815; vol. III, 1822), consisted of popular tales that for the most part were still familiar to the common people in Hesse. Other men than themselves had become fascinated by these tales, for the spirit of Herder, and of the Romantic movement, had been enlivening academic circles for some while; and the tales the Grimms collected do not seem to have been particularly difficult to secure. Indeed versions of some of the most magical tales, such as 'Snow White', 'Hansel and Gretel', and 'The Twelve Dancing Princesses', were taken down from the recitation of friends and next-door neighbours. But where the Grimms were remarkable was in what now seems to us most ordinary. The Grimms were the first substantial collectors to like folktales for their own sake; the first to write the tales down in the way ordinary people told them, and not attempt to improve them; and they were the first to realize that everything about the tales was of interest, even including the identity of the person who told the tale. Thus, although they put forward ideas about the antiquity and significance of the tales which subsequent research has not confirmed; and although they did not always adhere to the high standards they set themselves, and were willing to mend some of their tales, fitting two and more variants together to make what they believed to be the full story, their collection (which Wilhelm continued enlarging to the end of his life) stands as the pre-eminent commendation of the traditional tale; the work that was to inspire the serious collecting of folk and fairy tales in Britain and in the rest of the world; and – since the Grimms were in their way visionaries, as well as being dauntingly industrious – the work that laid the foundations of a new discipline, the scientific study of folklore and folk literature.

The contribution made by Hans Christian Andersen (1805–1875) to fairy-tale literature was wholly different. Born at Odense, in the Danish island of Fünen, the son of a sickly shoemaker and an illiterate washerwoman, he himself had a kind of fairy-tale life – as he never wearied of telling people – raising himself from a street-boy to the darling of Europe by the inventing of fairy tales. He had achieved only moderate success as an author, though he had impressed many people by his personality, when on 8 May 1835 a small sixty-four-page booklet was published, *Eventyr, fortalte for Børn* (Tales told for Children), containing four stories, amongst which were 'The Tinder Box' and 'The Princess on the Pea'. He wrote them, as he said, not in a literary style but in the way he would tell them to children, and referred to them as 'those trifles', being more excited at the time by the publication of his first novel *Improvisatoren*.

Hans Andersen was unlike the Grimms in that he was a creator not a collector. Even when he used traditional themes for his tales he made the stories his own, putting into them his own life and personality; yet some of his tales were of such immediate appeal that they, in their turn, soon came to be passed on orally (the Grimms published *Die Erbsenprobe* in 1843, not realizing it had come from Andersen), and some of his stories have even supplanted earlier traditional tales.[1] Andersen was in fact the first writer of fairy tales to come – as the Grimms with their professional background did not – from the humble class to whom story-telling was a living tradition. All the people who surrounded him in his childhood, other than his father, were people who relied on word of mouth, not books, for their knowledge.

[1] Andersen and the Grimms eventually became good friends. But when Andersen first introduced himself to Jacob, confident of his fame, the meeting was painfully disconcerting. Jacob had never heard of him.

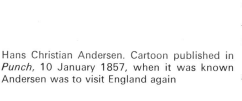

Hans Christian Andersen. Cartoon published in *Punch*, 10 January 1857, when it was known Andersen was to visit England again

Andersen's tales – there were eventually to be more than 150 of them – arrived in Britain in 1846, in which year no less than five collections appeared: *Wonderful Stories for Children*, translated by Mary Howitt (published in New York the following year); *A Danish Story-Book*, *The Nightingale and other Tales*, and *The Shoes of Fortune, and other Tales*, all translated by Charles Boner; and *Danish Fairy Legends and Tales*, translated by Caroline Peachey. With the arrival of Andersen's tales in the English language came an unfreezing of men's minds, an appreciation of fantasy literature and its limitless possibilities. Although the humour in Andersen's writing was not understood by the early translators, and he acquired a reputation for sentimentality which was undeserved, the way was now open for the fairy-tale literature that was to enthral the second half of the nineteenth century. Writers such as Frances Browne with *Granny's Wonderful Chair*, Charles Kingsley with *The Water-Babies*, Jean Inglow with *Mopsa the Fairy*, George MacDonald with *At the Back of the North Wind*, and even Lewis Carroll, largely wrote in the way they did, and certainly were greeted by the public as friends in the way they were, because of the introduction they had been given by two students in Cassel and a cobbler's son in Odense. Imagination, which had formerly brought terror to mankind, had become a source of delight.

One of Cruikshank's figures in
German Popular Stories, 1823,
re-engraved by John Byfield, 1849

Right: The beginning of Tom Thumb's
history. The newborn child is as
big as he will ever be—the size
of his father's thumb. Colour
wood-engraving by Kronheim & Co.,
after the design by H. W. Petherick,
from *Our Nurse's Picture Book*, 1869

'The History of Tom Thumb' is a glorious idea rather than a glorious story. Its attraction lies in the thought of the wonderful feats a manikin might perform who was so small he was not ordinarily noticed, and the ridiculous situations he might find himself in if, despite his lack of all inches but one, he was adventurous. The author of this tale, or the man who gave it shape and set it down seems to have been a Londoner, Richard Johnson (1573–1659?), whose initials appear on the

Title-page of the only known copy of *The History of Tom Thumbe,* 1621. The book gives the earliest surviving English text of a popular fairy tale.

Imprinted at London for *Tho: Langley.* 1621.

last page of the earliest surviving text. This is entitled *The History of Tom Thumbe, the Little, for his small stature surnamed, King Arthvrs Dwarfe: Whose Life and adventures containe many strange and wonderfull accidents, published for the delight of merry Time-spenders.* It is a forty-page booklet, printed in London for Thomas Langley in 1621, of which the only known copy is in the Pierpont Morgan Library, New York. It is also, it seems, the earliest extant printing of an English fairy tale.

How much the character of Tom Thumb, as portrayed in this story, was already traditional, and how much Richard Johnson (if Richard Johnson was indeed the author) invented or embroidered it, is uncertain. What is clear is that Tom Thumb was already well known by name. William Fulke referred to him in 1579 in *Heskins Parleament Repealed,* so did Thomas Nashe in *Pierce Pennilesse* in 1592; and more interestingly, Reginald Scot, writing 'Of vaine apparitions, how people have beene brought to feare bugges' listed 'Tom Thumbe' in his *Discoverie of Witchcraft,* 1584, along with 'bull-beggers, spirits, witches, urchens, elves, hags, fairies, satyrs, pans, faunes, sylens, kit with the canstick, tritons, centaures, dwarfes, giants, imps,' and suchlike bogies—creatures, he declared, with which servant maids had so affrighted people in their childhood 'that we are afraid of our owne shadowes'.

That some part of Tom's history was current before 1621 is evident from lines by James Field, prefixed to Coryate's *Crudities* in 1611:

Tom Thumbe is dumbe, vntill the pudding creepe
In which he was intomb'd, then out doth peepe.
Tom Piper is gone out, and mirth bewailes,
He never will come in to tell vs tales.

By this time, however, Johnson's *History* may already have been in circulation, since it is improbable that the 1621 printing was the first: the woodblock on the title-page bears all the marks of having had earlier use.

In the preface, too, 'R. J.' himself speaks of the antiquity of Tom's story, extolling it as a diversion of former times:

'The ancient Tales of Tom Thumbe in the olde time, haue been the onely reuiuers of drouzy age at midnight; old and young haue with his Tales chim'd Mattens till the Cocks crow in the morning; Batchelors and Maides with his Tales haue compassed the Christmas fire-blocke, till the Curfew Bell rings candle out; the old Shepheard and the young Plow boy after their dayes labour, haue carold out a Tale of Tom Thumbe to make them merry with: and who but little Tom, hath made long nights seeme short, & heauy toyles easie?'

Indeed incidents and situations in the tale are paralleled so closely in famous tales that had not at this time been recorded, that Tom's history almost seems to be the prototype fairy tale. Thus Tom, though no fairy himself, possesses that most useful means of fulfilling ambitions, a fairy godmother. Like Jack the Giant Killer he is on easy terms with royalty, while having little respect for the numbskull giants he encounters, particularly after his life has been simplified (as was Jack's) by the ability to make himself invisible, and to travel anywhere 'in a moment'. Tom even meets, like Jack, a giant who threatens (in vain of course) to grind his bones to make his bread. And the story deteriorates as it progresses, in so similar a manner to 'The History of Jack and the Giants', that one is almost persuaded it must emanate from the same storyteller.

Analysts of the folk tale like to point out that Tom's history is one of the swallow cycle; and that it is thus related to the story of Little Red Ridinghood who was devoured by a wolf, a kinship that others may find rather distant. It would seem more apt to describe Tom's history as a swallow cycle in itself, the little fellow being gulped down in turn by a cow, by a giant, and by a fish; and in extensions of the tale by a miller and by a salmon. In these repeated deglutitions the story is manifestly unimaginative; while some of the deliverances do little credit to seventeenth-century humour. Nineteenth-century editors, when presenting the story to the young, found certain modifications to

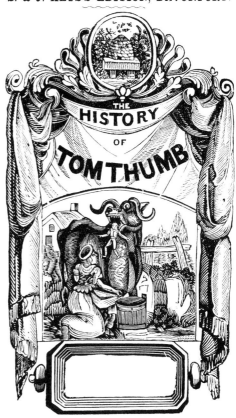

S. & J. KEYS'S EDITION, DEVONPORT.

The cover of a penny history of Tom Thumb printed at Devonport, *c.* 1835. The woodcut shows Tom being dropped from the cow's mouth, his usual manner of liberation in revised versions of the tale.

be necessary, and Tom was rarely permitted to pass beyond the cow's mouth, so that the evacuation could be comparatively seemly.

Tom Thumb has nevertheless remained a favourite character in English legendary lore; and his counterparts in Continental Europe such as *Le petit Poucet* in France (cf. 'Hop o' my Thumb' p. 128); *Daumesdick, Däumling,* and *Daumerling,* also swallowed by a cow, in Germany; and *Svend Tomling,* in Denmark, 'a man no bigger than a thumb, who would be married to a woman three ells and three quarters long', also have long histories. Further afield, the English imp may be

Tom Thumbe,

His Life and Death

Wherein is declared many Maruailous
Acts of Manhood, full of wonder,
and ſtrange merriments :

Which little Knight liued in King *Arthurs* time, and
famous in the Court of *Great-Brittaine.*

London Printed for *Iohn Wright.* 1630.

Title-page of *Tom Thumbe, His Life and Death,*
1630, showing Tom on King Arthur's horse. This
metrical rendering of the tale considerably added
to the story's popularity.

compared with *Vamuna* in India, and *Issun Boshi*
('Little One Inch') in Japan, who danced about in
an ogre's stomach, jabbing at it with his needle-
sword.

In Britain reprintings of the *History* have been
innumerable. (In America John Dunton was selling
an edition at his warehouse in Boston as early as
1686.) In 1630 a metrical version was in print,
*Tom Thumbe, His Life and Death: Wherein is
declared many Maruailous Acts of Manhood, full of
wonder, and strange merriments,* which takes in
Tom's last sickness, not described in the 1621
volume, though it may possibly have appeared in
the continuation of the story of which 'R. J.'
gave notice, but of which no copy has survived.
In 1711 William Wagstaffe parodied Addison's
appreciation of the ballad 'Chevy Chase' with
A Comment upon the History of Tom Thumb,
examining an edition of this metrical version which
he had found, he said, in 'the Library of a School-
Boy committed to my Charge'. In 1730 Henry
Fielding's tragedy *Tom Thumb* was produced at
the Haymarket Theatre, and subsequently con-
verted into an opera by Kane O'Hara. In mid-
eighteenth century, when books for juvenile
entertainment first appeared, Tom Thumb became
a most prolific author. Diminutive volumes with
titles such as *Tommy Thumb's Song Book* (1744),
Tommy Thumb's Little Story Book (*c.* 1760), and
Tom Thumb's Folio for Little Giants (*c.* 1767),
became a commonplace. In fact Tom's name was
more employed in nursery literature than that of
any other national hero.

In 1791 Ritson observed that it was needless to
dwell on the popularity of Tom Thumb's story.
'Every city, town, village, shop, stall, man,
woman, and child, in the kingdom, can bear
witness to it.' Today, when a new product comes
on the market, whether dwarf vegetable, small
cigar, or miniature transistor, it is liable to be
branded a 'Tom Thumb'; and any midget who
wishes to capitalize on his diminutiveness finds it
profitable to relate himself to Tom Thumb, as
Charles Stratton (1837–1883), 'General Tom
Thumb', discovered to his own and his sponsor's
satisfaction in the middle of the last century.

THE HISTORY OF
TOM THUMBE

Of the birth and Parentage of *Tom Thumbe*,
with his description and bignesse.

In the old time, when King *Arthur* ruled this land, the World was in a better frame then it is now: for then old plainnesse and ciuill society were companions for all companies: then, an vngarded Plowman might come vncontroled to a Royal Princes presence, and in those dayes the Countrey Husbandman was of the Kings Counsell, and in his russet Coate gaue as sound iudgement, as doe now many of our embrodred vpstarts in their robes of Tissue: for as then (in this Land) learning was geason,[1] and the chiefest discipline in the world was Martiall actiuitie.

Amongst many others of the Kings Councell, that attended in Court, there was a plaine Plowman, as then, called old *Thomas* of the Mountaine, which was the Kings owne Husbandman; for, as then, Princes maintained Shepheards, Neat-heards, Plough-men, & such like, to keepe their Cattel, and till their grounds, with like busines of houshold Husbandry. This *Thomas* of the Mountaine, being a man well growne in yeares, long marryed, hauing a wife (as he thought) sufficient to bring children; but not blessed with that wished happinesse, often complayned to her in this manner: saying, Oh Wife (quoth he) happy were I, if blessed with one Child: one Child though it were no bigger then my thumb, would make me happy: a child, of the very bignes of my thumb would bring me the greatest content in the world: Therfore would I haue thee (my deare wife) go to the Prophet *Merlin*, and of him learne the cause of thy barrennesse, and our wants in hauing children; he is a man, rather a diuell or spirit, cunning in all Arts and Professions, all sciences, secrets and discoueries, a coniurer, an inchanter, a charmer, hee consorts with Elues and Fayries, a Commaunder of Goblins, and a worker of Night-wonders: hee can shew the secrets of Nature, calculate childrens Birthes, and no doubt, but discouer the cause of thy barrennesse, and bee a meanes to procreate vs children: Away, and of him procure this good blessing of a child, be hee no bigger then my very Thumbe.

These reasons, and perswasions of olde *Thomas*, so encouraged and whetted on this longing woman his wife, that vp she got the next morning betime, and by the Sunnes rise, came to the Caue of old *Merlin*, which was the hollow trunke of a blasted Oke, all ouer growne with withered mosse, (for other house had hee none) whom shee found, as it were mumbling spels of incantation, making Characters in sand, with an Ebone staffe, to the great wonder of this poore affrighted Woman; who to satisfie her

[1]Scarce.

Husbands desire, deliuered the ful effect of her businesse and comming. To whom *Merlin* with a graue and solid countenance said as followeth:

> *Ere thrice the Moone her brightnes change,*
> *A shapelesse child by wonder strange,*
> *Shall come abortiue from thy wombe,*
> *No bigger then thy Husbands Thumbe:*
> *And as desire hath him begot,*
> *He shall haue life, but substance not;*
> *No blood, nor bones in him shall grow,*
> *Not seene, but when he pleaseth so:*
> *His shapelesse shadow shall be such,*
> *You'l heare him speake, but not him touch:*
> *And till the World to ending come,*
> *There shall be Tales told of Tom Thumbe.*

This *Ænygma*, or mysticall Riddle, no sooner deliuered, but home goes the merry old Wench to her husband, and tels of her good successe, and of the Oracle thus reuealed, how that within three moneths space *Merlin* had promised her a little sonne: against which time, the father not a little glad thereof, prouided all things fitting for such a purpose, so that no necessaries were wanting against his wiues lying in: but such a Child-bed lying in was neuer seene nor heard of; for thither came the Queene of Fayres to bee her Midwife, with her attendants the Elues and Dryades, with such like midnight dancing shadowes, who gaue most diligent assistance, at that painfull houre of this womans deliuerie. The child thus borne by the help of this midnights Midwife, the Queene of Fayres, had at the first minute it tooke life, the full and largest bignes that euer it grew to: which was (as his Father wished) the bignesse of his Thumbe; and therefore named *Tom Thumbe*, who neuer seemed older, nor yonger; bigger, nor smaller; stronger, nor weaker: but as he was at the first houre of his birth, so continued hee to the last minute of his life.

Of *Tom Thumbs* apparell, and of the sports he vsed amongst other Children.

Tom Thumbe, being thus by miracle begot & borne, in lesse then foure minutes grew to be a little man against which time the Queene of Fayres, his kind Midwife, & good Godmother, prouided him a very artificiall sute of apparell. First, a Hat made of an Oken Leafe, with one feather of a Tittimouse tayle sticking in the same for a plume: his Band and Shirt being both sowed together, was made of a Spiders Cobweb, only for lightnesse and soft wearing for his body: his cloth for his Doublet and Hose, the tenth part of a dramme of Thistledowne weaued together: his Stockings the outward Rinde of a greene Apple: his Garters two little hayres pulled from his Mothers eye-browes: as for his Shooes and Bootes, they were made of a mouses skin, tan'd into

Leather: the largenesse wherof was sufficient to make him twelue payre of Bootes, & as many shooes and Pantofles.[1] Thus furnisht forth like a proper young Gallant, hee aduentured foorth (though with great danger of the windes blowing him away) into the streets, amongst other children to play for Pins, Points,[2] Counters, and such like, but seldome played hee bankerupt: for like an inuisible Knight, he would at his pleasure (vnseene) diue into his play-fellows pockets: where (before) hauing lost, would there againe renew his stock, and now and then, when hee pleased, would he creep into their least cherrybags, and Pin-boxes. But on a time, it so hapned, that for these his nimble flights of actiuitie, he was most grieuously punished and imprisoned: for one of his play-fellowes kept him fast pind vp in his pinbox the whole time of schooling, without either meate, drinke, ayre, or light though indeed hee could haue fasted for euer without foode or sustenance, a gift that his Godmother the Queene of Fayries had giuen him at the houre of his birth: yet for all this, *Tom Thumbe*, hauing a desperate little spirit, like to his small bignesse, purposed to quittance these his former iniuries done by his craftie companions; for indeed many of them had serued him so.

How by art *Tom Thumbe* hung black Pots and Glasses on the beames of the Sunne, as vpon a line or cord: and of the successe.

Tom Thumb, remembring his former imprisonment in his companions pinboxes, and Cherry-bags, beate so together his nimble braines, that he deuised a pretty reuenge: It so fell out, as his playfellowes & acquaintance were playing together, hee got some of his mothers blacke Pots and Glasses, and most articifialy hangd them vpon a Sunne-beame, that shone in at the Schoole-house window, at a little creuice, that made it seeme like a small straight line or cord, vpon which hee orderly, to the others imagina-tions, hung vp his Pots and Glasses all on a row.[3] Which pretty trick when the rest saw, they likewise got of their mothers Pots & glasses, and in proffering to doe the like, they broke them all in pieces: for which doings, they had not onely the mockage of *Tom*, but thereby wonne to themselues euery one a sound breching: and euer after that, to their more disgrace, there was a Rime made amongst the Schoole-boyes, as hereafter followeth.

If thou wilt from whipping,
    keepe safely thy bum,
Take heed of the pastimes,
    here taught by Tom Thumbe:

Young Schollers are knauish
    and apter to learne
A tricke that's unhappy,
    then good to discerne.

[1] Slippers.

[2] Metal-tagged laces used to fasten clothes. At this time points were both playthings and wealth to children, along with pins and counters.

[3] This 'pleasant game', notes Palgrave, 'is borrowed from the pseudo-hagiography of the Middle Ages. It is found not only in one of the spurious gospels, but also in the legend of St Columbanus, who, as we are told, performed a similar miracle by hanging his garment on a sunbeam.'

How *Tom Thumbe* fell into his Mothers pudding Bowle:
and of the first originall of those Puddings
now called *Tom Thumbs*.

Tom Thumbe for these aforesaid merry tricks, was denied the fellowship of his Schoole-fellowes and companions, which made him with great griefe stay at home in his fathers house, and to be gouerned onely by his mothers direction. But it so fell out, that about Christmas time, his father had killed a Hogge, and his mother was to make Puddings. And hauing all things ready: as Bloud, Oatemeale, Suet, Salt and Spice all mingled, and well seasoned together in a greate Bowle of wood; vpon the side whereof, *Tom* was to sit (in stead of a Candlesticke) to hold the Candle, and giue her light, which he did so mannerly, as if hee had bin brought vp a Candle holder. But now marke the euent: ether *Tom* fell asleepe, or else being a little too nimble, or of too light a timberd body, that of a suddaine hee tipt and fell into the Pudding batter, quite ouer head and eares Candle and all, the which his mother spying, made hast with all speed to recouer him, but there shee found the Candle but not her Sonne: for whome after shee had searched a long time, and not finding him, supposed him to be drowned: with griefe she ouerpassed her losse in a short time, (I might say a minutes space) especially considering him to be a child (for his littlenesse,) more disgracefull, then comfortable. So falling againe to her businesse, shee tooke vp her small Sonne, and in stead of a piece of fat, put him at vnawares into one of her Puddings, which was of the largest size: the which, with many others, shee cast into a kettle then boyling ouer the fire. But now *Tom* feeling the scalding liquor, and being in the middle of this Pudding, made such a rumbling and tumbling vp and downe the Kettle, that all the rest flew ouer into the fire, choosing rather to be roasted, then sodden: Some without skins, some without fashion, some brok in pieces, some halfe sod, some one way, some another as if the Diuell and old *Merlin* had beene amongst them.

This accident, or rather hurlyburly, amongst *Toms* mothers puddings, made her thinke that they were either bewitcht or fore-spoke by some vnlucky tongue. Wherevpon, at that very instant time, comes to the doore, a sturdy beging Tinker, and asked an almes for good Saint *Iohns* sake: which the Old Woman heareing, (&

perceuing the vnrulines of that pudding in the Kettle) runs to the same, and gaue it to the Tinker: who being therewith well pleased, into his budget he puts it, and hyes him away as fast as his legs can beare him. But farre had he not gone, but the Pudding beganne to rumble and tumble in the Tinkers budget, as it had done before in the Pudding Kettle: which so affrighted the poore Tinker, that in going over a stile, hee farted for very feare. Marry gip, good man Tinker, quoth *Tom Thumbe*; are you farting ripe with a wannion?[1] hereupon the tinker (as he thought) hearing the Diuell at his backe, threw downe budget, Pudding, tooles and all, and ran away as fast as his legges could beare him, not once looking backe, till hee was out of all the hearing of *Tom Thumb*, or the sight of his budget.

The Tinker being thus gone, and *Tom Thumbe* freed from his greasie Leather imprisonment, hee eate himselfe at libertie from his blacke bondage, and returned home againe to his mothers house: where afterwards he told what had hapned, and how he was carryed away bound vp in the Puddings belly; which happy escape and aduenture not a little reioyced his old Father, and Mother, betwixt whom, and amongst many others, there arose a name & title, belonging to al puddings of the like roundnesse and thicknesse, and to be called *Tom Thumbes*: Which name to the honour of all Puddings, continues to this day.

How his mothers Red Cow, at one bit ate vp *Tom Thumbe*, as he sate vnder a Thistle.

These fearefull dangers before rehearsed, being thus happily ouerpassed, durst not by his mother of a long time bee suffered to depart out of her presence, but either she lockt him in her Cupbord for feare of losing him, or else tyed him to a Brickbat with a Packthrid, doubting the wind should blow him away: or else kept him in her pocket for his more securitie: But yet for all this, another mischance befell him. For on a time, as his mother went a milking, *Tom* had a great desire to goe with her, and to see that kinde of womanly housewifery: Whereupon, she tooke vp her Sonne and put him into her empty Milke-payle, and so bore him to the fielde: where being come, and the day very cold, shee set him downe vnder a Thistle for a shelter to keepe him warme, and so goes a milking of her Kine: but before shee had dispatched halfe her businesse, there comes a Red Cow, and at one bit eates vp this little man, her Sonne, Thistle and all: But whether it was for cowardlinesse or valor to sit still, I knowe not, but poore *Tom* was eaten vp at one mouthfull, where without chewing he went as easily downe into the Cowes belly, as if he had beene made of a docke leafe. But now all this while his mother not missing him, but still milked on till her payle grew full, & then being ready to goe home, she looked for her sonne *Thomas*, where she

[1] With a vengeance.

Woodcuts from Mozley and Sons' penny edition of
The Life and Adventures of Tom Thumb, c. 1840

neither found him nor the thistle where she left him. Whereupon she went vp and downe calling for *Tom*, but no *Tom* was heard of. At last with great earnestnes (being much affrighted with this losse,) she went crying amongst her Kine, Where art thou *Tom?* Where art thou, *Tom?* Here, Mother (quoth he) in the Red Cowes belly: in the Red Cowes belly, mother, still cryed he, vntill such time as she perceiued his place of abiding, where (no doubt) but *Tom* was in a pitifull taking, but the poore Cow in a farre worse, hauing such a nimble timberd fellow dancing Trench-more[1] in her belly. But to conclude, the poore beast could not be deliuered of her troublesome burthen, till a laxatiue drinke cast into her belley, had turned him out in a Cowturd. Who all besmeared as he was, went home with his mother to be made cleane. This was another of *Tom Thumbes* most dangerous aduentures, which he most happily escaped.

How *Tom Thumbe*, in stead of a wheat corne, was carried away in a Rauens mouth.

Another time *Tom Thumbe*, being desirous to helpe his Father driue the plowe, and in seedes-time to see the manner of his sowing wheate, the which the olde man agreed to, and taking his litle sonne vp, he put him into his pocket, and being come to the field where his land lay, he set *Tom* in one of his horses eares, and so droue all the rest round about the Land, as if hee had gone by their sides, so propper, so fine, and so nimble a light fellow was this *Tom Thumbe*, that the horses eare serued for a shelter to keepe him from raine and foule weather, and likewise preserued him as well from drowning in a beasts footestep, as from the windes blowing him away, and many times from loosing himselfe in Chaffe and Prouender, where surely he had beene eaten vp amongst horses: but yet for all these great cares thus taken by his Father, another most strange and dangerous euent behappened him, for as his father went a sowing wheat vp and down the land, *Tom Thumbe* was appointed to scarre away Crowes, who with a cudgell made of a Barley straw, for that purpose, stood most manfully in the middle of the land, crying, Shooe, shooe, Crow, shooe; but amongst the rest, there came a huge blacke Rauen, that in stead of a wheate corne, carried poore *Tom* quite away, where he was not of a long time heard of, either by Father or Mother: which great losse of this their little Son they long time afterward mourned for, with many a sad and heauy lamentation, spending whole dayes and weekes, and weary iourneys in seeking him vp and downe, but all in vaine; there was not a Crowes nest in a whole countrey but they searched, nor a Church steeple within ten miles, nor a Pidgeon-hole but they looked

[1]A boisterous country dance.

into, nor a Counterpit[1] amongst boyes, nor hardly a cherrypit was forgotten: but all lost labour, *Tom* was not to be found, but vtterly lost and gone for euer, without all hope of recouery to be got againe; whose want (as I said before) bred in his old Parents hearts most heauy and long lamentations: where wee will leaue them now mourning, and tell of their lost litle sonnes succeeding fortunes and aduentures.

How *Tom Thumbe* fell in at a Chimney top, and what happened to him there.

Tom Thumbe, being thus taken vp by a Rauen (as you heard) in stead of a graine of wheat, was carried in her beake ouer a great forrest, where in all the way of this her long flight, *Tom Thumbe* did nothing but cry, Shough, shough Crowe, shough, in this maner affrighting the poore Rauen in her flight, that she durst neither swallow him downe her maw, nor let him fall out of her beake, vntill such time, as what with faintnesse in flying, or almost starued with hunger, being quite tyred with this her heauy burthen and long iourney, she was constrained to rest on the top of an olde Castle wall moted round about with an exceeding deepe riuer, which belonged to an ancient and neuer conquered Giant, that onely there inhabited without any other company: This Rauen (as I said) resting on the top of the Castle, and being ouerwearied, *Tom Thumbe* with a nimble skip suddenly escaped both from her beake and tallons, and with much lightnesse leapt vp to the top of the Castle chimney, where being set, and looking downe, he espied the Gyant sitting by his fire, boyling, broyling and roasting the ioynts & quarters of men, deuouring them all one after another, legs, armes & heads bit by bit till they were all eaten vp at last: which fearful sight so amazed *Tom Thumbe*, that he knew not what to doe, nor tell how to get away; to escape was impossible: for the Castle wall was too high for him to get downe, and the riuer too deepe for such a little fellowe to wade ouer: so, being in these fearefull and dangerous doubts, of a sodaine came a puffe of winde, and blew poore *Tom* downe into the Gyants Chimney, where he grew almost besides his wits, to see himselfe by the fire side: whom when the Gyant saw, thinking him to be some Fairy, or a spirit come thither by miracle, ran with an eager fury to catch him; but so nimble and quicke was this little fellowe, that the Gyant had no feeling of him, for when he caught him in his hand, hee slipt out betweene his fingers, and being in his armes, he crept out betweene his elbowes; so that neither strength nor policy could take him. Thus for that time escaped little *Tom*, where for his more securitie, he crept into a mouse-hole, and there safely for that night slept hee freely from the Gyants intended cruelty.

How *Tom Thumbe* became the Gyants man, and what happened to him in that seruice.

Tom Thumbe being thus safe in lodging, (I meane in the Mouse hole) put the Gyant in a great wonder, maruelling what was become of him, for which cause hee went

[1] Hole into which counters were pitched.

The giant determines to find out whether Tom is edible. Illustration by Alfred Crowquill (A. H. Forrester) for an edition of *Tom Thumb* published 1844

supperlesse to bed, but could not sleepe all that night following for thinking of *Tom Thumbe*, which he deemed to bee some strange creature, in that he had so nimbly escaped his clutches: therefore in the middle of the night, hee rose vp and tooke his clubbe, (which was the whole arme of an Oke) and went vp and downe the Castle in the darke, (for light had he none) crying with a roaring voyce, in this maner following,

> Now fi, fee, fau, fan,
> I feele smell of a dangerous man:
> Be he aliue, or be he dead,
> Ile grind his bones to make me bread.[1]

These fearefull speeches, thus thundred out by this Gyant, put poore *Tom* into a pittifull taking not knowing what to doe, nor how to behaue himselfe; yet at last considered, it was but misery to be thus imprisoned in this litle closet of darknesse, and thought it better (then to lye there) to aduenture foorth and submit himselfe to the Gyants mercy, which most willingly he accepted of, and employed this his new litle man, about his houshold businesse: wherevpon *Tom* became very diligent & seruiceable: for the Gyant had no other Cat to catch Mise and Rats, but *Tom;* no other broome to sweepe cobwebs from any corner of his house but *Tom;* no other key to open his lockes, but *Tom;* so *Tom* was very fitting and nimble for any businesse whatsoeuer. But now marke the euent: the Gyant on a time had a litle roastmeat to be laid to the fire, & *Tom* must be the turn-spit: whereupon, sitting in the Chimney-corner vpon a litle chip of wood to turne the spit, holding a spoone before him to keepe the heate from his face, (for indeede the spoone couered his whole body) the Gyant now thinking to take *Tom* at the aduantage, and to know whether hee was a humane creature, or a spirit, of a sudden catched at *Tom*, purposing to grinde the poore fellowes bones and body into pieces; but *Tom* hauing more then an ordinary nimblenesse in himselfe, did, (when the Gyant tooke hold of him) giue a skippe downe (vnchewed) into his throat, and so into his belly, and there kept such a rumbling and tumbling in his guts, as if hee would haue gnawne a hole quite thorow: it little booted the Gyant to rest in quiet, for he thought the Diuell or his dam had plaide at Tennis in his paunch: therefore in a fury hyed he vp to the toppe of his Castle wall, where he disgorged his stomacke, and cast out his burthen,

[1]See footnote to 'Jack the Giant Killer', p. 63.

at least three miles into the Sea, (vpon the bankes whereof this Castle stood) where *Tom Thumbe* was most brauely entertained by a Fishe, which swallowed him downe aliue, in which watry dwelling he remained, till the same Fishe was taken, and giuen for a present to King *Arthurs* Table, where this noble & aduenturous little Gallant was found, and for the strangenesse of his stature, accepted of for his Highnesse Dwarfe, and so by this means *Tom Thumbe* became a Courtier.

From Mozley's edition of
Tom Thumb, c. 1840

Of *Tom Thumbes* behauiour in Court, and the honours by him atchieued there.

Tom Thumbe being now in Court, became a companion for Ladies and Gentlewomen, and so braue minded that not any in King *Arthurs* Palace gained more fauours then hee did, insomuch that the Ladies and Gentlewomen could seldome bee without him; for his company was so pleasing, that many times they gaue him leaue to sleepe vpon their knees, and now and then in their pockets, with many such like priuate places, and withall to sit vpon their pinpillowes, and play with their pinnes, and to runne at tilt against their bosomes with a bul-rush; for bigger weapon was hee not able to manage. But now marke what happened: vpon a time King *Arthur* appointed a royall triumph in his Court, with great reuelling and masking to be holden amongst his Knights, where Sir *Lancelot-du-Lake*, Sir *Triamor*, and Sir *Tristram*, all of the round Table, performed many noble acts of Cheualry: amongst which worthy Gallants, *Tom Thumbe* would not sit out, and being then in great fauour, to his vtmost skill, would approue himselfe a right Courtier; whereupon, amongst them all, in presence of the King, Queene, and others of the Nobilitie, hee requested one of the Maydes of Honour to hold foorth her hand, where, vpon the Palme thereof he daunced a most excellent Galliard, to the wonderfull and great admiration of all the beholders; for which noble performance, were many rich guifts bestowed vpon him, as well by strangers as Peeres of the Land; amongst the rest, the King himselfe gaue him a gold Ring from his owne finger, the which *Tom Thumbe* wore for a girdle, as a fauour about his middle, for it was the iust compasse of his body to hoope it in round.

How *Tom Thumbe* grew daily into more fauour with the King, and of a boone obtained of his Highnesse.

King *Arthur* seldome sate amongst his Knights of the round Table, but *Tom Thumbe* was in company, either amongst their spangled feathers, or sitting vpon the pommel of the Kings own chaire, such great delight had his Highnesse in his company, that he seldome rode abroad, but *Tom* was cockered vpon his saddle-bow, where alwaies when it rained, would he creepe in at a button-hole of the Kings doublet to keepe himselfe dry; where being settled so neere his Highnesse heart, that he continually obtained what hee asked for, and now hauing opportunity fitting to beg a boone, and withall remembring his old father and mother, whom he had not of a long time seene, he requested of the King to giue him a burthen of money, no more then his backe could carry, from his Treasury, therewithal to relieue his father & mother in their old dayes: which request no sooner obtained, but away goes *Tom Thumbe*, and loades himselfe with a burthen of money from the Kings Treasury, which was in all, no more but a poore three-pence, the whole waight that his body could carry at one time: so trauelling two dayes and two nights, with long labour, he gat some thirty yardes from King *Arthurs* Court, some part of the way towards his Fathers house, that being all the iourney he was able to goe in fourty eight houres, bearing so huge and heauy a burthen vppon his shoulders: so from time to time, and from iourney to iourney, he came at last (though with great wearinesse) to his Fathers doore, not in all distant from King *Arthurs* Pallace, aboue three quarters of a mile; whom when his Father and Mother beheld, for very ioy they swouned; but recouering themselues, his Mother tooke him vp in her handkercher for feare of hurting his bones, and carried him into the great hall, where she set him in a Wal-nut-shell (in stead of a chaire) by a good fire to warme himselfe. Where after a little refreshing, and much reioycing, hee deliuered vp the great masse of treasure giuen him by King *Arthur*, which hee had brought with such long iournies, and great paines to his father & mother. The money receiued, they got him to supper, where the cloath was laid vpon his mothers hand, &

the seruice was the curnell of a hazell-nut, of which he eate but the third part, and the rest serued him sufficiently for foure meales after, yet grew he sometimes sicke by eating so much at one time.

Thus after that *Tom Thumbe*, with his Father and Mother, had ryoted for certaine moneths, Time called him away to his charge in Court: but not knowing how to get thither, by reason of a great Flood that was risen by a few Aprill drops, hee grewe into a very great melancholly, and made most heauy lamentations. Whereupon his Father hauing a ready, and quicke fore-casting wit, but a farre stronger breath, tooke a birding trunke of Wood,[1] and put his sonne *Thomas* therein, and at one blast: blew him into King *Arthurs* Court: Where (after this his great iourney) hee was entertained with Triumphs and much Reuelling.

Of the gifts that the Queene of Fayries gaue her god-sonne: and of the rare and excellent vertues thereof.

Tom Thumbes renowne and honours, growing to the full height of Fame in this Kingdome, caused people to come from all parts of the Land to visit him: some with one present, some with another, to bestow vpon him. Amongst the rest, his olde Godmother the Queene of Fayries came for to see him, and to witnesse what Fame and good Fortunes had befallen him.

But so it happened, that she found her little God-sonne asleepe (in the Kings Garden) vpon the toppe of a Red Rose new blowne. And being then iust highnoone-tide, (her chiefest time of liberty to worke wonders in) she stood inuisibly before him, stroaking downe the sweaty droppes with her vnfelt hand from his little forehead, which cast him into a most sweete and pleasurable dreame, and withall bestowed foure of the most rarest guifts of the world vpon him, which she left there lying by against his awaking. First, an inchanted Hat, the which by wearing hee should know, what was done in all parts of the world. A Ring likewise inchanted, that hauing it vpon his finger, hee might goe if hee pleased into any place vnseene, and walke inuisible. Thirdly, a Girdle, that by wearing it, should change him into what shape soeuer he desired. And lastly, a payre of shooes, (that being on his feete) would in a moment carry him to any part of the earth, and to be any time where hee pleased. Thus with a feruency of loue blessed shee him, and departed. Whereupon *Tom Thumbe* awaked, as out of a golden slumber, & found these aforesaid guifts as his good Godmother had left him, the which being well considered of, (and as it was reuealed to him in his sleepe) he first tooke the Hat & put it vpon his head: whereupon he was presently inspired with the knowledge of al things in the world; and at that very instant knew, what was done in K. *Arthurs* Court, and what the King himself was a doing. Next, putting on the ring, he went as he wished inuisible, and caught birds as they sate in bushes: fowles in the

[1] A birding trunke is a blow-gun for shooting birds.

ayre, & such like. Then putting on the Girdle, hee wisht himselfe a Gyant, then a Dwarfe, then a fish, then a worme, then a man, &c. Lastly, putting on the Shooes, which no sooner on his feete, but he was carried as quicke as thought into another world, where hee sawe wonders, as men without heads, their faces on their breasts, some with one legge, some with one eye in the forehead, some of one shape, some of another: then by and by was he come backe againe into King *Arthurs* Court.

How *Tom Thumbe* riding forth to take the ayre,
met with the great *Garagantua*, and of
the speach that was betweene them.

Tom Thumbe on a time being weary, crept into a Ladies pocket, and there rested himselfe, this Lady forgetting of her seruant *Thomas*, suddenly pulled foorth her handkercher, and with her handkercher *Tom Thumbe:* she blowing her nose with it so frighted poore *Thomas*, that the little Gentleman fell in a sownd, but they fetched him againe with the hundred part of an Aquauity drop: yet for all their care that they tooke hee was troubled with a great Palsie, and none of the Kings Physitions could cure him. The King grieued to see his little Gentleman in this taking, and for his recouery spared no cost, for he sent for the chiefe Physition to King *Twaddell*, which was King of the Pigmies, (which King and his subiects are but two foote high from the ground,)[1] this Physition being litle of body, but great of skill, soone found out his disease and cured him.

  Tom Thumbe being cured rod foorth in his Coach one day to take the ayre, his Coach was made of halfe a Wal-nut-shell, the wheeles were made of foure button-mouldes, and foure blew flesh-flyes drewe it: Riding in this maner by the Wood side he chanced to meete the great *Garagantua*,[2] who was riding also to solace himselfe, his horse being of that great bignesse, as is described in the booke of his honourable deedes, and himselfe being in height not inferiour to any steeple. *Tom Thumbe* seeing of him, asked what he was? *Garagantua* answered him, that he was the onely wonder of the world, the terror of the people, and the tamer of man and beast: stay there said *Tom Thumbe*, for I am to be wondred at as much as thy selfe any waies can bee: for I am not onely feared, but also loued: I cannot onely tame men and beastes, but I also can tame thy selfe. Hereat *Garagantua* fell into such a laughter that the whole earth where hee stood shooke which made *Tom Thumbe* in all hast to ride away, and to beate his winged steades into a false Gallop.

  Garagantua seeing him in this feare desired him to stay, and they would talke

---

[1]In the sixteenth and seventeenth centuries a name for a very small person, such as might be a subject of King Twaddell (or Twadle), was *twattle*, a term presumably related. Cotgrave in his French-English *Dictionarie*, 1611, defined *Nain* as 'a dwarfe, or dandiprat, an elfe, or twattle; one that's no higher then three horse-loaues.'

[2]Although Rabelais had not yet been translated, Garagantua or Gargantua was well known to the Elizabethans, and personified largeness and great voraciousness. Thus in *As You Like It*, III ii, 'You must borrow me Gargantuas mouth first'; and in Ben Jonson's *Every Man in His Humour*, II i, 'Your Garagantua breech cannot carry it away so'.

Tom Thumb entertaining the king and queen. From *The History of Tom Thumb*, one of 'Nelson's Oil Colour Picture Books for the Nursery', *c*. 1864

familiarly, who was the better man, and could doe the most wonders. Hereto *Tom Thumbe* consented, and caused his Coach to stand, and they began to dispute dialogue maner as followeth. Dwarfe, quoth *Garagantua*, I can blow downe a Steeple with my breath, I can drowne a whole Towne with my pisse, I can eate more then a hundred, I drinke more then a hundred, I carry more then a hundred, I can kill more then a hundred: all this can I do, now tell what thou canst doe?

I can doe more then this, saide *Tom Thumbe*, for I can creepe into a keyhole, and see what any man or woman doe in their priuate chambers, there I see things that thou art not worthy to know. I can saile in an egge-shel, which thou canst not: I can eate lesse then a Wren, and so saue victuals: I can drinke lesse then a Sparrow, therefore I am no drunkard: I cannot kill a Rat with my strength, and therefore am no murtherer: these qualities of mine are better then thine in all mens iudgements, and therefore great monster I am thy better.

Hereat *Garagantua* was madde and would with his foote haue kicked downe the whole wood, and so haue buried *Tom Thumbe: Tom* seeing of it, with his skill so inchanted him that he was not able to stur, but so stood still with one leg vp, till *Tom Thumbe* was at his lodging: Hereat *Garagantua* was much vexed, but knew not how to helpe himselfe.

How *Tom Thumbe* after conference had with
great *Garagantua* returned, and how he
met with King *Twadle*.

Tom Thumbe being somewhat well at ease by taking of the fresh aire returned backe againe to the Court of King *Arthur*, who no sooner being come, but great preparation was made for the entertainement of so tall a person, as that the officers of the house with all their seruants were in a sweat to prouide for this tall Sir *Thomas Thumbe* his dinner.

This entertainment being ended, K. *Arthur* sent for *Tom Thumbe*, & being come, withdrew themselues into a priuate roome, where *Tom* told King *Arthur* what strang accidents befell to him in meeting of great *Garagantua*, and of their conference together; as likewise of their exployts: and afterward how by his skill he enchanted him in the wood where they met, and there left him: whereat K. *Arthur* was wonderfully amazed, hearing of the strength of that mighty Gyant *Garagantua*.

Then he told K. *Arthur* how he met with K. *Twadle* being King of the Pigmes, a man of mighty stature in comparison of *Tom Thumbe*, being not two foote high, this stout King did he ouerthrow at Tilt both horse and man: and all these things did he performe by vertue that was in the guifts which his godmother the Queene of Fairies did bestow vpon her godsonne *Tom Thumbe*: which was his Hat of knowledge, his Ring which made him goe inuisible, his Girdle which made him bee what he wisht to be either man or beast, & lastly his shooes, which being on his feet was on a sudden in any part of the world, & in the twinkling of an eye was in King *Arthurs* Court againe.

JACK THE GIANT KILLER

Sir Francis Palgrave's pronouncement (generally attributed to Sir Walter Scott) that, 'Jack, commonly called the Giant Killer,' landed in England 'from the very same keels and warships which conveyed Hengist and Horsa, and Ebba the Saxon,' has often been echoed by the nursery historians. Certainly the tenor of Jack's tale and details of more than one of the tricks with which he outwits the giants, have prototypes in Northern mythology. In the Prose Edda of Snorri Sturluson, written about 1220, the giant Skrymir is as wary of Thor, his travelling companion, as was Jack when staying the night with the Welsh giant. Before going to sleep he makes a mound in his sleeping-place—prudently as it turns out—to represent his head. When Thor with his mighty hammer strikes, as he thinks, Skrymir's head, Skrymir who is in fact Utgard-Loki, the king of Utgard, inquires if a leaf has fallen from a tree. When Thor strikes again Skrymir wonders whether an acorn has fallen. And when Thor strikes yet again, delivering the fiercest blow of which he is capable so that the head of the hammer sinks in to the handle, Skrymir complains only that a bird has dropped something on his face.

A similar incident occurs in the Swedish tale of 'The Herd-Boy and the Giant'. When the herd-boy rests for the night in the giant's home he takes the precaution of placing a milk churn in his bed, and himself hides behind the door. The next day the giant is astonished to see him alive and well. 'I thought I struck thee dead with my club' is his morning greeting; and the pert lad replies: 'I rather believe I felt in the night as if a flea had bitten me'.

In the same tale the herd-boy sits down with the giant to eat porridge, first tying a bag to his chest, as Jack did; and he puts two spoonfuls of porridge in his bag for every spoonful he eats. When the giant asks how so small a person can eat so much, the lad confides that, when full, he slits his stomach so that he can eat as much again; and taking a knife he rips open the bag so that the porridge pours out. The dolt of a giant (in fairy tales all giants are stupid) is entranced by the trick, takes a knife to his own stomach, and kills himself.

This tale, it would seem, shares an ancestor with that of 'The Valiant Little Tailor', a story that in itself has wide distribution, and was collected in Hesse by the Grimm brothers. In fact it will be appreciated that in the domain of folklore the bamboozling of giants, ogres, ghouls, griffins, dragons, the minotaur, and other fearsome creatures, is so pleasant to the youthful imagination as to be of universal expression, particularly if the gratitude of a well-endowed maiden is to be the reward. Thus world-wide analogues offer no surety of Jack's antiquity—any more than do his possession of a cloak of invisibility, cap of knowledge, shoes of swiftness, and sword of sharpness, all second-hand articles which he seems to have acquired from Tom Thumb or from Northern mythology.

That stories about giants, and man-eating giants in particular, were rife around British hearths in days of old is apparent enough. King Arthur's bloody encounter with the giant of St Michael's Mount, the granite island fortress that may still be visited off the toe of Cornwall, is related both in Sir Thomas Malory's *Le morte Darthur*, printed by Caxton in 1485, and, even earlier, in Geoffrey of Monmouth's popular *Historia Regum Britanniae*, written in the twelfth century. In *The Complaynt of Scotland* published in 1549, one of the tales the shepherds told was 'the tayl of the giantis that eit quyk men'. In *King Lear*, written probably in 1605, Edgar, mouthing snatches of old verse during his assumed madness, lets drop the lines:

> Childe Rowland to the darke Tower came,
> His word was still, fie, foh, and fumme,
> I smell the blood of a Brittish man.

And nine years before *King Lear*, Thomas Nashe, in *Haue with You to Saffron-Walden*, not only showed that he, too, knew the giant's fulmination, but gave a warning that we ourselves, perhaps, should take to heart:

'O, tis a precious apothegmaticall Pedant, who will finde matter inough to dilate a whole daye of the first inuention of Fy, fa, fum, I smell the bloud of an Englishman.'

Be this as it may, since the *cante-fable* which associates a Childe Rowland with the giant's rhyme is almost certainly of modern composition, and possibly a hoax, it would seem safe to think that Shakespeare knew a tale of blood-sniffing giants, such as those who made sport for nimble Jack.

The difficulty is that no mention of Jack the Giant Killer (or of Jack and the Beanstalk) has been found in sixteenth and seventeenth-century literature; and although a strong tradition of magical giant-killing tales has been found among the hill folk of British stock in the southern Appalachians,[1] no telling of the tale has been recorded in English oral tradition.

The story of Jack the Giant Killer, as we know it, appears to consist of a number of classic anecdotes strung together by an astute publisher in the not-so-long-ago. The earliest-known edition, styled *The History of Jack and the Giants*, was issued in two parts. Only the second part seems to exist, or to have existed (for, in keeping with its enchanted subject, the copy in the British Museum has vanished), but the record has it that it was printed by J. White of Newcastle in 1711, and that it contained, as its title-page set forth, a full account of Jack's

Victorious Conquests over the North Country Giants; destroying the inchanted Castle kept by Galligantus, dispers'd the fiery Griffins; put the Conjuror to Flight, and released not only many Knights and Ladies, but likewise a Duke's Daughter, to whom he was honourably married.

The suggestion that this continuation of the tale, at least, had been first published only a few years earlier is difficult to confute. *The History of Jack and the Giants* does not seem to have been one of the series of chapbooks listed in the late seventeenth century. It does not occur, where it might be expected, in William Thackeray's catalogue of 'small Books, Ballads and Histories' produced for sale by chapmen about 1689. It has not been found in several lists examined of petty books published in the first years of the eighteenth century. Nor does Jack seem to have been one of the folk heroes in the popular repertoire of Robert Powel, the puppet showman, who was operating at this time in Covent Garden. On the other hand *Jack and the Gyants* is referred to in *The Weekly Comedy*, 22 January 1708, as being 'formerly printed in small Octavo';[2] and Nicholas Amherst,

[1] See Isabel Gordon Carter, 'Mountain White Folklore: Tales from the Southern Blue Ridge', *Journal of American Folklore*, vol. XXXVIII, 1925, pp. 340–74; also Richard Chase, *The Jack Tales*, Cambridge, Mass., 1943.

[2] This reference occurs in a dialogue, notable only for its facetiousness, in which a speaker is making play with a hypothetical situation, so that when he says 'formerly' he apparently refers not to the past but to present reality.

Left: Jack's slaughter of Giant Blunderbore and friend, depicted by Alfred Crowquill in *Aunt Mavor's Nursery Tales*, 1858

Right: Jack dispatches the Cornish giant. Colour wood-engraving from Routledge's Shilling Toy Book *Jack the Giant Killer, c.* 1872

in the tenth number of *Terrae-Filius*, February, 1721, speaks of history professors 'who never read any thing' but Tom Thumb and Jack the Giant Killer. Indeed it is apparent that as the eighteenth century grew older Jack became a familiar character to all and sundry. A 'comi-tragical farce' entitled *Jack the Gyant-Killer* was performed at the Haymarket in 1730. Make-belief letters from Jack the Giant Killer were a feature of *A Little Pretty Pocket-Book*, 1744, the first book that John Newbery produced for the young. A political satire probably by Henry Brooke, *The last Speech of John Good, vulgarly called Jack the Giant-Queller*, was published about 1745.

Further, Henry Fielding, in the first chapter of *Joseph Andrews* (1742) speaks of

> 'John the Great, who, by his brave and heroic actions against men of large and athletic bodies, obtained the glorious appellation of the giant-killer.'

Dr Johnson admitted to Mrs Thrale that in an idle moment he had been reading Jack the Giant Killer, and hazarded that 'so noble a narrative' might rouse in him the soul of enterprise. Boswell declared that when a boy he had been much entertained by Jack the Giant Killer; and when he was twenty-three he bought himself a new copy from the printer in Bow Church-Yard. And William Cowper, born 1731, who was another who loved 'giant-killing Jack', commented on such a tale in his *Conversation*:

> A story, in which native humour reigns
> Is often useful, always entertains.

The text which follows is almost certainly that with which these literary giants were familiar two hundred years ago. It comes from a chapbook edition published in Shrewsbury, the first part being printed by J. Eddowes, the second part by J. Cotton and J. Eddowes. John Cotton and Joshua Eddowes are known to have been in partnership, supplying cheap literature to hawkers, from 1761 to 1765, and they may have been in business together before this, for Cotton, who seems to have died in 1765, had been in business in Shrewsbury since 1746, and Eddowes since 1749. Further, the text of their *History of Jack and the Giants* almost certainly derives, with little alteration, from a chapbook of the beginning of the century. The text is longer than that in the illustrated metropolitan editions, the style is more archaic, and the wording of the subtitle of Part II is convincingly similar to that of John White's edition of 1711.

Covers of three of the numerous penny and twopenny editions of *Jack the Giant Killer* issued in the middle years of the nineteenth century. These examples were printed in, respectively, London, Devonport, and Edinburgh.

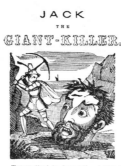

THE HISTORY OF
JACK AND THE GIANTS

PART THE FIRST

In the Reign of King *Arthur*, near the Lands-End[1] of *England*, namely, the County of *Cornwall*, there lived a wealthy Farmer, who had one only Son, commonly known by the Name of JACK the GIANT-KILLER: He was brisk, and of a lively ready Wit, so that whatever he could not perform by Force and Strength, he compleated by ingenious Wit and Policy, never was any Person heard of that could worst him; nay, the very Learned many times he baffled, by his cunning and sharp ready Inventions. For Instance, when he was no more than 7 Years of Age, his Father, the Farmer, sent him into the Field to look after the Oxen, which were then feeding in a pleasant Pasture: a Country Vicar, by chance one Day coming a-cross the Fields, called to *Jack*, and asked him several Questions; in particular, *How many Commandments are there? Jack* told him *There were Nine.* The Parson replied, *There are Ten.* Nay, quoth *Jack*, Mr. Parson, *you are out; it's true there were Ten, but you broke one with your Maid* Margery. The Parson replied, *Thou art an arch Wag*, Jack. Well, Mr. *Parson*, quoth *Jack*, You have asked me one Question, and I have answered it, I beseech you let me ask you another. *Who made these Oxen?* the Parson replied, *God made them, Child:* Now you are out again, quoth *Jack;* for God made them Bulls, but my Father and his Man *Hobson* made Oxen of them. These were the witty Answers of *Jack*. The Parson finding himself outwitted trudged away, leaving *Jack* in a Fit of Laughter.

In those Days the Mount of *Cornwall* was kept by a huge and monstrous Giant, eighteen Foot in Height, and about three Yards in compass, of a fierce and grim Countenance, the Terror of all the neighbouring Towns and Villages; his Habitation was a Cave in the midst of all the Mount. Never would he suffer any living Creature to inhabit near him: His Feeding was upon other Men's Cattle, which often became his Prey; for whensoever he wanted Food, he would wade over the main Land, where he would furnish himself with whatsoever he found; for the People at his Approach would forsake their Habitations, then would he seize upon their Cows and Oxen, of which he would make nothing to carry over on his Back half a Dozen at a Time; and as for their Sheep and Hogs, he would tie them round his Waste like Bandaliers.[2] This he for many Years had practised, so that great Part of the County of *Cornwall* was much impoverished by him.

But one Day *Jack* coming to the Town-Hall when the Magistrates were sitting in Consultation about this Giant, he asked them *What reward they would give to any Person*

[1] Cornishmen continue to speak of 'the Land's End', while the rest of the country refers to 'Land's End'.
[2] Bandaliers are here the little cases, each containing a charge for the musket, which soldiers hung from their shoulder belt.

that should destroy him? They replied, *he should have all the Giant's Treasure in recompence.* Quoth *Jack,* then I myself will undertake the Work.

Jack having undertaken the Task, he furnishes himself with a Horn, Shovel and Pick-ax, and over to the Mount he goes in the beginning of a dark Winter Evening, where he fell to work, and before Morning had digged a Pit two and twenty Feet deep, and almost as broad, covering the same over with long Sticks and Straw; then strowing a little of the Mould upon it, it appeared like the plain Ground; this done, *Jack* places himself on the contrary Side of the Pit, just about the dawning of the Day, when putting his Horn to his Mouth, he blew the same *Tan-tive, Tan-tive,* which unexpected Noise roused the Giant, who came running towards *Jack,* saying: *You incorrigible Villain, are you come here to disturb my Rest, you shall pay dearly for this; Satisfaction I will have, and it shall be this, I will have you whole, and broil you for my Breakfast.* Which Words were no sooner out of his Mouth, but he tumbled headlong into the Pit, whose heavy fall made the very Foundation of the Mount to shake. *O Giant,* quoth Jack, *where are you now; in faith you are gotten into* Lob's Pound,[1] *where I will plague you for your threatening Words: What do you think now of broiling me for your Breakfast, will no other Diet serve you but poor* Jack? Thus having tantalized the Giant for a while, he took him such a considerable Blow upon the Crown of his Head with his Pick-ax, that he tumbled down, and with a dreadful Groan died; this done, Jack threw the Earth in upon him, and so buried him. And then going and searching his Cave, he found much Treasure. Now when the Magistrates which employed him, heard the Work was over, they sent for him, declaring, that he should henceforth be called, *Jack the Giant-Killer,* and in Honour thereto, presented him with a Sword, together with an embroidered Belt, on which these Words were wrought in Letters of Gold.

Here's the right valiant Cornish *Man,*
Who slew the Giant Cormilan.[2]

The News of *Jack's* Victory was soon spread over the *Western* Parts, so that another Giant named *Blunderboar,* hearing of it, vowed to be revenged on *Jack,* if it ever was his Fortune to light on him; this Giant kept an inchanted Castle, situated in the midst of a loansome Wood. Now *Jack* about four Months after, walking by the Borders of the same Place, in his Journey towards *Wales,* he grew weary, and therefore sat himself down by the Side of a pleasant Fountain, where a deep Sleep suddenly seized him; at which Time the Giant coming there for Water found him, and by the Lines written

---

[1]Lob's pound was a popular name in the sixteenth, seventeenth, and eighteenth centuries for a prison, or any place of confinement.

[2]Giant Cormilan is alternatively named in eighteenth-century texts Cormelian, Cormoran, and Corinoran (possibly the Corinaeus of Geoffrey of Monmouth).

'Jack finds three ladies tied up by the hair of their heads.' Illustration by Hugh Thomson from *Jack the Giant Killer,* 1898

JACK FINDS THREE LADIES TIED UP BY THE HAIR OF THEIR HEADS

upon his Belt knew him to be *Jack*, who killed his Brother Giant; and therefore without making any Words, he snatches him upon his Shoulder for to carry him home to his inchanted Castle; now as they passed through a Thicket, the rustling of the Boughs awakened *Jack*, who finding himself in the Clutches of the Giant, he was strangely surprized, but it was but the Beginning of his Terror; for entering within the first Walls of his Castle, he beheld the Ground covered with Bones and Skulls of dead Men; the Giant telling *Jack* that his Bones would enlarge the Number of what he see there.

This said, he brought him into a large Parlour, there he beheld the bloody Quarters of some that were lately slain.

And in the next Room were Hearts and Livers, which the Giant, to terrify *Jack* told him, that Mens Hearts was the choicest of his Diet, for he commonly, as he said, eat them with Pepper and Vinegar, adding, that he did not question but that his Heart would make him a dainty Bit. This said, he locks poor *Jack* into a upper Room, leaving him there while he went to fetch another Giant, living in the same Wood, that he might partake of the Pleasure that they should have in the Destruction of poor *Jack*. Now while he was gone, dreadful Shrieks and Cries affrighted poor *Jack*, especially a Voice which continually cry'd,

> *Do what you can to get away,*
> *Or you'll become the Giant's Prey;*
> *He's gone to fetch his Brother, who*
> *Will Kill, and likewise Torture you.*

This dreadful Noise so amazed poor *Jack* that he was ready to run distracted, then going to a Window he opened a Casement where he beheld afar off the two Giants coming together. Now, quoth *Jack* to himself, my Death or Deliverance is at hand. There were strong Cords in the Room by him, of which he makes two, at the Ends of which he makes a Noose, and while the Giant was unlocking the Iron-Gate he threw the Ropes over their Heads, and drew the other End a-cross a Beam, which he pulled with all his main Strength, till he had throttled them, and then fastning the Ropes to the Beam he returned to the Window, where he beheld the two Giants black in the Face; then sliding down by the Rope, he came to their Heads, where the helpless Giants could not defend themselves, and drawing out his Sword, slew them both, and delivered himself from their intended Cruelty; then taking the Keys, he entered the Castle, where, upon strict Search, he found three fair Ladies, tied by the Hair of their Head, almost starved to death, who told *Jack*, *That their Husbands had been slain by the Giant, and they were kept many Days without Food, in order to feed upon the Flesh of their murdered Husbands, which they could not, if they were to Starve to death.* Sweet Ladies, quoth *Jack*, I have destroyed the Monster, with his brutish Brother, by which I obtained your Liberties; this said, he presented them with the Keys of the Castle, and so proceeded for his Journey in *Wales*.

Jack having but little Money, thought it prudent to make the best of his Way by Travelling hard, and at length losing his Road was belated, and could not get a Place of Entertainment, till coming to a Valley placed between two Hills, he found a large House in that lonesome Place, and by reason of his present Necessity, he took Courage to knock at the Gate, where to his Amazement, there came forth a monstrous Giant with two Heads, yet he did not seem to be so fiery as the others had been, for he was a *Welsh* Giant, and what he did was by private and secret Malice, under the false Shew of Friendship; for *Jack* telling his Condition he bid him Welcome, shewing him a Room with a Bed in it, where he might take his Night's Repose, whereupon *Jack* undresses, and as the Giant was walking away to another Apartment, *Jack* heard him mutter these Words to himself.

> *Tho' here you lodge with me this Night,*
> *You shall not see the Morning Light,*
> *My Club shall dash your Brains out quite.*

Say'st thou so, quoth *Jack*, that's like one of your *Welsh Tricks*, yet I hope to be cunning enough for you; then getting out of his Bed and feeling about in the dark, he found a thick Billet, which he laid in the Bed in his stead, and laid himself in a dark Corner of the Room, when in the dead of the Night came the *Welsh* Giant with his Club, and struck several heavy Blows upon his Bed, where *Jack* had laid the Billet, and then returned to his Chamber, supposing he had broken all the Bones in his Skin.

The next Morning *Jack* came to give him Thanks for his Lodging. Quoth the Giant, How have you rested? did you not feel something in the Night? No, nothing, quoth *Jack*, but a Rat, which gave me three or four Slaps with her Tail.

Soon after the Giant arose, and went to his Breakfast with a Bowl of Hasty-Pudding, containing four Gallons, giving *Jack* the like Quantity, who being loth to let the Giant know he could not eat with him, got a large Leathern Bag putting it artificially under his loose Coat, into which he secretly conveyed the Pudding, telling the Giant he would shew him a Trick; then taking a large Knife ript open the Bag, which the Giant supposed to be his Belly, and out came the Hasty-Pudding, which the Giant seeing cried out, *Cotsplut, hur can do that Trick hurself*: then taking a sharp Knife he ript open his own Belly from the Bottom to the Top, and out dropt his Tripes and Trolly-bubs, so that hur fell down dead. Thus *Jack* outwitted the *Welsh* Giant, and proceeded forward on his Journey.

King *Arthur's* Son desired of his Father to furnish him with a certain Sum of Money, that he might go seek his Fortune in the Principality of *Wales*, where a beautiful Lady lived, whom he heard was possessed with seven Evil Spirits; the King, his Father, counselled him against it, yet he would not be persuaded from it, so that he granted what he requested, which was one Horse loaded with Money, with another for himself to ride on.

Thus he went forth without any Attendance, and after several Days travel he came to a Market-town in *Wales*, where he beheld a vast Concourse of People gathered together, the King's Son demanded the Reason of it, and was told, *That they had*

'Taking a sharp knife he ripped open his own belly.' Engraving from *Tabart's Popular Stories*, 1804

arrested a Corps for many large Sums of Money, which the Deceased owed when he died. The King's Son replied, *It is Pity that Creditors should be so cruel.* Go bury the Dead, said he, and let his Creditors come to my Lodging, and their Debts shall be discharged.

Accordingly they came, and in such great Numbers, that before Night he had almost left himself Pennyless; now Jack the Giant-Killer being there, and seeing the Generosity of the King's Son, he was highly taken with him, and desired to be his Servant; it was agreed upon, and the next Morning they set forward; when riding out at the Town's End, an old Woman called after him, crying out, *He has owed me Two-pence this seven Years, pray Sir, pay me as well as the rest.* He put his Hand in his Pocket and gave it her, it being the last he had left.

Then the King's Son turning to *Jack*, said, I cannot tell how to subsist in my intended Journey. For that quoth Jack, take you no Thought nor Care, let me alone, we will not want; now *Jack* had a small Spil in his Pocket, and at Noon it served to give them a Refreshment, which done they had not a Penny left between them; the Afternoon they spent in Travel and familiar Discourse, 'till the Sun began to grow low, at which Time the King's Son said, *Jack*, since we have no Money, where can we think to lodge this Night? *Jack* replied, Master, we will do well enough, for I have an Uncle lives within two Miles of this Place, he is a huge and monstrous Giant with three Heads, he'll fight five hundred Men in Armour, and make them flee before him.

Alas! quoth the King's Son, what should we do there, he'll certainly chop us up in a Mouthful, nay we are scarcely enough to fill one of his hollow Teeth.

It is no Matter for that quoth *Jack*, I myself will go before and prepare the Way for you, therefore tarry and wait my Return.

He waits, and *Jack* rides full speed, when coming to the Gate of the Castle, he knocked with that Force which made the Neighbouring Hills resound.

The Giant, with a Voice like Thunder, roared out, who is there? He was answer'd, None but your poor Cousin *Jack:* Quoth he, what News with my poor Cousin *Jack?* He replied, dear Uncle, heavy News God-wot. Prithee what heavy News can come to me? I am a Giant, and with three Heads, and besides, thou knowest I can fight five hundred Men in Armour, and make them fly like Chaff before the Wind. O, but quoth *Jack*, here is the King's Son a coming with a thousand Men in Armour to kill you, and destroy all that you have. O Cousin *Jack*, that is heavy News indeed; I have a large Vault under Ground, where I will immediately run and hide myself, and thou shalt lock, bolt, and bar me in, and keep the Keys till the King's Son is gone.

Now *Jack* having secured the Giant, he returns and fetches his Master, and were both heartily merry with Wine, and of the Dainties which the House afforded. That Night they rested in pleasant Lodgings, while the poor Giant lay trembling in a Vault under the Ground.

In the Morning *Jack* furnished his Master with a fresh Supply of Gold and Silver, and then set him three Miles forward of his Journey, concluding he was then pretty well out of the Smell of the Giant, and then returned and let his Uncle out of his Hole, who asked *Jack* what he should give him for his Care, in Regard to see his Castle was not demolished. Why, quoth *Jack*, I desire nothing but the old rusty Sword, Coat and Slippers, which are at your Bed's-head. Quoth the Giant thou shalt have them, and prithee keep them for my Sake, for they are Things of excellent Use. The Coat will keep you invisible, the Cap will furnish you with Knowledge, the Sword cut in sunder whatever you strike, the Shoes are of extraordinary Swiftness; they may be Serviceable to you, and therefore take them with all my Heart. *Jack* takes them, and so follows his Master.

Jack having overtaken his Master, they soon arrived at the Lady's House, and finding the King's Son to be a Suitor, prepared a Banquet for him, which being ended, she wiped his Mouth with a Handkerchief, saying, you must show me this Tomorrow Morning, or else lose your Head. And with that put it into her Bosom.

The King's Son went to Bed right sorrowful, but *Jack's* Cap of Knowledge instructed him how to obtain it; in the Middle of the Night she calls upon her Familiar to carry her to *Lucifer*. *Jack* whipt on his Coat of Darkness, with his Shoes of Swiftness, and was there before her, for by Reason of his Coat they could not see him.

When she entered, she gave the Handkerchief to *Lucifer*, who laid it upon a Shelf, from whence *Jack* took it and brought it to his Master, who shewing it to the Lady the next Day, saved his Life.

The next Night she saluted the young Prince, telling him, He must show her the Lips to-morrow Morning that she kiss'd last this Night, or lose his Head. He replied, if you kiss'd none but mine, I will. 'Tis neither here nor there, said she, if you do not, Death is your Portion.

At Midnight she went as before, and was angry with *Lucifer* for letting the Handkerchief go. But now, said she, I shall be too hard for the young Prince, for I will kiss thy Lips, which she did.

Jack standing by, with his Sword of Sharpness, cut off the Devil's Head, and brought it under his invisible Coat to his Master, who laid it at the End of his Bolster, and in the Morning when she came up, he pulled it out by the Horns, and shewed her the Devil's Lips, which she kiss'd last.

Thus having answered her twice, the Inchantment broke, and the Evil Spirit left her, at which Time she appeared in all her Beauty, a sweet and virtuous Creature.

They were married the next Morning, and soon after returned with Joy to the Court of King *Arthur*, when *Jack* for his good Service, was made one of the Knights of the Round Table.

THE SECOND PART OF JACK AND THE GIANTS

Jack, having been successful in all his undertakings, and resolving not to be idle for the future, but to perform what service he could for the honour of his king and country; he humbly requested the king his master, to fit him forth with a horse and money to travel in search of strange and new adventures: For, saith he, there are many Giants yet living in the remote parts of this kingdom, and the dominion of *Wales;* to the unspeakeable damage of your majesty's liege subjects; wherefore, may it please you to give me encouragement, and I doubt not but in a short time to cut them off root and branch, and so rid the relm of those cruel Giants and devouring monsters in nature. Now, when the king had heard his noble propositions, and had duly considered the mischievous practices of those blood-thirsty Giants, he immediately granted what honest *Jack* requested; and, on the first day of *March*, being thoroughly furnished with all necessaries for his progress, he took his leave, not only of king *Arthur*, but likewise of all the trusty and hardy knights belonging to the round-table, who after much satisfaction and friendly greeting, parted; the king and nobles to their country palace, and *Jack* the Giant-killer to the eager pursuit of fortune's favour; taking with him the cap of knowledge, sword of sharpness, shoes of swiftness, and likewise the invisible coat, the better to perfect and compleat the dangerous enterprizes that lay before him.

Jack travel'd over vast hills and mountains, when at the end of three days he came to a large and spacious wood, through which he must needs pass; where, all on a sudden, to his amazement, he heard dreadful shrieks and cries; whereupon, casting his eyes around, to observe what it might be, beheld a Giant, with a worthy knight and his lady, whom he held by the hair of their heads in his hands, with as much ease, as if they had been but a pair of gloves; the sight of which melted honest *Jack* in tears of pity and compassion; wherefore, alighting from his horse, which he left tied to an

Woodcuts from a penny edition of *Jack the Giant Killer*, printed at Banbury, c. 1840

oak-tree, and then putting on his invisible coat, under which he carried his infallible sword, he came up to the Giant, and tho' he made several passes at him, yet nevertheless it could not reach the trunk of his body, by reason of his height, tho' he wounded his thighs in several places; but at length, giving him with both hands a swinging stroke, cut off both his legs, just below the knee, so that the trunk of his body made not only the ground to shake, but likewise the trees to tremble with the force of his fall; at which, by meer fortune, the knight and his fair lady escaped his rage. Then had *Jack* time to talk with him, setting his foot on his neck, saying, thou savage and barbarous wretch, I am come to execute upon you, the just reward of your villany. And with that, running him through and through, the monster sent forth a hideous groan; and so yielded up his life into the hands of the valiant conqueror *Jack* the Giant-killer, while the noble knight and virtuous lady were both joyful spectators of his sudden downfall, and their own deliverance. This being done, the courteous knight and his fair lady not only returned him hearty thanks for their deliverance, but also invited him home, there to refresh himself after the dreadful encounter, as likewise to receive some reward by way of gratitude for his good service; I cannot (says *Jack*) be at ease till I find out the den which was this monster's habitation. The knight hearing this, waxed right sorrowful, and replied, noble stranger, it is too much to run a second hazard: For note, this monster lived in a den under yonder mountain, with a brother of his, more fierce and fell than himself; and therefore if you should go thither, and perish in the attempt, it would be the heart-breaking both of me and my lady; therefore let me persuade you to go with us, and desist from any further pursuit. Nay, quoth *Jack*, if there be another, say; were there twenty, I would shed the last drop of blood in my body, before one of them should escape my fury; and when I have finished this task, I will come and pay my respects to you. So taking direction to their habitation, he mounted his horse, leaving them to return home, while he went in pursuit of the deceased Giant's brother.

Jack had not rid past a mile and a half before he came in sight of the cave's mouth, near to the entrance of which he beheld this other Giant, sitting upon a huge block of timber, with a knotted iron club lying by his side, waiting (as he supposed) for his brother's return with his barbarous prey, his goggling eyes appearing like terrible flames of fire: his countenance grim and ugly, for his cheeks appeared like a couple of large flitches of bacon: Moreover, the bristles of his beard seemed to resemble rods of iron-wire; his locks hung down upon his brawny broad shoulders like curled snakes or hissing adders. *Jack* alighted from his horse, and put him into a thicket, then with his coat of darkness he approached something nearer to behold this figure, and said softly, O! are you there? it will not be long e'er I take you by the beard. The Giant all this while could not see him, by reason of his invisible coat; so that coming up close to him, valiant *Jack* fetching a blow at his head with his sword of sharpness, (and missing something of his aim) cut off the Giant's nose, whose nostrils were wider than a pair of Jack-boots. The pain was terrible, and so he put up his hands to feel for his nose, and when he could not find it, he raved and roared louder than claps of thunder; and though he turned up his glaring eyes, he could not see from whence the blow came, which had

Jack astonishes the Welsh two-headed giant with the amount of hasty pudding he is able to consume. Illustration by Richard Doyle in 1842, when the artist was eighteen years old

done him that great diskindness; yet nevertheless, he took up his iron-knotted club and began to lay about him like one that was stark staring mad. Nay, quoth *Jack*, if you are for that sport, then I will dispatch you quickly, for fear an accidental blow fall: then, as the Giant rose from his block, *Jack* makes no more to do, but runs his sword up to the hilt in the Giant's fundament, where he left it sticking for a while, and stood himself laughing (with his hands a kimbow) to see the Giant caper and dance the canaries,[1] with the sword in his arse, crying out, he should die, he should die with the griping of the guts. Thus did the Giant continue raving for an hour or more, and at length fell down dead, whose dreadful fall had like to have crushed poor *Jack*, had he not been nimble to avoid the same. This being done, *Jack* cut off both the Giants' heads, and sent them to king *Arthur* by a waggoner which he hired for the same purpose; together with an account of his prosperous success in all his undertakings.

Jack having thus dispatched these two monsters, resolved to enter the cave in search of the Giants' treasure; he passed along through many turnings and windings, which led him at length to a room paved with free-stone, at the upper end of which, was a boiling cauldron; and, on the right hand stood a large table, where he supposed the Giants used to dine; then he came to an iron gate, where was a window secured with bars of iron, thro' which he looked, and there beheld a vast many miserable captives; who, seeing *Jack* at a distance, cried out with a loud voice, alas! Young man, art thou come to be one among us in this miserable den? Aye, quoth *Jack*, I hope I shall not tarry long here: but, pray tell me what's the meaning of your captivity? why, said one, young man, I'll tell you. We are persons that have been taken by the Giants that kept this cave, and here are kept till such time as they have occasion for a feast more than ordinary, and then the fattest among us is slaughtered, and prepared for their devouring jaws; it is not long since they took three for the same purpose; nay, many are the times they have dined on murdered men. Say you so, quoth *Jack*, well, I have gave them both such a dinner, that it will be long enough, e'er they'll have occasion for any more. The miserable captives were amazed at his words. You may believe me, quoth *Jack*, for I have slain them with the point of my sword; and, as for their monstrous heads, I sent them in a waggon to the court of king *Arthur*, as trophies of my unparalelled victories.

And, for testimony of the truth, he said, he unlocked the iron gate setting the miserable captives at liberty; who all rejoiced like condemned malefactors, at the sight of a reprieve; then, leading them all together to the aforesaid room, he placed them round the table, and set before them two quarters of beef, also bread and wine, so that he feasted them very plentifully: Supper being ended, they searched the Giant's coffers, where finding a vast store of gold and silver, *Jack* equally divided it amongst them; they all returned him hearty thanks for their treasure, and miraculous deliverance. That night they went to their rest, and in the morning they arose, and departed; the captives to their respective towns, and places of abode; and *Jack* to the knight's house, whom he had formerly delivered from the hands of the Giants.

[1]The canaries was a lively Spanish dance popular in the sixteenth, seventeenth, and eighteenth centuries.

It was about sun-rising, when *Jack* mounted his horse, to proceed on his journey; and by the help of his directions he came to the knight's house something before noon, where he was received with all demonstration of joy imaginable by the knight and his lady; who, in honourable respect to *Jack*, prepared a feast, which lasted many days, inviting all the gentry in the adjacent parts; to whom the worthy knight was pleased to relate the manner of his former danger, and miraculous deliverance by the undaunted courage of *Jack* the Giant-killer; and, by way of gratitude, he presented him with a ring of gold, on which was engraved by curious art, the picture of the Giant, dragging a distressed knight and his fair lady, by the hair of the head; with this motto:

> We are in sad distress you see,
>   Under a Giant's fierce command;
> But gain'd our lives and liberty,
>   By valiant *Jack's* victorious hand.

Now, among the vast assembly then present, was five aged gentlemen, who were fathers to some of those miserable captives, which *Jack* had lately set at liberty; who, understanding that he was the person that had performed such miraculous wonders, they immediately paid their venerable respects: After which, their mirth increased, and the smiling bowls went freely round, to the prosperous success of the victorious conqueror: But, see in the midst of all this mirth, a dark cloud appeared, which daunted the hearts of this honourable assembly, &c. Thus it was; a messenger came, and brought the dismal tidings of the approach of one *Thunderdel*, a huge Giant with two heads; who, having heard of the death of his two kinsmen the two Giants aforesaid, was come from *Northern Wales* in search after *Jack;* to be revenged of him, for their miserable downfall, and was within a mile of the knight's house, the country people flying before him from their houses and habitations, like chaff before the wind. When they had related this, *Jack*, not a whit daunted, said, let him come, I am prepared with a tool to pick his teeth: and you, gentlemen and ladies, walk but forth into the garden and you shall be the joyful spectators of this monstrous Giant's death and destruction. To which they consented, every one wishing him good fortune in that dangerous enterprize.

The situation of the knight's house, take as follows; it was placed in the midst of a small island, incompast round with a vast moat, thirty foot deep and twenty foot wide, over which lay a drawbridge, whereof *Jack* employed two men to cut it on both sides, almost to the middle, and then dressing himself in his coat of darkness, likewise putting on his shoes of swiftness, he marches forth against the Giant, with his sword of sharpness, ready drawn; yet, when he came close up to him, the Giant could not see *Jack*, by reason of his invisible coat, which he had on, yet nevertheless he was sensible of some approaching danger, which made him cry out in these following words,

Fee, fau, fum,
I smell the blood of an *English* man,
Be he alive, or be he dead,
I'll grind his bones to make my bread.[1]

Sayest thou so, quoth *Jack*, then thou art a monstrous miller indeed; but how, if I should serve thee as I did the two Giants of late? in my conscience I should spoil your practice for the future. At which time the Giant spoke out with a voice like roaring thunder; Art thou that villain which destroyed my two kinsmen? Then I will tear thee with my teeth, suck thy blood, and what is more, I'll grind thy bones to powder. You will catch me first, quoth *Jack;* and with that threw off his coat of darkness that the Giant might see him clearly; and then run from him, as if through fear. The Giant, with foaming mouth and glaring eyes followed after, like a walking castle, making the foundation of the earth, as it were, to shake at every step. *Jack* led him a dance three or four times round the moat belonging to the knight's house, that the gentlemen and ladies might take a full view of this huge monster in nature, who followed *Jack* with all his might, but could not overtake him by reason of his shoes of swiftness, which carried him faster than the Giant could follow; at length, *Jack*, to finish the work, took over the bridge, the Giant pursuing him with his iron club upon his shoulder;

---

[1]Numerous versions exist of 'Fe, fau, fum', perhaps the most famous war cry in English literature, for example:

Fee, faw, fum,
I smell the blood of an earthly man;
Let him be alive or dead
Off goes his head.

And,

Fe, fi, fo, fum,
I smell the blood of an Englishman;
If he have any liver and lights
I'll have them for my supper tonight.

The formula is common to most British tales of blood-loving giants, including that of Red Etin, the uncouth Scottish monster 'with the thre heydis', who was apparently well known in former times (referred to in 1528), and who seems to have made his entrance invariably with the welcoming words:

Snouk but and snouk ben,
I find the smell of an earthly man;
Be he living, or be he dead,
His heart this night shall kitchen my bread.

See also the Forenote to this tale.

SONG BOOK.   57

FEE, FAW, FUM.

FEE, Faw, Fum,
I smell the Blood
Of an Earthly Man.
Let him be alive or dead,
Off Goes his Head.

ADAGIO.

OH,

but, coming to the middle of the draw-bridge, that, with the weight of his body, and the dreadful steps that he took, broke down, and he tumbled souse into the water, where he roared and wallowed like a whale. *Jack*, standing upon the side of the wharf, laughed at the Giant, and said, you would grind my bones to powder; here you have water enough, pray, where is your mill? The Giant fretted and fumed to hear him scoff at that rate; and, tho' he plunged from place to place in the moat, yet could not get out to be revenged on his adversary. *Jack*, at length got a cart rope and cast it over the Giant's two heads, with a slip knot, and, by the help of a team of horses, dragged him out again, with which he was near strangled: and, before he would let him loose, he cut off both his heads with his sword of sharpness, in the full view of all the worthy assembly of knights, gentlemen, and ladies, who gave a joyful shout when they saw the Giant fairly dispatched. Then, before he would either eat or drink, he sent his heads also after the other, to the court of king *Arthur;* which being done, *Jack*, with the ladies, returned to their mirth and pastime, which lasted for many days.

After some time spent in triumph, mirth and pastime: *Jack* grew weary of riotous living, wherefore taking his leave of the knights and ladies, he set forward in search of new adventures; through many woods and groves he passed, meeting with nothing remarkable, till at length coming near the foot of an high mountain, late at night; he knocked at the door of a lonesome house, at which time an ancient man, with a head as white as snow, arose and let him in. Father, said *Jack*, have you any entertainment for a benighted traveller that has lost his way? yes, said the old man, if you will accept of such commendations as my poor cottage will afford, thou shalt be right welcome. *Jack* returned him many thanks for his civility, therefore down they sat together, and the old man began to discourse him as follows. Son, said he, I am sensible that thou art the great conqueror of Giants, and it lies in thy power to free this part of the country, from an intolerable burthen which we groan under; for, behold, my son, on the top of this high mountain, there is an inchanted castle, kept by a huge and monstrous Giant, named *Galigantus;* who, by the help of an old conjuror, betrays many knights and ladies into his strong castle; where by magick art, they are transformed into sundry shapes and forms: but, above all I lament the miserable misfortune of a duke's daughter, whom they fetched from her father's garden, by magick art, and brought her through the air in a mourning chariot, drawn as it were by two fiery dragons, and having secured her within the walls of the castle, she was immediately transformed into the shape of a white hind, where she miserably mourned her misfortune; and tho' many worthy knights have endeavoured to break the inchantment, and work her deliverance, yet none of them could accomplish this great work, by reason of two dreadful Griffins, who are fixed by magick art; at the entrance of the castle-gate, which destroyed them at the first approach, so soon as they had fixed their eyes upon them: but you, my son, being furnished with an invisible coat, may pass by them undiscovered; where on the brazen gates of the castle, you shall find it engraved in large characters, by what means the inchantment may be broken. The old man having ended his discourse,

Jack gave him his hand, with a faithful promise, that in the morning he would venture his life for the breaking of the inchantment, and freeing the lady, together with the rest that were miserable partners in her calamity.

Having refreshed themselves with a small morsel of meat, they lay down to rest; and in the morning *Jack* arose, and put on his invisible coat, cap of knowledge, and shoes of swiftness, and so prepares himself for the dangerous enterprize. Now, when he had ascended up to the top of the mountain, he discovered the two fiery Griffins: he passed on between them without any fear, for they could not see him by reason of his invisible coat. Now, when he was got beyond them, he cast his eyes around him, where he found upon the gates a golden trumpet, hung in a chain of fine silver, under which these lines were engraved:

> *Whoever shall this trumpet blow,*
> *Shall soon the Giant overthrow;*
> *And break the black Inchantment strait,*
> *So shall all be in happy State.*

Jack had no sooner read this inscription, but he blew the trumpet, at which time the vast foundation of the castle trembled, and the Giant, together with the conjuror was in a horrid confusion, biting their thumbs, and tearing their hair, knowing their wicked reign was at an end; at which time *Jack* standing at the Giant's elbow, as he was stooping to take up his club, at one blow with his sword of sharpness cut off his head. The conjuror seeing this, mounted immediatly in the air, and was carried away in a Whirlwind. Thus was the whole inchantment broke, and every knight and lady, that had been for a long time transformed into birds and beasts, returned to their proper shapes and likenesses again; and as for the castle, though it seemed at first to be a vast place of strength and bigness, it vanished away like a cloud of smoak; whereupon a universal joy appeared amongst the released knights and ladies. This being done, the head of *Galigantus* was likewise according to his accustomed manner, conveyed to the court of king *Arthur*, as a present to the king. The very next day having refreshed the knights and ladies at the old man's habitation, who lived at the foot of the mountain, he set forward for the court of king *Arthur*, with those knights and ladies which he had so honourably delivered. When coming to the King and having related all the Passages of his fierce Encounters, his Fame rung through the whole Court, and as a Reward of his good Service, the King prevailed with the aforesaid Duke to bestow his Daughter in Marriage on honest *Jack*, protesting that there was no Man living so Worthy of her as he; all which the Duke very honourably consented to. So married they were, and not only the Court, but likewise the Kingdom was filled with Joy and Triumph at the Wedding. After which the King (as a Reward for all his good Services done for his Nation) bestowed upon him a noble Habitation, with a very plentiful Estate thereunto belonging, where he and his Lady lived the Residue of their Days in great Joy and Happiness.

'Le Nain Jaune' was incorporated in the story of 'Don Fernand de Tolède' in Madame d'Aulnoy's *Contes Nouveaux ou Les Fées à la Mode*, vol. IV, 1698, which was translated into English 'by several hands' in *A Collection of Novels and Tales, Written by That Celebrated Wit of France, The Countess D'Anois*, in 1721.

In the story the Countess shows her skill at embodying features and motives of traditional fairy lore in a tale that is original; and in maintaining interest in the well-being of the principal characters, despite virtually the entire action being magical. Only the beginning of the tale is worldly, where a beautiful princess, over-indulged by her mother, is indifferent to the twenty kings who have come to court her—a frigidity which makes her mother fear she will become an old maid, she being already fifteen, an age when princesses, both in the real world at this time and in fairy tale, were expected to be giving matrimony their serious consideration. Thereafter Madame d'Aulnoy introduced rapid journeys through the air, evil people who are ugly but who have the unfair ability to appear beautiful, a sword of invincibility, an engagement ring made of a single red hair (red hair being a fairy characteristic) which it is impossible to remove, and cakes made to pacify guardian lions on the way to the Desart Fairy, such as Psyche had to take to pacify Cerberus when she arrived at Proserpine's dark palace.

How closely Madame d'Aulnoy was attuned to fairy tradition, may be seen by comparing the first book, completed 1589, of Spenser's *Faerie Queene*, in which Duessa, the false sorceress, daughter of Deceit and Shame, and of Archimago, the wicked magician, beguiled the Red Cross Knight with her 'forged beauty', and led him away from Truth; and how Duessa conveyed the Knight to the Palace of Pride, which, like the Desart Fairy's stately palace, was filled with multitudes of

The Yellow Dwarf depicted by Gordon Browne in 1887. Lower illustration shows the unhappy ending of the original version of the tale when the dwarf kills the King of the Gold Mines

Right: Woodcuts from a penny chapbook, *The History of the Yellow Dwarf*, printed in Glasgow, 1852

beautiful people:

a noble crew
Of Lords and Ladies stood on every side,
Which with their presence fayre the place much
    beautifide.

Duessa, in her normal state, was a filthy, foul old woman, with 'neather partes misshapen, monsterous'. It is the nether parts, especially the feet, which fairies find impossible to transform as they can the rest of their bodies. Thus the Desart Fairy is able to change her appearance so completely that at first the young King of the Gold Mines believes he is in the presence of a lovely nymph, but her griffin feet betray her. Even the Devil himself cannot disguise his cloven hoofs; and Solomon, when warned that the Queen of Sheba was really a jinn, was instructed that he could ascertain this by inspecting her legs, which would be like an ass's legs, covered with coarse hair.

Despite its unhappy ending the tale of the Yellow Dwarf has been one of the most popular of Madame d'Aulnoy's stories, particularly as a pantomime. *Mother Bunch and the Yellow Dwarf* was performed at Astley's Royal Amphitheatre in 1807; *The Yellow Dwarf; or, Harlequin King of the Gold Mines*, was performed at Sadler's Wells in 1820; *The Yellow Dwarf; or, Harlequin Knight of the Lion*, was presented at Vauxhall Gardens in 1829; and at the end of the century one of the places where *The Yellow Dwarf* was performed was on the West Pier at Brighton in 1899. However, the tale was not always to end unhappily. When Walter Crane illustrated the story in 1875 the dwarf duly suffered the fate the wicked should expect in a fairy tale. He darted forward to seize the magic sword, but the princess uttered a loud shriek, and the king turned round in time to snatch the sword from the ground:

'With one blow he slew the wicked Dwarf, and then conducted the Princess to the sea-shore, where the friendly Syren was waiting to convey them to the Queen. On their arrival at the palace, the wedding took place, and Toutebelle cured of her vanity, lived happily with the King of the Gold Mines.'

THE YELLOW DWARF

There was a Queen, who, tho she had many Children, could get but one to live, which was a beautiful Daughter; and being left a Widow, and without hopes of having any more, was so much afraid of losing her, that she never gave her any Correction for what Faults she committed: insomuch that that admirable Person, who knew her own Beauty, and that she was born to a Crown, was so vain and proud of her growing Charms, that she despised all the World besides. The Queen her Mother contributed, by her Caresses and Complaisance, to persuade her none were deserving of her; she was dress'd every day either like a Pallas or Diana, follow'd by her Nymphs: and in short, the Queen, to give the finishing Stroke to her Vanity, call'd her *All-Fair;* and having had her Picture drawn by the best Painters, sent it to all the Kings with whom she was in Alliance, who, when they saw it, were not able to resist the inevitable power of her Charms; some fell sick, others run mad, and those who escap'd either Sickness or Madness, came to her Court, and as soon as they saw her became her Slaves.

Never was any Court more gallant and polite; twenty Kings studied to please her, who, after they had spent immense Sums upon an Entertainment upon her, thought themselves fully recompens'd if she said any thing was pretty in them. The Adorations that were paid her over-joy'd the Queen her Mother; not a day pass'd over her head but she had thousands of Songs and fine Copies of Verses sent by all the most famous Poets in the World. In short, *All-Fair* was the only Subject of the most renown'd Authors, both in Prose and Verse. The Princess was about fifteen; there were none who did not desire to marry her, but they durst not pretend to that Honour, it was so difficult a Task to touch an Heart of that stamp. Her Lovers murmur'd very much against her Cruelty, and the Queen, who wanted to have her married, knew not how to gain her Consent; sometimes she would say to her, 'Will you not abate somewhat of that intolerable Pride, that makes you contemn all the Kings that come to our Court? I will chuse one for you, shew me in this some Complacency.' 'I am already happy, *reply'd* All-Fair, in the easy Indifference I now live in; if I should once lose that, you would perhaps be angry.' 'I should be angry if you loved any one beneath you, *answer'd the Queen;* but you cannot have more deserving Princes than those that now ask you.' In short, the Princess was so prepossess'd of her own Merit, that she thought it greater than what it was; and by this Resolution of hers to live a Maid, began to grieve her Mother so much, that she repented, but too late, that she had humour'd her so much.

The Queen, uncertain what to do, goes all alone to find a celebrated Fairy, that was call'd the *Desart Fairy;* but as it was an hard thing to see her, because she was guarded by two Lions, unless she made a Cake for them of Millet, Sugarcandy, and Crocodiles

A Victorian ending to the tale: the Yellow Dwarf comes to grief when the princess attacks his beard with magic scissors. Colour wood-engraving by Edmund Evans, after the design by 'Phiz' (Hablot K. Browne), from *Grimm's Goblins*, 1861

Eggs, she prepared one herself, and put it into a little Basket, which she hung upon her Arm: but being wearied with walking farther than she was used to, she laid herself down under the shade of a Tree to rest herself, and there insensibly fell asleep, and when she awaked found only her Basket, and her Cake gone; and, to compleat her Misfortune, heard the Lions coming. 'Alas! *cry'd she*, what will become of me? I shall be devour'd.' And having no power to stir, she lean'd against the Tree she had slept under, when hearing somebody say, *Hem, hem!* she look'd about on all sides, and raising her Eyes, perceiv'd a little Man in the Tree, about half a Yard in height, eating Oranges, who said to her, 'O Queen, I know you, and the fear you are in lest these Lions should devour you; I cannot blame you, they have devour'd a great many, and, to your misfortune, you want a Cake.' 'I must resolve on Death, *reply'd the Queen sighing;* but alas! I should not be so much griev'd was my dear Girl but married!' 'What! Have you a Daughter? *said the yellow Dwarf, who was called so from his Complexion and the Orange-tree he liv'd in:* Indeed I am very glad of that, for I have sought after a Wife both by Sea and Land; now if you will promise me I shall have her, I will secure you both from Lions, Tygers and Bears.' The Queen look'd at him, as much frighten'd at his horrible little Figure as at the Lions, and musing some time, return'd no Answer. 'What, do you hesitate, Madam? *cry'd he*, it seems you are not very fond of Life.' At the same time the Lions appear'd on the top of a small Hill, running towards her; at which sight the Queen, who trembled like a Dove when she sees a Kite, cry'd out with all her might, 'Good Sir Dwarf, *All-Fair* is yours.' 'Oh! *said he with an Air of Disdain, All-Fair* is too fair, I will not have her.' 'O Sir, *continu'd the afflicted Queen*, don't refuse her, she is the most charming Princess in the World.' 'Well, *said he*, I will take her out of Charity; but remember the Gift you make me.' And thereupon the Orange-tree open'd, and the Queen was let into it, and so escaped from the Lions. She was so vex'd she could find no Door to that Tree, when at last she perceiv'd one that open'd into a Field full of Nettles and Thistles, surrounded with a muddy Ditch; in the middle thereof stood a little thatch'd House, out of which the yellow Dwarf came in a pleasant Air, wooden Shoes, a coarse yellow Stuff Jacket, and without any Hair to hide his large Ears. 'I am glad, good Mother-in-law, *said he to the Queen*, to see you in this my Abode, where your Daughter is to live with me; she may keep an Ass to ride out on with these Nettles and Thistles, and may secure herself from the Injuries of the Weather under this rustick Roof; she will have this Water to drink, and may eat some of these Frogs that are fatten'd in it: besides, I shall always bear her Company, and never shall leave her.'

When the unfortunate Queen came to consider on the deplorable Life this Dwarf promised her dear Child, she was not able to support the terrible Idea, but fell into a

Engraving from *The Child's Own Book*, 1830

Swoon, and had not the power to say one word; and while she was in that Condition, was convey'd to her own Bed, in a fine Suit of Night-clothes of the newest Fashion. As soon as the Queen came to herself, she remembred what had happen'd, but knew not how to believe it, seeing she was in her own Palace, in the midst of all the Ladies of her Court, and her Daughter by her Bed-side: but the fine Night-clothes, which were of a curious Lace, amaz'd her as much as the Dream she fancy'd she had had; and thro the Excess of her Disquiet she fell into such an extraordinary Fit of Melancholy, that she hardly either spoke, eat, or slept. The Princess, who lov'd her at her heart, was much griev'd, and often ask'd her what was the matter; when the Queen, to deceive her, told her sometimes it proceeded from her ill State of Health, and other times from some of the neighbouring Princes Threatnings to make War against her. Tho *All-Fair* found these answers very plausible, however she knew there was something more in the bottom, which the Queen endeavour'd to hide from her; and being no longer able to endure her Uneasiness, resolved to go to the Desart-Fairy, to ask her advice whether or no she should marry, since she was so much press'd to it: she took care to make a Cake to appease the Lions, and pretending to go to bed earlier than ordinary, went down a pair of back Stairs in a white Veil that reach'd to her Feet, to set forward on her Journey.

When the Princess came to the fatal Orange-tree, she saw it so loaded with Fruit, that she had a great mind to gather some; whereupon, she set down her Basket, and pluck'd some and eat them; but when she went to look for her Basket and Cake, and found them taken away, her Grief was inexpressible, and turning about, espy'd the little frightful Dwarf, who said to her, 'What makes you cry, Child?' 'Alas! who can forbear? *replied she*, I have lost my Basket and Cake, which were so necessary in my Journey to the Desart-Fairy's.' 'What want you with her? *answered this little Monkey*, I am her Relation and Friend, and am as knowing to the full.' 'The Queen my Mother, *replied the Princess*, is grown very melancholy, which makes me fear for her Life; I fancy I may be the cause of it, since she has desired me to marry, and I must own to you, I have not yet found any one that I think deserving enough of me: These are the Reasons that have engaged me to speak with the Fairy.' 'Princess, give yourself no further trouble, *said the Dwarf*, I am more proper to inform you about these things: The Queen your Mother is vex'd, that she has promised you in Marriage.' 'The Queen promised me in Marriage! *said she, interrupting him;* undoubtedly you are mistaken, she would certainly have told me of it: I am too much concern'd in that Affair, to be engaged without my own Consent.' 'Beautiful Princess, *said the Dwarf, throwing himself at her feet;* I flatter myself this Choice will not be displeasing to you, when I tell you I am destin'd to that Happiness.' 'My Mother chose you for a Son-in-Law! cry'd All-Fair, *falling back some Steps;* was ever any Folly like yours?' 'I am not very fond of the Honour, *said he, in a Passion;* but here are the Lions, who will revenge my Affront.'

At the same time the Princess heard the Lions roaring: 'What will become of me!

said she; must I thus end my Days!' The wicked Dwarf look'd at her, and with a malicious Smile said, 'You shall have the Glory of dying, and not bestowing your shining Merit on a poor miserable Dwarf, such as I am.' 'Pray be not angry, *said the Princess, lifting up her hands;* I'd rather marry all the Dwarfs in the World, than die after so frightful a manner.' 'Observe me well, Princess, *said he,* before you give me your Word, for I do not pretend to surprize you.' 'I have already, *reply'd she;* but the Lions approach

'"Observe me well, Princess, before you give me your word," said the Yellow Dwarf.'
Illustration by Walter Crane, 1875

towards me, save me, or I shall die with fear.' In short, she fell into a Swoon, and without knowing how she got there, found herself in her own Bed, in the finest Linen and Ribbons possible, with a Ring of one single red Hair so fast upon her Finger, that she could not get it off.

When the Princess saw all this, and remembred what had pass'd before, she grew so melancholy, that all the Court were surprized and uneasy at it; the Queen was most alarm'd of all, and ask'd a thousand times what was the matter, but she was determin'd in herself to conceal her Adventure from her. At last the States of the Kingdom, impatient to have their Princess married, assembled, and address'd the Queen to make choice of an Husband for her out of hand; the Queen told them, it was what she had most at heart, but that her Daughter was very much against it: however, she advised them to go to her, and talk with her about it, which they did immediately. *All-Fair*, whose Pride was somewhat abated, since her Adventure with the Yellow Dwarf, thought it would be the best way to marry some potent Prince, with whom that little Ape would not dare to dispute so glorious a Conquest; and gave them a favourable Answer, and consented to marry the King of the Golden Mines, who was a powerful and handsome Prince, who loved her with a violent Passion, and who never till then durst entertain any hopes. We may easily guess at the Excess of his Joy, and his Rival's Rage, when the News was declared. There were great Preparations made against the Nuptials, and the King of the Gold Mines launched out such prodigious Sums of Money, that the Sea was full of Ships, that were sent to the remotest Parts for the greatest Rarities. In short, that Prince discover'd such lively and delicate Sentiments, that she began to have some Passion for him. Thus were they both happy, when one day the King, who was both gallant and in love, took the liberty to discover his Tenderness to her in the Garden, in Verses of his own making; among which, he repeated these Lines:

> *The verdant Leaves bud out when you appear,*
> *And all the Trees their brightest Liverys wear;*
> *The Flow'rs spring forth by your indulgent Heat,*
> *And am'rous Birds their little Songs repeat:*
> *In this blest Place, distant from Care and Crowns,*
> *All Nature smiles, and you her Goddess owns.*

In the midst of all this Joy, the King's Rivals, who were in the utmost despair at his Good-fortune, and sensible of the most piercing Grief, left the Court, and return'd to their own Dominions, not being able to be Eye-witnesses to the Princess's Marriage; but before they went, they took their leaves of her in so obliging a manner, that she could not but pity them. 'O! Madam, *said the King of the Gold Mines*, what do you rob me of, by granting your Pity to Lovers, who are over and above recompenced for their pains by one single Look from you!' 'I should be angry, *reply'd the Princess*, if you were insensible of the Compassion I have shewn those Princes, to whom I am lost for ever; it is a Proof of your Delicacy, which I approve of: But, Sir, their Conditions are far different from yours; you ought to be pleased with what I have done for you, they have no reason to be so, therefore you should restrain your Jealousy.' The King of the Golden Mines was so confounded at the obliging manner that the Princess took a thing that might very well have displeased her, that he threw himself at her feet, kiss'd her hand, and ask'd a thousand pardons.

At last the long-wish'd-for Day came, and the Nuptials were proclaim'd, by sounding of Trumpets, and all other Ceremonies; the Balconies were all adorn'd with Tapestries, and the Houses bedeck'd with Flowers. The Queen was so overjoy'd, that she was hardly in bed, and got to sleep, but she rose again to give the necessary Orders, and to chuse out the Jewels the Princess was to wear that day. She was cover'd almost over with Diamonds, and on her Gown, which was a silver Brocade, were twelve Suns form'd with Diamonds. But nothing appear'd so bright as that Princess's natural Charms; a rich Crown was set upon her Head, her Hair hung down almost to her feet, and the Majesty of her Shape distinguish'd her from all the Ladies that attended on her. The King of the Gold Mines shew'd himself no less accomplish'd and magnificent; Joy and Chearfulness appear'd in all his Actions: none approach'd him, but he loaded them with his Gifts and Presents; for he had order'd some thousands of Tons of Gold, and velvet Sacks, imbroider'd with Pearls, full of Guineas, to be placed in the Hall, where all that put forth their Hands, received Handfuls of Gold; insomuch that this part of the Ceremony drew there great Crouds of People, that would have been insensible of all the other Pleasures.

As the Queen, King, and Princess, were going out into a long Gallery, they saw a Box move towards them, in which there sat a large old Woman, at whose Age and Decrepidness they were not so much surprized, as at her Ugliness: she lean'd upon a Crutch, had a black taffety Ruff on, a red velvet Hood, and a Fardingale all in Rags; and after having taken two or three Turns about, without speaking a word, she stopt in the middle of the Gallery, and shaking her Crutch in a threatening manner, cry'd out, 'Ho, ho! you Queen and Princess, do you think to falsify, unpunish'd, your Words, which you gave my Friend the Yellow Dwarf; I am the Desart-Fairy, and don't you know, that if it had not been for him and his Orange-tree, you had been devour'd by my Lions. These Insults to Fairys shall not be allow'd; think presently on what you design, for I swear by my Coif, you shall marry him, or I will burn my Crutch.' 'Ah! Princess, *said the Queen in Tears*, 'what is this that I hear? what have you promised?' 'Ah! Mother, *reply'd the Princess, full of Grief*, what have you promised?' The King of the Gold Mines, enraged at what had pass'd, and that this wicked old Woman should come to oppose his Happiness, drew his Sword, and going up towards her, pointed it to her Throat, 'Wretch, *said he*, be gone from hence, or I'll revenge thy Malice on thy Life.' He had no sooner pronounced these words, but the upper part of the Box flew off with great noise, and out came the Yellow Dwarf, mounted on a large *Spanish* Cat, and placed himself between the Desart-Fairy and the King of the Gold Mines: 'Rash Youth, *said he*, think not to commit this Violence on the illustrious Fairy, thy Rage should light on me; I am thy Rival and thy Enemy: the false Princess, who was going to bestow herself on thee, has given me her Word, and receiv'd mine; see if she has not a Ring of my Hair upon her Finger, by that you may judge of my Right to her.' 'Hideous Monster, *said the King*, hast thou the Boldness to call thyself the Adorer of this Divine Princess, and to pretend to so glorious a Possession? Thou art such a Baboon, such an odious Figure, that I had sacrificed thee before now, hadst thou been worthy of so honourable a Death.' The Dwarf piqued to the very Soul at those words, clap'd his Spurs in the Cat's Sides, which made such a mewing, and flying about, as frighten'd all but the King; who hemmed in the Dwarf so close, that he drew a large Cutlash, with which he was arm'd, and defying the King to a Combat, went down into the Court of the Palace, making a terrible noise. The enraged King follow'd him as fast as possible; and when they stood opposite to each other, ready to begin the Combat, the Sun on a sudden turn'd as red as Blood, and it grew as dark as pitch; it thunder'd and lighten'd, and by the Flashes of the Lightning, the King and all the Court, who were got into the Balconies, perceiv'd two Giants vomiting Fire on each side of the Dwarf: All which was not capable of daunting the magnanimous Heart of this young Monarch, who shew'd a wonderful Intrepidity in his Looks and Actions, that encouraged all who were concern'd for his Safety, and gave the Dwarf and his Enemies some Confusion. But all his Courage was not proof against what he saw the Princess endure; when the Desart-Fairy, with her Head cover'd with Snakes, like *Tisiphone*, and mounted on a wing'd Griffin, struck her so hard with a Lance she carried in her Hand, that she fell into the Queen's Arms all over Blood. This tender Mother, who was touch'd to the very Soul to see her Daughter in this Condition, made most sad Complaints; and for the King, he lost both all his Reason and Courage, left the Combat, and ran to the Princess, to succour her, or die with her: but the Yellow Dwarf would not give him time to get to her, but flew on his *Spanish* Cat into the Balcony where she was, and took her out of her Mother's Arms, and from all the Ladies, and then leaping upon the top of the Palace, disappear'd with his Prey.

The King, confused and motionless, look'd on such an extraordinary Adventure with the utmost despair, since it was not in his power to help it; when, to compleat his Misfortunes, he found a Mist before his Eyes, and himself lifted up by some extraordinary Power in the Air. For the wicked Fairy, who came to assist the Yellow Dwarf in taking away the Princess, had no sooner set her Eyes on the King of the Gold Mines, but her Heart grew sensible of that young Prince's Merit, and that he might be her Prey; she therefore carried him to the bottom of a frightful Cavern, and there loaded him with Chains fix'd to a Rock, hoping that the Dread of an approaching Death might make him forget *All-Fair*, and engage him to do as she would have him. As soon as he arrived there, she restored him his Sight, and borrowing, by the Fairy-Art, all those Charms and Graces that Nature had deny'd her, appear'd to him like a lovely Nymph, that was come that way by chance. 'What is this that my Eyes behold? *said she:* What have you done, charming Prince, that you are kept here?' Whereupon the King, deceiv'd by these false Appearances, reply'd; 'Alas! fair Nymph, I know not what the infernal Fury that brought me hither, would have; for tho, when she took me away, she depriv'd me of my Sight, and has not since appear'd, yet I knew by her Voice, that she was the Desart-Fairy.' 'Oh! Sir, *cry'd the false Nymph*, you are in the hands of a Woman, who will never let you go till you marry her; 'tis what she has done by several Heroes: she is the most obstinate Woman in the World in these Affairs.' But while she pretended to bear a share in the King's Affliction, he perceiv'd her Griffin-feet, which was always a Mark by which the Fairy was known in all her Metamorphoses, and which she could not change; and seeming to take no notice of it, but speaking in an Air of Confidence, said, 'Indeed, I have no Aversion for the Desart-Fairy, but I cannot bear that she should protect the Yellow Dwarf, and keep me chain'd thus like a Criminal: What have I done? I love, 'tis true, a charming Princess, and had I my Liberty, it would engage me in gratitude to love her.' 'Do you use Sincerity?' *said the pretended Nymph.* 'Doubt you of it? *reply'd the King:* I am a Novice in the Art of Dissembling; and I must own to you, a Fairy has much more to flatter my Vanity with, than a Princess; but if I loved her to Distraction, and she confined me, I should hate her.'

Deceiv'd by these Words, the Desart-Fairy resolv'd to transport him to a Place, as agreeable as this was horrible; and to that end, obliged him to get into her Chariot, which was then drawn by Swans, whereas it was generally drawn by Bats. But in what a Condition was this Prince, when as he was traversing the waste Space of Air, he saw his dear Princess in a Castle of polish'd Steel, the Walls of which cast such a Reflection when the Sun shin'd, that there was no going near it; she was laid in a Grove by a Brook-side, leaning her Head on one hand, and wiping away her Tears with the other: and as she was looking up to Heaven to ask Relief, she saw the King pass along with the Desart-Fairy, who, as she had made use of her Art to seem handsome to that young Monarch, she appear'd to the Princess the most charming Person in the World. 'What, *cry'd she*, am I not unfortunate enough, to be in this inaccessible Castle, whither this ugly Dwarf has brought me; but to add to my Misfortunes, I must be tormented with Jealousies? Must I be inform'd by such an extraordinary Adventure of the Infidelity of the King of the Gold Mines, who has certainly thought, that by losing the sight of me, he was freed from his Oaths? But who can this formidable Rival be, whose fatal Beauty surpasses mine?' While she was saying these words, the amorous King felt a mortal Pain, in being carried away with such swiftness from the dear Object of his Vows: had he not known the Fairy's Power, he would certainly have tried to have got from her, either by killing her, or some other means that his Love and Courage would have suggested to him; but how could he attempt any thing at this time?

The Fairy also perceiv'd the Princess, and sought in the King's Eyes to penetrate into the Effect that sight might produce in his Heart. 'None can inform you so well as myself of what you want to know, *said he to her;* the unexpected meeting with that unhappy Princess, for whom I had once some respect, before I was acquainted with your Charms, gave me some small disturbance; but you have so much a greater Sway over me, that I would sooner die, than be false to you.' 'Ah! Prince, *said she*, may I flatter myself with having inspir'd you with such favourable Sentiments for me.' 'Time shall convince you, Madam, *reply'd he;* but if you would make me sensible, that I have any part in your Esteem, deny not *All-Fair* your Assistance.' 'Do you know what you ask? *answer'd the Fairy, knitting her Brow, and frowning:* 'What would you have me make use of my Knowledge against the Yellow Dwarf, who is my best Friend, to force a proud Princess, whom I must look upon as my Rival, out of his hands? No, I cannot bear the thoughts of it.' At that the King sigh'd inwardly, but durst return no Answer. At last they came to a large Meadow, enamelled with various Flowers, and surrounded by a deep River, into which there ran several small Brooks, which formed Meanders about little Holts of Trees, where there was always a fresh Air: at a small distance stood a stately Palace, the Walls of which were of transparent Emeralds, and as soon as the Swans that drew them alighted, thousands of beautiful Persons came to receive the Fairy with Acclamations of Joy, and Songs in praise of her Charms and her Choice; which overjoy'd the Fairy, to hear them mention her Amours. She led the King into the most magnificent Apartment that had ever been seen in the memory of Fairies, and leaving him there, and thinking she was not sure she had captivated him, she got into an obscure Place, from whence she might observe all his Actions; and he fancying she would watch him, went to a large Glass, and said to it, 'Faithful Adviser, permit me to study out Ways to render myself agreeable to the charming Fairy, whom I adore; for great is my Desire to please.' And thereupon he painted, powder'd, and patch'd, put on a magnificent Suit of Clothes that lay ready for him, and adjusted himself the best he could.

Upon this the Fairy went in unto him, so much transported with Joy, that she could not moderate it. 'I shall not forget, *said she*, the care you have taken to please me; you have found out the true and only way: you see, Sir, it is not so difficult, when People please.' The King, who thought that saying fine things to the Fairy was the best Card he could play, spared no soft Expressions at this juncture, and by that means got leave to take a Walk on the Sea-shore, which the Fairy, by her Art, had render'd so dangerous and boisterous, that no Pilots were so bold as to venture to sail in it; so that she was under no Apprehensions of her Prisoner's escaping, who thought it a great Assuagement to his Pains, to muse along, and think of his dearest Princess, without being interrupted by his hateful Goaler. When he had walk'd some time, kiss'd the Sand, and invoked the Powers of the Sea, he heard a Voice, which made him give great Attention, and observing the Waves to swell, and regarding them stedfastly, he perceiv'd a beautiful Mermaid arise, with a Looking-glass in one hand, and combing her Hair, which was gently agitated by the Winds, with the other. At this sight the King was very much surpriz'd, but much more, when it came and said to him; 'I know the sad Condition you are reduced to, by your Separation from your Princess, and the Desart-Fairy's Passion for you; if you approve of it, I will carry you away from this fatal Place, where, perhaps, you may languish out thirty or forty Years.' The King knew not what Answer to return, not but he desir'd to be deliver'd from his Captivity, but for fear the Fairy had assumed a new Form to deceive him: and as he hesitated, the *Syren*, who guess'd at his Thoughts, said, 'Fear not, this is no snare laid for you, I am too much an Enemy to the Desart-Fairy, and the Yellow Dwarf, to serve them: I see your unfortunate Princess every day, her Beauty and Merit raises my Pity; and I tell you again, if you have any Confidence in me, I will assist you to get away.' 'I have so much in you, *cry'd the King*, that I will do whatever you bid me; but since you have seen my Princess, tell me some news of her.' 'We shall lose too much time in talking, *reply'd the* Syren; come along with me, and I will carry you to the Steel-Castle, and leave on this Shore a Figure so like you, that the Fairy shall be deceiv'd by it.'

She presently cut down some Sea-Rushes, and bundling them together, and blowing upon them, said, 'My good Friends, I order you not to stir off from this Beach, till the Desart-Fairy comes and takes you away.' Whereupon a Skin grew soon over the Rushes, and they became so like the King of the Gold Mines, that it was surprizing; they were clothed like the King, and looked pale and·dead, as if he had been drown'd. After this the *Syren* made the King sit upon her Fish's Tail, and both sail'd away in a rolling Sea, with all imaginable Satisfaction. When they were at some distance from the Shore, the Syren said, 'I will now tell you how the wicked Dwarf carried the Princess away; he set her behind him on his Spanish Cat, and notwithstanding the Blood she lost by the Wound she receiv'd from the Desart-Fairy, which made her swoon away, he never stop'd to give her Assistance, till he had her safe in his Steel-Castle, where he was receiv'd by some of the most beautiful Persons in the World, which he had transported thither, who all shew'd a great desire to serve the Princess; who was put into a Bed of Cloth of Gold, embroider'd with large Pearls.' 'O! *cry'd the King of the Gold Mines*, he has married her; I swoon and die away.' 'No, *said she*, assure yourself the Princess's Constancy is too firm to admit of that.' 'Then go on,' *reply'd he*. 'What I have more to tell you, is, *continu'd the* Syren, she was in the Grove you pass'd over, and saw you with the Desart-Fairy, who was so painted, that she seem'd to her of a much superior Beauty to herself, and her Despair is not to be comprehended, since she fancies you love her.' 'I love her! *cry'd the King*: Just Heavens! how much is she deceiv'd? What ought not I to do, to make her sensible how much she is mistaken?' 'Consult your own Heart, *answer'd the* Syren, *with a gracious Smile;* People that are deeply engaged have no need of Advice on that account.' And just as she made an end of these Words, they arriv'd at the Steel-Castle, which on the Sea-side the Dwarf had not fortified with those burning Walls.

'I know, *said the* Syren, the Princess is by the same Brook-side, where you saw her as you pass'd by; but as you will have a great many Enemies to fight with before you can come to her, take this Sword, with which you may undertake any thing, and face the greatest Dangers, provided you never let it go out of your hand. Farewel,

I shall retire under that Rock you see there; if you have any need of me, to conduct you farther with your Princess, I shall not fail you, for the Queen her Mother is my best Friend, and 'twas on her account that I have thus served you.' After these words she gave him the Sword, which was made of one entire Diamond, that gave as great a Lustre as the Sun; upon the receiving it, he could use no words expressive enough for an Acknowledgment, but desir'd her to make it up in thinking all that a generous Mind was capable of.

But to return to the Desart-Fairy: When she saw that her Lover did not return, she hasten'd after to find him, running all along the Shore, attended with an hundred young Damsels, loaded with Presents for him; some brought great Baskets full of Diamonds, some golden Vessels of admirable Work, some Ambergrease, Coral, and Pearls, and some carried great Pieces of Stuffs upon their Heads, of prodigious Richness; others, Flowers, Fruits, and Birds; in short, every thing that might be acceptable. But in what a sad Condition was the Fairy, when following this noble Troop, she saw the Rushes in the shape of the King of the Gold Mines; she was so amazed and grieved, that she gave a terrible Shriek, that made the Hills echoe again, and seem'd more furious than *Megara*, *Alecto*, and *Tisiphone* together: she threw herself upon the Body, cry'd, howled, and tore fifty of the Persons that were with her in pieces, as a Sacrifice to the *Manes* of the dear deceased. Then she call'd eleven of her Sister-Fairies, to help her to erect a stately Mausoleum to this young Hero; who were all as much deceiv'd as herself by the *Syren*, who was more powerful than they. But while they were providing Porphyry, Jaspire, Agate, Marble, Statues and Devices in Gold and Brass, to immortalize the Memory of the King, whom they thought to be dead, he thank'd the lovely *Syren*, conjuring her to grant him her Protection; which she engaging him she would, he had nothing to do but advance towards the Steel-Castle.

Thus guided by his Love, he went forward, and looking carefully about, perceiv'd his adorable Princess; but was not long without Employment, for four terrible *Sphinxes* flew at him, and had torn him into a thousand pieces, had it not been for the *Syren's* Sword, which glitter'd so in their Eyes, that they fell down at his Feet without any Strength; and he gave each a mortal Wound, and so proceeded on, till he met with six Dragons, whose scaled Skins were harder than Iron: whatever fear such Creatures might have put some into, he was intrepid, and with his Sword cut them all asunder, and thought he had surmounted the utmost Difficulties, when he met with the greatest of all; which was four and twenty Nymphs, holding in their Hands long Garlands of Flowers, with which they stop'd his Passage: 'Whither are you going, Sir? *said they;* we are appointed to guard this Place, and if we let you pass, it will be bad both for you and us, therefore pray be not obstinate: sure you would not imbrue your victorious Arm in the Blood of so many young innocent Damsels, who have done you no wrong.' At these words the King, who was a great Admirer of the Fair Sex, and had profess'd himself always their Protector, was so confounded to think that he must force his Passage thro them, that he knew not what to resolve on; when he heard a Voice say,

'Strike, strike, or you lose your Princess for ever.' Whereupon, without making any Reply, he threw himself into the midst of the Nymphs, giving them no quarter, and soon dispersed them. This being the last Obstacle he had to meet with, he went into the Grove, where the Princess lay pale and languishing by a Brook-side; and upon his approaching trembling towards her, she flew from him with as much Indignation, as if he had been the Yellow Dwarf. 'Condemn me not, Madam, *said he*, before you hear me; I am neither false, nor guilty of what you imagine, but only an unfortunate Wretch, that has displeased you with Repugnance to himself.' 'Ah! barbarous Man, *cry'd she*, I saw you traversing the Air with a beautiful Person; was that against your Consent?' 'Yes, Princess, *said he*, it was: the wicked Desart-Fairy, not satisfied with chaining me to a Rock, took me with her in her Chariot, and convey'd me to a distant Part of the World, where I should have languish'd out my Days, without hope of any Succour, had it not been for a kind *Syren*, that brought me hither. I come, my Princess, to deliver you out of the hands of those that detain you here; refuse not the Assistance of the most faithful of Lovers.' Thereupon he threw himself at her feet, and catching hold of her Gown, unfortunately let fall the formidable Sword, which the Yellow Dwarf, who lay hid behind some small Shrub, no sooner saw out of the King's Hand, but, knowing its Power, he ran and seized it.

The Princess, at the sight of the Dwarf, gave a terrible Shriek; but all her Complaints served only to exasperate the little Monster, who by two cabalistical Words conjur'd up two huge Giants, that loaded the King with Irons. 'I am now, *said the Dwarf*, Master of my Rival's Fate; however, I will grant him his Life and Liberty, on condition he consents to my Marriage.' 'No, I will die a thousand Deaths first,' *cry'd the amorous King in a Rage.* 'Alas! *reply'd the Princess*, the Thoughts of that is the most terrible of all.' 'Nothing shocks me so much, *answer'd the King*, as that you should become a Victim of this Monster.' Then said the Princess, 'Let us die together.' 'No, my Princess, *said the King*, let me have the Satisfaction of dying for you.' 'I'd sooner consent, *said she*, to the Dwarf's Desires.' 'Oh! cruel Princess, *interrupted the King*, should you marry him before my face, my Life would ever after be odious to me.' 'No, it shall not be before thy face, *reply'd the Dwarf*, for a beloved Rival I cannot bear.' At those words he stabbed the King to the heart; whose Death the Princess was not able to survive, but fell on her dear Prince's Body, and poured out her Soul with his. Thus died these two illustrious, but unfortunate Lovers, before the *Syren* could apply any Remedy, all her power lying in the fatal Sword.

The wicked Dwarf was better pleased to see his Princess void of Life, than in the Arms of another; and the Desart-Fairy being inform'd of this Adventure, conceiv'd as great an Hatred against the Memory of the King of the Gold Mines, as Love for his Person, and destroy'd the Mausoleum she had erected. And for the kind Mermaid, who was grieved at this Misfortune, she could obtain no other Favour of Fate, but to change them into two Palm-Trees; which preserving a faithful and lasting Passion for each other, caress and unite their Branches together.

'La Belle au bois dormant' was the first tale in Perrault's *Histoires ou contes du temps passé*, 1697; and it is a tale so finely told it is no surprise that the retellings which folklorists have subsequently found in oral tradition have been flat or foolish in comparison. The story of 'Dornröschen', for instance, collected by the Grimm brothers in Hesse at the beginning of the nineteenth century, which is undoubtedly derived from Perrault's text, however reluctant the Grimms were to recognize it, possesses little of the quality of the French tale. Yet it is evident from a story in Basile's *Pentamerone* (Day 5, tale 5), 1636, that the tale Perrault immortalized was not the whole story; or rather, that his tale was in part defective.

In this seventeenth-century Neapolitan story a great king commands the wise men of his country to assemble and tell him the future of his newborn daughter, named Talia. The wise men confer, and agree that peril will come to her from a splinter in some flax. To safeguard his child, the king orders that no flax, or any similar material, shall enter his palace. But one day when Talia has grown up, she is standing at a window and an old woman passes by who is spinning. Due to the king's injunction, the princess has never seen anyone spinning, and she asks if she may try it. No sooner has she taken the distaff in her hand, and begun to draw out the thread, than a splinter gets under her finger-nail, and she falls dead. Her father, striken with grief, places Talia's body on a velvet chair, and locking the gates of the palace, which is in the middle of a wood, abandons it for ever. Some time later (we are not told how much later) a king is out hunting, and his falcon flies into a window of the palace. Since the bird does not return he follows it, explores the building, and is astonished to find it deserted except for the princess whom he takes to be asleep. He cannot rouse her, yet falls in love with the insensible body as did the prince who came upon Snow White laid out in her coffin; but being less courteous, he rapes her, leaves her, and forgets her. Nine months later Talia gives birth to twins, a boy and a girl. The infants are looked after by fairies, and feed at their mother's breast. One day one of the infants mistakenly sucks at her finger, the finger that has been pricked, and draws out the splinter, restoring Talia to life. (Compare, again, with the story of Snow White; and with the further tale from the *Pentamerone* summarized in the forenote to Snow White.) Some while after this, the king, hunting again in the same locality, recollects his adventure with the fair sleeper, revisits the palace, and apparently is not abashed to find Talia awake, and with two children. He tells her what happened; they form—to quote a nineteenth-century translation—'a great league and friendship'; and he remains several days.

At this point the plot rises above Perrault's, whose seemingly unnecessary appendage, in which the king's mother turns out to be an ogress yearning to eat her grandchildren—an appetite usually attributed to stepmothers—is here shown to be an essential part of the story incorrectly transmitted. In Basile's tale it is revealed that the sport-loving king was already married. When he returns home after his compact with Talia, his wife—the queen—soon guesses the reason for his dallying elsewhere, and gains the information that he has begotten two children—whose names, incidentally, are 'Sun' and 'Moon' (cf. Le Jour and L'Aurore, the two children in Perrault's tale). Her jealousy, and consuming desire to kill her husband's bastards, is thus understandable, even if not pardonable. By a trick she obtains possession of the children, and consigns them to the cook, with orders for their throats to be cut and their flesh to be made into a savoury hash. This she encourages the king to eat, repeatedly assuring him 'You are eating what is your own'. Happily the cook has as tender a heart as has the 'clerk of the kitchen' in Perrault's tale,

and the dainty dish set before the king was made from the meat of two kids, although when the treachery is discovered the king at first believes he has eaten his own children. Talia, too, like Sleeping Beauty, narrowly escapes death. The Queen orders her to be burnt alive. Talia plays for time (in a more convincing manner than did Bluebeard's wife), suggesting that she first undresses, to which the Queen agrees, not out of pity but because Talia's clothes are embroidered with gold and pearls. Talia removes first her gown, then her skirt, then her bodice, and is about to take off her petticoat when the king, her lover, makes his appearance.

That a story such as this was current years before the *Pentamerone* is apparent from the fourteenth-century prose romance *Perceforest*, a vast work, printed in France in 1528 and translated into Italian in 1531, which seeks to link the legends of Alexander the Great and King Arthur of Britain. Here, in a chapter entitled 'Histoire de Troylus et de Zellandine', the deities Venus, Lucina, and Themis, are said to have been invited to the banquet given in honour of the birth of the king's daughter Zellandine. Themis—with less reason than the uninvited Eris before her—feels slighted because she has not been given a knife like the other guests; and shows her displeasure in the now familiar fashion of putting a curse on the innocent princess. The exact nature of the curse is not known, so no attempt can be made to shield the princess from its effect; but her fate was to be the same as Beauty's:

'She took from the hands of one of the maidens a distaff full of flax and began to spin, but she had not finished the first thread when, overcome with sleep, she took to her bed and slept so soundly that no one could rouse her; she neither drank nor ate, nor did her form and colour fade, so that everyone marvelled how she could live in that state.'

Years later, when Prince Troylus finds his way to

the sleeping princess in her tower, he behaves in the same unrestrained and casual manner as did the king who came upon Talia's sleeping body. Thus when Zellandine awakes she, too, finds herself with child.

The tale of Sleeping Beauty in embryo, and perhaps even a hint of its significance, may be seen in the story of Brynhild in the *Vǫlsunga Saga;* for when Brynhild was banished to earth, and the decree made that she should wed like any other member of her sex, her uppermost fear, it will be remembered, was that she might find herself mated to a coward. To ensure this would not happen Odin placed her in a deserted castle, and surrounded it with a massive barrier of flame. He then touched her with the thorn of sleep so that her youth and beauty would be perfectly preserved, no matter how much time elapsed before a hero arose courageous enough to make his way through the barrier of flame and enter the castle. Further it was ordained that when such a man removed the armour from her insensible body he would instantly fall in love with her, and she, waking with this action, would fall in love with him, as indeed happened when Sigurd accomplished the feat.

Perrault's story 'La Belle au bois dormant' was first translated into English by Robert Samber, and the text that follows is from his *Histories, or Tales of past Times*, 1729. The story is notable amongst Perrault's tales in that it early achieved separate chapbook publication in England. *Sleeping Beauty* is, for instance, the only one of Perrault's tales listed among the 150 'Histories' published by Cluer Dicey and Richard Marshall in 1764. *Sleeping Beauty* has also a long history as a pantomime (in 1840 it was the first of Planché's extravaganzas to be produced at Covent Garden); and pantomime producers have always known, what apparently Perrault did not know, that the way to wake Sleeping Beauty was with a kiss:

Princess. 'Ah! was that you, my Prince, my lips who prest!'
Prince. 'She wakes! she speaks! and we shall still be blest!
 You're not offended?'
Princess.   'Oh, dear, not at all!
 Aren't you the gentleman who was to call?'

THE
SLEEPING BEAUTY
IN THE WOOD

There was once upon a time a King and a Queen, who were so sorry that they had no children, so sorry that it was beyond expression. They went to all the waters in the world, vows, pilgrimages, every thing was tried and nothing came of it. At last however the Queen was with child, and was brought to bed of a daughter: There was a very fine Christening; and the Princess had for her godmothers all the Fairies they could find in the kingdom (of whom they found seven) that every one of them might give her a gift, as was the custom of Fairies in those days; by this means the Princess had all the perfections imaginable.

After the ceremonies of the Christening were over, all the company return'd to the King's palace, where there was prepared a great feast for the Fairies. There was placed before every one of them a magnificent cover with a case of massive gold, wherein was a spoon, knife and fork, all of pure gold set with diamonds and rubies. But as they were all sitting down to dinner, they saw come into the hall an old Fairy, whom they had not invited, because it was now above fifty years since she had been seen out of a tower, and they thought her either dead or enchanted. The King order'd her a cover, but could not give her a case of gold as the others, because they had seven only made for the seven Fairies. The old Fairy fancied she was slighted, and mutter'd some threats between her teeth. One of the young Fairies, who sat by her, heard her, and judging that she might give the little Princess some unhappy gift, went as soon as they rose from table and hid herself behind the hangings, that she might speak last, and repair as much as possibly she could the evil that the old Fairy might do her.

In the mean while all the Fairies began to give their gifts to the Princess. The youngest gave her for gift that she should be the most beautiful person in the world; the next, that she should have the wit of an angel; the third, that she should have an admirable grace in every thing she did; the fourth, that she should dance perfectly well; the fifth, that she should sing like a nightingale; and the sixth, that she should play upon all kinds of musick to the utmost perfection.

The old Fairy's turn coming next, with a head shaking more with spite than old age, she said, that the Princess should have her hand pierced with a spindle and die of the wound. This terrible gift made the whole company tremble, and every body fell a crying.

At this very instant the young Fairy came out from behind the hangings, and spoke these words aloud: Assure yourselves, O King and Queen, that your daughter shall

The old fairy ill-wishing the infant princess. Illustration, probably by J. D. Watson, from Routledge's Shilling Toy Book *The Sleeping Beauty in the Wood*, 1872

not die of this disaster: It is true, I have not power to undo intirely what my Ancient has done. The Princess shall indeed pierce her hand with a spindle; but instead of dying, she shall only fall into a profound sleep which shall last a hundred years, at the expiration of which a King's son shall come and awake her.

The King, to avoid the misfortune foretold by the old Fairy, caused immediately proclamation to be made, whereby every body was forbidden on pain of death to spin with a distaff and spindle, or to have so much as any spindle in their houses. About fifteen or sixteen years after, the King and Queen being gone to one of their houses of pleasure, the young Princess happen'd one day to divert herself in running up and down the palace, when going up from one apartment to another, she came into a little room on the top of the great tower, where a good old woman was spinning with her spindle. This good woman had never heard of the King's proclamation against spindles. What are you doing there, said the Princess? I am spinning, my pretty child, said the old woman, who did not know who she was. Ha! said the Princess, this is very pretty, how do you do it? Give it to me, that I may see if I can do so: She had no sooner taken it into her hand, than, whether being very hasty at it, somewhat unhandy, or that the decree of the Fairy had so ordained it, it ran into her hand, and she fell down in a swoon.

The good old woman not knowing very well what to do in this affair, cried out for help: People came in from every quarter in great numbers, they threw water upon the Princess's face, unlaced her, struck her on the palms of her hands, and rubbed her temples with *Hungary-water*[1]; but nothing would bring her to herself.

And now the King, who came up at the noise, bethought himself of the prediction of the Fairies, and judging very well that this must necessarily come to pass since the Fairies had said it, caused the Princess to be carried into the finest apartment in the palace, and to be laid upon a bed all embroider'd with gold and silver; one would have taken her for a little Angel, she was so very beautiful; for her swooning away had not diminished one bit of her complexion; her cheeks were carnation, and her lips like coral: She had only her eyes shut, but they heard her breathe softly, which satisfied them that she was not dead. The King commanded that they should not disturb her, but let her sleep quietly till her hour of awaking was come.

The good Fairy, who had saved her life by condemning her to sleep an hundred years, was in the kingdom of *Matakin* twelve thousand leagues off, when this accident befel the Princess; but she was inform'd of it in an instant by a little dwarf, who had boots of seven leagues, that is, boots with which he could tread over seven leagues of ground at one stride. The Fairy came away immediately, and she arrived about an hour after in a fiery chariot, drawn by dragons. The King handed her out of the chariot, and she approved every thing he had done; but as she had a very great foresight, she thought when the Princess should awake she might not know what to do with

---

[1] A distilled water made of rosemary flowers infused in rectified spirit of wine, named after a queen of Hungary, for whose use it was first prepared.

herself, being all alone in this old palace; and this was what she did. She touched with her wand every thing that was in the palace (except the King and the Queen) governesses, maids of honour, ladies of the bed-chamber, gentlemen, officers, stewards, cooks, under-cooks, scullions, guards with their beef-eaters, pages, footmen; she likewise touch'd all the horses that were in the stables, as well pads as others, the great dogs in the outward court, and pretty little *Mopsey* too the Princess's little Spaniel bitch that lay by her on the bed.

Immediately upon her touching them they all fell asleep, that they might not awake before their mistress, and that they might be ready to wait upon her when she wanted them. The very spits at the fire, as full as they could hold of partridges and pheasants, also slept. All this was done in a moment; the Fairies are not long in doing their business.

And now the King and the Queen having kissed their dear child without waking her, went out of the palace, and put forth a proclamation, that no body should dare to come near it. This however was not necessary; for in a quarter of an hour's time, there grew up all round about the park, such a vast number of trees, great and small, bushes and brambles twining one within another, that neither man nor beast could pass through: so that they could see nothing but the very top of the towers of the palace and that too, not unless it were a good way off. No body doubted but the fairy shewed herein an extraordinary piece of her art, that the princess, while she slept, might have nothing to fear from the Curious.

At the expiration of the hundred years, the son of the King then reigning, and who was of another family from that of the sleeping Princess, being gone a hunting on that side of the country, asked what those towers were that he saw in the middle of a great thick wood: Every one answered according as they had heard. Some said, that it was an old castle haunted by spirits; others, that all the sorcerers and witches of the country kept there their Sabbath, or weekly meeting. The most common opinion was, that an *Ogre* liv'd there, and that he carry'd thither all the little children he could catch hold of, that he might eat them up at his leisure, without any body's being able to follow him, as having himself only the power to pass through the wood. Now an *Ogre* is a giant that has long teeth and claws, with a raw head and bloody bones, that runs away with naughty little boys and girls, and eats them up.

The Prince was in a brown study, not knowing what to believe, when an old country-man spoke to him after this manner. May it please your Royal Highness, it is now above fifty years since I heard my father say, who heard my grandfather say, that there then was in this castle a Princess, the most beautiful that ever was seen, that she must sleep there an hundred years, and should be waked by a King's son, for whom she was reserved. The young Prince was all on fire at these words; and believing, without weighing the matter, that he could put an end to this fine adventure, and pushed on by love and honour, resolv'd that moment to look into it.

Scarce had he advanced towards the wood, when all the great trees, the bushes and brambles gave way of themselves to let him pass through: he walked up to the castle that he saw at the end of a large Avenue which he went into; and what a little surprized him, was, that he saw none of his people could follow him, because the trees closed again, as soon as he had passed through them. However, he did not cease from continuing his way: a young and amorous Prince is always valiant. He came into an outward court, where every thing he saw might have frozen up the most fearless person with horrour; there reigned all over a most frightful silence; the image of death every where shewed it self, and there was nothing to be seen but stretch'd out bodies of men and animals, that appear'd as if they were dead. He knew however very well, by the ruby faces and pimpled noses of the beef-eaters, that they were only asleep; and their goblets, wherein still remained some drops of wine, shewed plainly, that they fell asleep in their cups.

He then crossed a court pav'd with marble, went up the stairs, and came into the guard chamber, where the guards were standing in their ranks, with their muskets upon their shoulders, and snoring as loud as they could. After that, he went through several rooms full of gentlemen and ladies, all asleep, some standing, others sitting. At last, he came into a chamber all gilt with gold, where he saw upon a bed, the curtains of which were all open, the finest sight that ever was seen, a Princess, that appear'd to be about fifteen or sixteen years of age, and whose bright resplendent beauty had somewhat in it luminous and divine. He approached with trembling and admiration, and fell down before her upon his knees.

And now, as the enchantment was at an end, the Princess awaked, and looking on him with eyes more tender than the first view might seem to admit of; is it you my Prince, said she to him, you have waited a great while.

The Prince charm'd with these words, and much more with the manner they were spoken in, knew not how to shew his joy and gratitude; he assured her that he lov'd her better than he did himself. Their discourse was not well connected, they wept more than they spoke, little eloquence, a great deal of love. He was more at a loss than she, and we need not wonder at it; she had time to think on what to say to him; for it is very probable, (tho' history mentions nothing of it) that the good fairy, during so long a sleep, had given her very agreeable dreams. In short, they talked four hours together, and yet they did not say half the things they had to say.

In the mean while, all the palace awaked; every one thought upon their particular business; and as all of them were not in love, they were ready to die for hunger: the ladies of honour being as sharp set as other people, grew very impatient, and told the Princess aloud, that supper was serv'd up. The Prince helped the Princess to rise, she was intirely dress'd, and very magnificently, but they took care not to tell her, that she was drest like my great grandmother, and had a point band peeping over a high collar; she looked not a bit the less beautiful and charming for all that. They went into the great hall of looking-glasses, where they supped, and were served by the Princess's officers; the violins and hautboys played old tunes, but very excellent, tho' it was now above a hundred years since they had played; and after supper, without losing any time, the Lord Almoner married them in the chapel of the castle, and the chief lady of honour drew the curtains; they slept very little; the Princess had no occasion, and the Prince left her the next morning to return into the city, where his father must needs have been in pain for him: the prince told him, that he lost his way in the forrest as he was hunting, and that he had lain at a collier's cottage, who gave him cheese and brown bread.

The King his father, who was a good man, believed him; but his mother could not be persuaded this was true; and seeing that he went almost every day a hunting, and that he always had an excuse ready for so doing, though he had lain out three or four nights together, she began to suspect he had some little amour, for he lived with the Princess above two whole years, and had by her two children, the eldest of which, who was a daughter, was named *Morning*, and the youngest, who was a son, they called *Day*, because he was a great deal more handsome and beautiful than his sister. The

Queen spoke several times to her son, to inform herself after what manner he past his life, and that in this he ought in duty to satisfy her: but he never dared to trust her with his secret, he feared her though he loved her, for she was of the race of the *Ogres*, and the King would never have married her, had it not been for her vast riches; it was even whispered about the court, that she had *Ogreish* inclinations; and that when she saw little children passing by, she had all the difficulty in the world to refrain falling upon them: And so the Prince would never tell her one word.

But when the King was dead, which happened about two years afterward, and he saw himself lord and master, he declared publickly his marriage; he went in great cere-mony to conduct his Queen to the palace. They made a magnificent entry into the capital city, into which she rode between her two children.

Some time after, the King went to make war with the Emperor *Cantalabutte* his neighbour. He left the government of the kingdom to the Queen his mother, and earnestly recommended to her care his wife and children. He was obliged to continue his expedition all the summer, and as soon as he departed, the Queen-mother sent her daughter in law and her children to a country house in the woods, that she might with greater ease put in execution her horrible desires. Some few days afterwards she went thither her self, and said to her clerk of the kitchen, I have a mind to eat little *Morning* for my dinner to morrow. Ah! Madam, said the clerk of the kitchen! I will have it so, said the Queen (and this she spoke in the tone of an *Ogresse*, who had a strong desire to eat fresh meat) and I will eat her with *Sauce Robert*.★ The poor man knowing very well that he must not play tricks with an *Ogresse*, took his great knife, and went up into little *Morning's* chamber: she was then four years old, and came up to him jumping and laughing to take him about the neck, and ask him for some sugar candy. Upon which he began to weep, the great knife fell out of his hands, and he went into the back yard, and killed a little lamb, and dress'd it with such good Sauce, that his mistress assured him she had never eaten any thing so good in her life. He had at the same time taken up little *Morning*, and carried her to his wife, to conceal her in the lodging he had at the bottom of the Court-yard.

About eight days afterwards, the wicked Queen said to the clerk of the kitchen, I'll sup upon little *Day:* he answered not a word, being resolved to cheat her, as he had done before; he went to find out little *Day*, and saw him with a little file in his hand, with which he was fencing with a great monkey; he was then only three years of age, he took him up in his arms, and carried him to his wife, that she might conceal him in his lodging along with his sister, and drest in the room of little *Day* a young kid very tender, which the *Ogress* found to be wonderfully good.

This was very well hitherto; but one evening this wicked Queen said to the clerk of the kitchen, I'll eat the Queen with the same sauce as I had with her children. It was now that the poor clerk of the kitchen despaired of being able to deceive her. The

---

★*Sauce Robert* is a *French* sauce, made with onions shred, and boiled tender in butter, to which is added, vinegar, mustard, salt, pepper, and a little wine. [Translator's note.]

Sleeping Beauty in a ninepenny children's book *Histories or Tales of Past Times*, seventh edition, 1777

young Queen was past twenty, not reckoning the hundred years that she had slept: her skin was somewhat hard, though fair and white; and how to find in the yard a beast so firm, was what puzzled him: he took then a resolution, that he might save his own life, to cut the Queen's throat; and going up into her chamber with intent to do it at once, he put himself into as great a fury as he could possibly, and came into the young Queen's chamber with his dagger in his hand, he would not however surprize her, but told her, with a great deal of respect, the orders he had received from the Queen-mother. Do it, do it, said she, holding out her neck as white as snow or alabaster, execute your orders, and then I shall go and see my children, my poor children, whom I so much and so tenderly loved: for she thought them dead ever since they had been taken away without her knowledge. No, no, Madam, said the poor clerk of the kitchen, all in tears, you shall not die, and yet you shall see your children again, but then you must go home with me to my lodgings, where I have conceal'd them, and I shall deceive the Queen once more, by giving her in your stead a young hind. Upon which he conducted her immediately to his chamber; where leaving her to embrace her children, and cry along with them, he went and dress'd a hind, which the Queen had for her supper, and devoured it with the same appetite, as if it had been the young Queen: she was very well pleas'd with her cruelty, and she had invented a story to

Sleeping Beauty in Mrs Craik's *The Fairy Book* 1863. Engraving by C. H. Jeens after Joseph Noel Paton

tell the King at his return, how the mad wolves had eaten up the Queen his wife, and her two children.

One evening, as she was, according to her custom, rambling round about the courts, and palace-yards, to see if she could smell any fresh meat; she heard in a ground room little *Day* a crying, for his *Mama* was going to whip him, because he had been very naughty, and she heard at the same time little *Morning* begging pardon for her brother, telling her *Mama*, he would be good, and would never do so any more. The *Ogresse* knew presently the voice of the Queen and her children, and being quite mad that she had been thus deceived, she commanded next morning, by break of day, with a most horrible voice, which made every body tremble, that they should bring into the middle of the great court, a large tub, which she caused to be filled with toads, vipers, snakes, and all kind of serpents, in order to have thrown into it the Queen and her children, the clerk of the kitchen, his wife and maid; who she had given orders should be all brought thither with their hands tied behind them. They came accordingly, and the executioners were just going to throw them into the tub, when the King, whom they did not expect so soon, enter'd the court on horseback; for he came post, and asked with the utmost astonishment, what that horrible spectacle meant? No one dared to tell him, when the *Ogresse*, all enraged to see what had happen'd, threw her self head foremost into the tub, and was devoured in an instant by the ugly creatures she had ordered to be thrown into it for others. He could not but be very sorry, for she was his mother, but he soon comforted himself with his beautiful wife, and his pretty children.

Woodcuts, almost certainly by Thomas Bewick,
which appeared in *A New Year's Gift for Little
Masters and Misses*, 1777

LITTLE RED RIDINGHOOD

The tale of Little Red Ridinghood is remarkable both for its extraordinary popularity, and for the fact that no version of the story has been found prior to Perrault's manuscript of 1695, and its subsequent publication in *Histoires ou Contes du temps passé*, 1697.

Despite the naivety of the tale, or perhaps because of it, Little Red Ridinghood rapidly became known to English children in the eighteenth century even when they did not possess a copy of Perrault's tales. It was anthologized in, for instance, *A Pretty Book for Children; or, An Easy Guide to the English Tongue*, first issued about 1744, and in *The Top Book of All, for Little Masters and Misses*, published about 1760; while some of the earliest of the woodcuts attributed to Thomas Bewick (born 1753) depict scenes from the story. Moreover, Charles Dibdin, as early as 1803, made *Red Ridinghood: or, The Wolf Robber* the subject of a pantomime; and Charles Dickens confessed that Little Red Ridinghood was his first love. If only he could have married her, he felt, 'I should have known perfect bliss'; and he bitterly deplored 'the cruelty and treachery of that dissembling Wolf who ate her grandmother without making any impression on his appetite, and then ate her, after making that ferocious joke about his teeth.'

If the conjectures of the symbolists and mythologists, who see in this tale either a seduction scene or the Dawn being devoured by the Night, can be dismissed, which they can, it will be appreciated that the final dialogue alone, between the wolf and the little heroine, is what raises the story to the classic level. It is a dialogue that can be compared with that in the *Elder Edda*, of the thirteenth

'Too much talking is hurtful.' A pop-up three-dimensional scene from the *Theatrical Picture-book, c.* 1870

Advertisement for Fry's Cocoa, 1891

be killed or saved, and if saved by whom, and if swallowed whether she alone, or her grandmother as well, should be allowed to survive the ordeal. Thus Mrs Craik, author of *John Halifax, Gentleman*, a mother of much good sense, who rendered the fairy tales 'anew' in 1863, did not feel the tale required a happy ending. In Madame de Chatelain's *Merry Tales for Little Folk*, 1868, on the other hand, the wolf was just about to spring at Little Red Ridinghood when a wasp stung his nostril, which gave a signal to a tomtit, which warned a huntsman, who let fly an arrow 'that struck the wolf right through the ear and killed him on the spot'. In Felix Summerly's edition, in the early 1840s, in which the story is set firmly on English soil 'near the forest in Hampshire, which is called the "New Forest"', Little Red Ridinghood screamed as loudly as she could, 'and in rushed her father and some other faggot makers, who, seeing the wolf, killed him at once'. In a version traditional in Brittany in the nineteenth century the tale ended as nastily as can be imagined. The wolf puts the grandmother's blood in bottles, and induces the unsuspecting heroine to drink her ancestress. In a version of the story that the Grimm brothers collected, however, the wolf, replete after its dinner of grandmother and little girl, falls asleep. A huntsman passing by hears the wolf's thunderous snores, goes into the house, sees the wolf in bed, guesses what has happened, and rips open the wolf's stomach with a pair of scissors. Out jumps the little girl ('How dark it was inside the wolf!'), followed by the exhausted but otherwise unharmed grandmother, and the wolf is then dispatched.

It will be recalled that a wolf is also the villain in the somewhat similar story of 'The Three Little Pigs'. The wolf is commonly the villain, too, in traditional fables, and frequently so in children's games such as 'What's the time, Mr Wolf?', 'Wolf and the Lamb', and 'Sheep, Sheep, come home'. The suggestion that the term 'wolf' for a woman-hunter comes from Red Ridinghood's misadventure seems improbable. The term only acquired this significance in the United States about 1930, and earlier referred to a more specialized type of human predator.

The story of Red Ridinghood first appeared in English in *Histories, or Tales of past Times*, 1729.

century, where Loki has to explain to the giant Thrym why his would-be bride Freyja, who is Thor in disguise, possesses such unladylike characteristics.

'I have never seen a bride eat so much and drink so much,' remarks Thrym, when 'she' has tucked into an ox and eight salmon.

'It is because she has had such a longing to see you, she has not eaten for eight days,' explains Loki.

'Why are Freyja's eyes so ghastly?' asks Thrym, catching a glimpse of them beneath her veil.

'It is because she has had such a longing to see you,' replies Loki, 'she has had no sleep for eight nights.'

The deception succeeds, so that Thor manages to slaughter the giant; and Perrault was in no doubt, either, about Red Ridinghood's fate. His story ends with unsentimental abruptness: 'Et en disant ces mots, ce méchant Loup se jetta sur le petit chaperon rouge, & la mangea'.

Subsequent tellers of the tale, however, have disagreed about whether Red Ridinghood should

THE LITTLE
RED RIDING-HOOD

There was once upon a time a little country girl, born in a village, the prettiest little creature that ever was seen. Her mother was beyond reason excessively fond of her, and her grandmother yet much more. This good woman caused to be made for her a little red Riding-Hood; which made her look so very pretty, that every body call'd her, *The little red Riding-Hood*.

One day, her mother having made some custards, said to her, Go my little *Biddy*, for her christian name was *Biddy*, go and see how your grandmother does, for I hear she has been very ill, carry her a custard, and this little pot of butter. *The little red Riding-Hood* sets out immediately to go to her grandmother, who lived in another village. As she was going through the wood, she met with *Gossop Wolfe*, who had

Little Red Ridinghood much astonished by her grandmother's altered appearance. Illustration by Gustave Doré, 1872

The wolf about to have his first meal of the day. *Favourite Stories for the Nursery*, 1900

a good mind to eat her up, but he did not dare, because of some faggot-makers that were in the forrest.

He asked of her whither she was going: The poor child, who did not know how dangerous a thing it is to stay and hear a Wolfe talk, said to him, I am going to see my grandmamma, and carry her a custard pye, and a little pot of butter my mamma sends her. Does she live far off? said the Wolfe. Oh! ay, said *the little red Riding-Hood*, on the other side of the mill below yonder, at the first house in the village. Well, said the Wolfe, and I'll go and see her too; I'll go this way, and go you that, and we shall see who will be there soonest.

The Wolfe began to run as fast as he was able, the shortest way; and the little girl went the longest, diverting her self in gathering nuts, running after butterflies, and making nose-gays of all the little flowers she met with. The Wolfe was not long before he came to the grandmother's house; he knocked at the door *toc toc*. Whose there? Your grand-daughter, *The little red Riding-Hood*, said the Wolfe, counterfeiting her voice, who has brought you a custard pye, and a little pot of butter mamma sends you.

The good grandmother, who was in bed, because she found herself somewhat ill, cried out, Pull the bobbin, and the latch will go up. The Wolfe pull'd the bobbin, and the door open'd; upon which he fell upon the good woman, and eat her up in the tenth part of a moment; for he had eaten nothing for above three days before. After that he shut the door, and went into the grandmother's bed, expecting *the little red Riding-Hood*, who came some time afterwards, and knock'd at the door *toc toc*, *Who's there?* The *Little red Riding-Hood*, who hearing the big voice of the Wolfe, was at first afraid; but believing her grandmother had got a cold, and was grown hoarse, said, it is your grandaughter, *The little red Riding-Hood*, who has brought you a custard pye, and a little pot of butter mamma sends you. The Wolfe cried out to her, softening his voice as much as he could, Pull the bobbin, and the latch will go up. The *little red Riding-Hood* pull'd the bobbin, and the door opened.

The Wolfe seeing her come in, said to her, hiding himself under the clothes. Put the custard, and the little pot of butter upon the stool, and come into bed to me. *The little red Riding-Hood* undressed her self, and went into bed, where she was very much astonished to see how her grandmother looked in her night-cloaths: So she said to her, *Grandmamma, what great arms you have got!* It is the better to embrace thee my pretty child. *Grandmamma, what great legs you have got!* it is to run the better my child.

Grandmamma, what great ears you have got! It is to hear the better my child. *Grandmamma, what great eyes you have got!* It is to see the better my child. *Grandmamma, what great teeth you have got!* It is to eat thee up. And upon saying these words, this wicked Wolfe fell upon *the little Red Riding-Hood*, and eat her up.

Red Ridinghood's death avenged. Illustration by W. Tomlinson from Grandmama Goodsoul's edition of the story, *c.* 1880

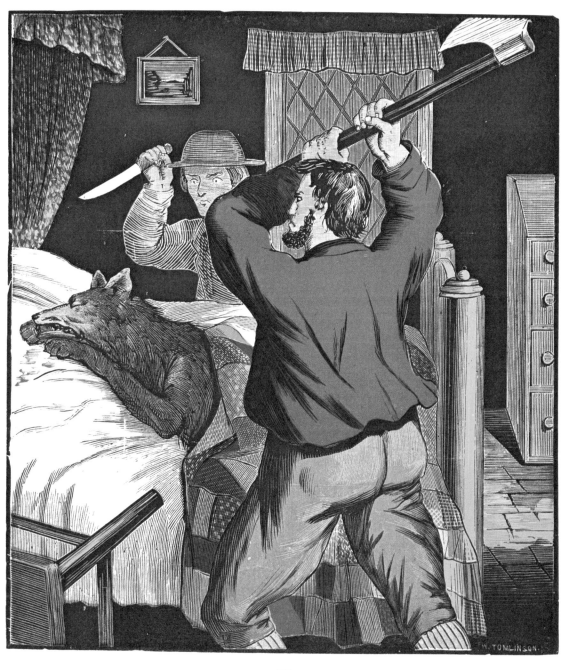

DIAMONDS AND TOADS

The theme of this tale is one of the most popular in the world, that of the proud and privileged being brought low, and the meek and down-trodden being raised above them. A proud widow possesses two daughters, the elder of whom is so disagreeable that her mother loves her to distraction, while the younger daughter is so lovely and obliging she is made the servant of the other two, and has to fetch water twice a day from a well that is a mile and a half distant. One day at the well she meets an old woman who asks for and receives a drink. Her reward is that for every word she speaks a flower or jewel shall come from her mouth. The elder sister follows her, but not her example in courtesy. She is rude to the old woman at the well; and her gift is to be unable to say anything without speaking snakes and toads. For this her sister is blamed, and she is forced to run away; but happily she meets a prince who is struck by her beauty and proposes to her, though not before he has calculated that the outpouring of jewels from her lips will recompense him for her lack of dowry.

This tale appeared in Perrault's manuscript *Contes de ma mere LOye*, 1695, under the title 'Les Fées'. In Mlle Marie Jeanne L'Héritier de Villandon's *Œuvres meslées contenant l'Innocente tromperie*, 1695, a much embroidered version of the story appeared as 'Les Enchantements de L'Éloquence ou les Effets de la Douceur'; and possibly the tale was well known in France at this time, although Mlle L'Héritier seems to have heard the story from Perrault.

A version of the tale had in fact already appeared in the fourth part of the *Pentamerone*, 1634. In the story of the two cakes, 'Le Doie Pizzele', the two girls are cousins, one of them being as fair as she is good, the other as ill-featured as she is ill-natured. The fair one, Marziella, goes to fetch water at the well, taking a cake with her for sustenance. An old woman begs a bite of the cake, and having tasted Marziella's kindness, blesses her with three gifts: the breath of roses and jessamines, the footprints of violets and lilies, and the more practical ability to comb pearls and garnets from her hair. When the ill-natured cousin, Puccia, attempts to imitate her, similarly equipped with a cake, and is asked for a piece by the beggar woman, she cannot resist the retort that only fools give away their provisions—that 'one's teeth are nearer than one's relatives'. As a result her accomplishments are to foam at the mouth like a mule, to make thistles grow where she steps, and to produce lice when she combs her hair.

The conceit that jewels should materialize when the hair of a virtuous person is combed was not new in the seventeenth century. In the tale of the 'Damsel and the Snake', in Straparola's *Piacevoli notti* (Night 3, tale 3), published in 1550, Biancabella, the much-wronged Queen of Naples, was left in the forest with her hands cut off and her eyes put out, when an old woodman took pity on her, and brought her back to his home. His wife was indignant at his doing so, and wished to turn her out; but when one of his daughters obligingly combed Biancabella's tresses for her, pearls and rubies and other precious stones fell out; and when her maimed arms were washed in clear water, roses and violets appeared in abundance.

The tale of 'Diamonds and Toads' is said to have parallels in more than twenty countries; and a thousand variants on the theme of 'The Kind and the Unkind Girls' have been collected. One notable example is the tale the Grimm brothers found in Hesse, in which an ill-clad stepdaughter is sent out in mid-winter to gather a basket of fresh strawberries. She comes to a small house where live three dwarfs. When she has shared her crust of bread with them and swept the snow from their backdoor they give her these gifts, that every day she shall grow more beautiful, that a king shall marry her, and that her voice shall literally be golden. Each time she speaks, when she returns home, pieces of gold fall from her mouth. Her stepsister, however, who also visits the dwarfs, is as perverse as was Puccia. In consequence her fate is to grow uglier every day, to have a toad spring out of her mouth with each word she utters, and to die in misery.

A not dissimilar story, which has long been known in England, is the story of 'The Three Heads in the Well' (see p. 156); and it may be remarked that the torment of toads issuing from unwelcome places as a consequence of ungraciousness was a phenomenon familiar in Britain long before the arrival of Perrault's tale. A broadside ballad entitled *A most notable Example of an Ungracious Son, who in the pride of his heart denyed his owne Father, and how God for his offence turned his meat into loathsome Toades*, was published in the time of Elizabeth I, and subsequently reprinted a number of times. Indeed God has sometimes taken the role of rewarder and retributor even in fairy tales. In a Russian variant of 'Diamonds and Toads' God the Father plays the role of the fairy accompanied by three angels, and the denouement takes place in a church; while in the Grimms' story of 'The White Bride and the Black' the Lord, in the guise of a poor man, rewards a good stepdaughter with three wishes, but a malevolent mother and daughter he makes as black as night and as ugly as sin.

The text that follows is the first English translation of Perrault's 'Les Fées', which appeared in *Histories or Tales of past Times*, 1729, under the title 'The Fairy'. This is the tale now usually known as 'Diamonds and Toads'.

The embarrassment of having flowers and jewels drop from one's mouth. Illustration from a penny picture-book, *c.* 1865

THE FAIRY

There was once upon a time a widow, who had two daughters, the eldest was so much like her in face and humour, that whoever looked upon the daughter saw the mother. They were both so disagreeable and so proud, that no body could live with them. The youngest who was the very picture of the father for civility and sweetness of temper, was withal one of the most beautiful girls that ever was seen. This mother loved even to distraction her eldest daughter, and at the same time had a frightful aversion for the youngest. She made her eat in the kitchen and work continually.[1]

Amongst other things, this poor child was forced twice a day to draw water above a mile and a half off the house, and bring a pitcher full of it home. One day as she was at this fountain there came up to her a poor woman, who begged of her to let her drink: O ay with all my heart, Goody, said this pretty little girl; and rincing immediately the pitcher, she took up some water from the clearest place of the fountain, and gave it to her, holding up the pitcher all the while that she might drink the easier.

The good woman having drank what she had a mind to, said to her, You are so very pretty, my dear, so good and so mannerly, that I cannot help giving of you a gift (for this was a Fairy, you must understand, who had taken upon her the form of a poor countrywoman to see how far the civility and good manners of this pretty girl would go). *I will give you for gift**, continued the fairy, that at every word you speak there shall come out of your mouth either a flower or a jewel.

When this pretty girl came home, her mother scolded at her for returning so late from the fountain. I beg your pardon, mamma, said the poor thing, for staying so long, and immediately upon speaking these words there came out of her mouth two roses, two pearls, and two large diamonds. What is it I see there, said her mother all astonished, I think I see pearls and diamonds come out of her mouth: How comes this, child? (This was the first time she ever call'd her child.) The poor creature told her plainly all that had happen'd, not without dropping out of her mouth an infinite number of diamonds. Truly, said the mother, I must send thither my daughter. Come hither, *Fanny*, see what comes out of your sister's mouth when she speaks: Wou'd not you be glad to have the same gift given to you? You have nothing else to do but go and draw water out of the fountain, and when a certain poor woman comes to ask to drink a little, to give it her very civilly. It wou'd be a very pretty sight indeed, said this brute, to see me go to draw water: I will have you go, said the mother. So she went, but

[1]In the manuscript version of 1695 the sisters are stepsisters, the beautiful younger girl being the daughter of her father's first wife, as in Cinderella. This was doubtless the relationship in the traditional story; but Perrault probably altered it to make the situation less like that in the Cinderella story.
*These words the fairies make use of when they have a mind to do good or harm to any body. [Translator's note.]

'There came out of her mouth two snakes and two toads.' Colour wood-engraving by Kronheim, after the watercolour drawing by Kate Greenaway, from Aunt Louisa's London Toy Book *Diamonds and Toads*, *c.* 1869. This is one of the first books Kate Greenaway is known to have illustrated.

grumbled all the way, taking along with her the best silver tankard they had in the house. She was no sooner at the fountain than she saw coming out of the wood a lady most richly drest, who came up to her and asked to drink. Now you must know, that this was the very fairy that appeared to her sister, but had now taken upon her the air and dress of a Princess, to see how far the rudeness and ill manners of this girl would go.

Am I come hither, said the proud brute, for nothing else but to give you to drink? I have just now brought a silver tankard on purpose for my lady. You may drink out of it, I think, if you will.

You have not a grain of civility or good breeding in you, reply'd the Fairy, without putting herself into a passion: Well then, since you have so little manners and are so disobliging, *I give you for gift*, that at every word you speak there shall come out of your mouth a snake or a toad. As soon as her mother saw her coming she cry'd out, Well, daughter; Well, mother, answer'd the brute, and at the same time there came out of her mouth two snakes and two toads. O, mercy! cry'd the mother, what is it I see! It is her sister that has been the cause of all this; but she shall pay for it; and immediately she ran after her to beat her. The poor creature fled away from her and went to hide herself in the forest that was hard by.

The King's son, who was returning from hunting, met her, and seeing her so very pretty, asked her what she did there alone, and why she cry'd! *Alack-a-day! Sir, my mamma has turned me out of doors.* The King's son, who saw five or six pearls and as many diamonds come out of her mouth, desired her to tell him whence this happen'd. She accordingly told him the whole story; upon which the King's son fell in love with her; and considering with himself that such a gift as this was worth more than any marriage portion whatsoever in another, conducted her to the palace of the king, his father, and there married her. As for her sister, she made herself so odious that her own mother turn'd her out of doors, and the unhappy wretch having wandered about a good while without finding any body to take her in, went to a corner of a wood and died.

The elder daughter and the fairy, by Harry Clarke, 1922

The story of Bluebeard, 'La Barbe bleüe,' was set down by Perrault in *Histoires ou contes du temps passé*, 1697. Except for the magic key, upon which the blood persistently reappears after it has been scoured, the story contains no supernatural element; and the tale, as Perrault tells it, reads not so much as an imagined romance as a legend imperfectly recollected. An obvious gap occurs in the narrative, for instance, between the wife's entering the forbidden room and Bluebeard's unexpected return, a time when her house-party unaccountably vanishes. Likewise Bluebeard's willingness to wait quarter of an hour before adding her to his mortuary collection seems out of character, and is weakly excused. Although no earlier telling of the tale has been discovered, it may be taken for granted that one existed.

The fatal effects of curiosity, particularly female curiosity, have of course long been the subject of report. Lot's wife turned to salt when she looked back to see the destruction of Sodom. Pandora's inability to resist opening the box containing the blessings of the gods has meant that man has had to plod through life with the single blessing of hope. Psyche's overpowering curiosity brought about her undoing when she fetched a lamp so that she might know her husband's features. And forbidden chambers, too, are not unknown in pre-Perrault literature. In the *Pentamerone* (Day 4, tale 6), 1635, the ogress told the Princess Marchetta she might enter any room she wished but the one to which she was being given the key, and naturally she was unable to resist opening it. In 'The Tale of the Third Calender' in *The Arabian Nights' Entertainments* (Nights 60–62), Prince Agib was presented with a hundred keys to open a hundred doors, and had permission to open every one of them except the golden door, which he does, and by doing so loses not only an eye but the continuation of perpetual pleasure. However the reason he was entrusted with the key to the golden

door is made clear. He was given it as a test. It would, as the forty damsels told him, have been an affront to a Prince to question his discretion. However Bluebeard's motive, in giving his new young wife the key to the room whose opening will mean either her death or his, is less apparent.

In the tale of Bluebeard type collected by the Grimm brothers in Hesse, 'The Fitcher's Bird', a story which unlike Perrault's is definitely a tale of magic, it is clear the wizard gives his succession of women the key to the forbidden room to test them. When the third daughter of a poor man shows herself able to withstand the test, she is considered worthy to become his bride, indeed the wizard no longer has power over her, and is forced to do whatever she wishes. In an oral version of the tale, traditional in La Vendée, and recorded by Eugène Bossard in 1886, Bluebeard's bride gives a reasonable excuse (folkloristically) for not coming downstairs to be butchered. She explains she is putting on her wedding-dress. Wedding-clothes were formerly favoured as garments to be buried in, and, in the case of those to be executed, to die in. The wife is thus craftily deceiving Bluebeard, for she is making believe she is resigned to dying.

A tale analogous to Bluebeard in England is that of 'Mr Fox', known to have been current in the eighteenth century (recorded in the Malone-Boswell edition of Shakespeare, 1821). In this tale a lady who has become attracted by a wealthy but mysterious neighbour, visits his house when he is absent, comes upon a room full of skeletons and tubs of blood, and actually witnesses him dragging home a further female victim by the hair. A few days later when Mr Fox comes to dinner, and the guests are amusing themselves with extraordinary anecdotes, she recounts her experience as if it had been a dream. At each stage of the dreadful recital Mr Fox says 'It is not so, nor it was not so, and God forbid that it should be so'. This tale apparently predates Perrault. In *Much Ado About*

Nothing (I. i) Claudio remarks 'If this were so, so were it uttered', and Benedick comments 'Like the old tale, my Lord, "It is not so, nor t'was not so, but indeed, God forbid it should be so"'.

A further story collected by the Grimms, 'The Robber Bridegroom', closely resembles this English tale; and a considerable cycle of tales, including stories in French, German, Norwegian, Icelandic, Gaelic, Basque, Italian, and Greek, all involving forbidden chambers, were usefully analysed, although inconclusively, by Sidney Hartland in 1885.

Probably the identity of Bluebeard—assuming the story to have an historical basis—will always remain a mystery. The candidate most often put forward is Gilles de Rais (1404–1440), whose extraordinary life has attracted numerous biographers. Gilles, an orphan at an early age, and the possessor of vast domains in Brittany, was made a marshal of France at the age of twenty-five, fought beside Joan of Arc at Orleans, and maintained a life-style of such ruinous extravagance that in his

'The key, Madam!' Frontispiece by John Austen to *Tales of Passed Times*, 1922

thirties he resorted to black magic and the search for the Philosopher's Stone in an attempt to redeem his fortunes. In 1440 he was the central figure in a notorious trial. He was accused not only of heresy but of multiple murder. The number of his victims was put at 140; and Gilles was hanged, together with two accomplices. His story, one of the most horrible of all time, has had a lasting influence on Breton folklore; and local tradition at his bleak strongholds attests that he was the original Bluebeard. The facts remain, however, that Gilles had one wife only and she survived him, that his beard was red not blue, and that the majority of his victims were not women but young boys, his pleasure being to fondle them while they were being put to death.

A more likely candidate would seem to be another Breton, Comorre the Cursed, born nine hundred years earlier, about A.D. 500. According to an account published in 1531, Comorre, a local chieftain, had already put several of his wives to death when he sought in marriage Tryphine, daughter of Guérok, Count of Vannes. The Count, aware of Comorre's reputation, at first refused him his daughter, but after long negotiations was persuaded by Gildas the Good, Abbot of Rhuys, who acted as intermediary. According to later accounts, the marriage was at first harmonious, but one day Tryphine learned that her husband invariably killed his wives when he found they were with child; and Tryphine knowing herself to be *enceinte* straightway fled the castle. It appears, however, that when Comorre found she had deserted him he set out in pursuit, and catching up with her gave her a mighty blow with his sword (which according to legend severed her head from her body), and left her for dead. St Gildas, as the guarantor of the marriage, was immediately summoned; and whether by medical skill or by a miracle, brought her back to life and health—the records showing that she lived to found a convent, after giving birth to a son who, like herself, was eventually canonized.

In Comorre we thus have a man, the subject of traditional stories, and the reputed slayer of four wives, whose fifth wife discovered his dreadful secret, and was herself almost killed. Such a history would not of itself be enough to associate Comorre with Perrault's Bluebeard were it not for one peculiar circumstance. In 1850 some paintings were discovered beneath the whitewash on panelling in a chapel dedicated to St Tryphine at St Nicolas de Bieuzy. These paintings were thought at first to belong to the Middle Ages, and caused intense interest since they clearly showed Tryphine and six scenes from Perrault's story of Bluebeard. When, later, the paintings were found not to be ancient, and the actual year of their execution was ascertained to be 1704, interest in them waned. Nevertheless, looked at from the twentieth century, it seems remarkable that Perrault's story should have been associated with the legend of St Tryphine within eight years of its publication, and actually in the year following Charles Perrault's death when, of course, members of his family were still alive.

The first English translation, which follows, is that by Robert Samber, published in *Histories, or Tales of past Times*, 1729.

Bluebeard portrayed by Harry Clarke, 1922

THE BLUE BEARD

There was once upon a time a man who had several fine houses both in town and country, a good deal of silver and gold plate, embroider'd furniture, and coaches gilt all over with gold. But this same man had the misfortune to have a *Blue Beard*, which made him so frightfully ugly that all the women and girls ran away from him.

One of his neighbours, a lady of quality, had two daughters who were perfect beauties. He desired of her one of them in marriage, leaving to her the choice of which of them she would bestow upon him. They would neither of them have him, and sent him backwards and forwards from one another, being resolved never to marry a man that had a *Blue Beard*. That which moreover gave them the greater disgust and aversion, was that he had already been marry'd to several wives, and no body ever knew what were become of them.

The *Blue Beard*, to engage their affection, took them with my lady their mother, and three or four other ladies of their acquaintance, and some young people of the neighbourhood, to one of his country seats, where they staid full eight days. There was nothing now to be seen but parties of pleasure, hunting of all kinds, fishing, dancing, feasts and collations. No body went to bed, they past the night in rallying and playing upon one another: In short, every thing so well succeeded, that the youngest daughter began to think, that the master of the house had not a *Beard* so very *Blue*, and that he was a very civil gentleman.

Woodcuts from Dean's penny history
of Bluebeard, *c.* 1850

As soon as they returned home the marriage was concluded. About a month afterwards *the Blue Beard* told his wife, that he was obliged to take a journey into a distant country for six weeks at least, about an affair of very great consequence, desiring her to divert herself in his absence, send for her friends and acquaintance, carry them into the country, if she pleased, and make good cheer wherever she was: Here, said he, are the keys of the two great rooms that hold my best and richest furniture; these are of my silver and gold plate, which is not to be made use of every day; these open my strong boxes, which hold my gold and silver money; these my caskets of jewels; and this is the master-key that opens all my apartments: But for this little one here, it is the key of the closet at the end of the great gallery on the ground floor. Open them all, go into all and every one except that little closet, which I forbid you, and forbid you in such a manner, that if you happen to open it, there is nothing but what you may expect from my just anger and resentment. She promised to observe every thing he order'd her, who, after having embraced her, got into his coach and proceeded on his journey.

Her neighbours and good friends did not stay to be sent for by the new married lady, so great was their impatience to see all the rich furniture of her house, not daring to come while the husband was there, because of his *Blue Beard* which frighten'd them. They ran through all the rooms, closets, wardrobes, which were all so rich and fine that they seemed to surpass one another. After that, they went up into the two great rooms where were the best and richest furniture; they could not sufficiently admire the number and beauty of the tapestry, beds, couches, cabinets, stands, tables and looking-glasses, in which you might see yourself from head to foot; some of them were framed with glass, others with silver and silver gilt, the finest and most magnificent as ever were seen: They never ceased to extol and envy the happiness of their friend, who in the mean time no ways diverted herself in looking upon all these rich things, because of the impatience she had to go and open the closet of the ground floor. She was so much pressed by her curiosity, that without considering that it was very uncivil to leave her company, she went down a back pair of stairs, and with such an excessive haste, that she had like to have broken her neck two or three times.

Being come to the closet door, she stopt for some time, thinking upon her husband's orders, and considering what unhappiness might attend her were she disobedient; but the temptation was so strong she could not overcome it: She took then the little key and opened it in a very great trembling. But she could see nothing distinctly, because the windows were shut; after some moments she began to observe that the floor was all covered over with clotted blood, on which lay the bodies of several dead women ranged against the walls. (These were all the wives that the *Blue Beard* had married and murder'd one after another.) She thought that she should have died for fear, and the key that she pulled out of the lock fell out of her hand: After having somewhat recover'd her surprise, she took up the key, locked the door and went up stairs into her chamber to recover herself, but she could not, so much was she frightened.

Having observed that the key of the closet was stain'd with blood, she tried two or three times to wipe it off, but the blood would not come out; in vain did she wash it and even rub it with soap and sand, the blood still remained, for the key was a Fairy, and she could never quite make it clean; when the blood was gone off from one side, it came again on the other.

The *Blue Beard* returned from his journey the same evening, and said he had received letters upon the road, informing him that the affair he went about was finished to his advantage. His wife did all she could to convince him she was extremely glad of his speedy return. The next morning he asked for the keys, which she returned, but with such a trembling hand, that he easily guess'd what had happen'd. What is the matter, said he, that the key of the closet is not amongst the rest? I must certainly, said she, have left it above upon the table. Do not fail, said the *Blue Beard*, of giving it to me presently: After several goings backwards and forwards she was forced to bring him the key. The *Blue Beard* having very attentively consider'd it, said to his Wife, how comes this blood upon the key? I don't know, said the poor Woman paler than death. You don't know, replied the *Blue Beard*, I know very well, you were resolv'd to go into the closet, were you not? Very well, Madam, you shall go in, and take your place amongst the ladies you saw there.

Upon this she threw herself at her husband's feet, and begged his pardon with all the signs of a true repentance, and that she would never more be disobedient. She would have melted a rock, so beautiful and sorrowful was she; but the *Blue Beard* had a heart harder than the hardest rock! You must die, Madam, said he, and that

A facetious treatment of Bluebeard.
Hand-coloured illustration, *c.* 1845

presently. Since I must die, said she, looking upon him with her eyes all bathed in tears, give me some little time to say my prayers. I give you, said the *Blue Beard*, a quarter of an hour, but not one moment more.

When she was alone, she called out to her sister, and said to her, Sister *Anne*, for that was her name, go up, I desire thee, upon the top of the tower, and see if my brothers are not coming, they promised me that they would come to day, and if thou seest them, give them a sign to make haste. Her sister *Anne* went up upon the top of the tower, and the poor afflicted lady cried out from time to time, *Anne, sister Anne, dost thou see nothing coming?* And sister *Anne* said, *I see nothing but the sun that makes a dust, and the grass that grows green.* In the mean while the *Blue Beard*, holding a great cutlass in his hand, cried out as loud as he could to his wife, Come down presently, or I'll come up to you. One moment longer, if you please, said his wife, and immediately she cried out very softly, *Anne, sister Anne, dost thou see nothing coming?* And sister *Anne* said, *I see nothing but the sun that makes a dust, and the grass that grows green.* Come down quickly, cried the *Blue Beard*, or I'll come up to you. I am coming, answer'd his wife, and then she cried, *Anne, sister Anne, dost thou see nothing coming?* I see, replied sister *Anne*, a great dust that comes on this side here. *Are they my brothers?* Alas! no, my dear sister, I see a flock of sheep. Will you not come down? cried the *Blue Beard*. One moment longer, said his wife, and then she cried out, *Anne, sister Anne, dost thou see nothing coming?* I see, said she, two horsemen coming, but they are yet a great way off. God be praised, said she immediately after, they are my brothers; I have made them a sign as well as I can to make haste. *The Blue Beard* cried out now so loud, that he made the whole house tremble.

The poor Lady came down and threw herself at his feet all in tears with her hair about her shoulders: This signifies nothing, says the *Blue Beard*, you must die; then taking hold of her hair with one hand, and holding up the cutlass with the other, he was going to cut off her head. The poor lady turning about to him, and looking at him with dying eyes, desired him to afford her one little moment to recollect herself: No, no, said he, recommend thy self to God: for at this very instant there was such a loud knocking at the gate, that the *Blue Beard* stopt short of a sudden: They open'd the gate, and immediately enter'd two horsemen, who drawing their swords, ran directly to the *Blue Beard*. He knew them to be his wife's brothers, one a dragoon, the other a musqueteer, so that he ran away immediately to save himself: but the two brothers pursued him so close, that they overtook him before he could get to the steps of the porch, when they ran their swords through his body and left him dead.

The poor lady was almost as dead as her husband, and had not strength enough to rise and embrace her brothers. The *Blue Beard* had no heirs, and so his wife became mistress of all his estate. She made use of one part of it to marry her sister *Anne* to a young gentleman who had loved her a long while, another part to buy captains commissions for her brothers, and the rest to marry herself to a very honest gentleman, who made her forget the ill time she had pass'd with the *Blue Beard*.

PUSS IN BOOTS

The story of Puss in Boots as told by Perrault, 'Le Chat Botté', published in *Histoires ou contes du temps passé*, 1697, is the most renowned tale in all folklore of the animal as helper. The tale is unusual in that the hero little deserves his good fortune, that is if his poverty, his being a third child, and his unquestioning acceptance of the cat's sinful instructions, are not nowadays looked upon as virtues. The morality of the story has in fact troubled many editors in the past, George Cruikshank amongst them, who took exception to 'a system of imposture being rewarded by the greatest worldly advantages'. Certainly the Master

Cat can be acclaimed the prince of 'con' men, few swindlers having been so successful before or since. The cat was not, however, Perrault's creation.

In Basile's *Pentamerone* (Day 2, tale 4), 1634, is the tale of an old beggar in Naples who died so poor that his elder son was left nothing but a sieve, the younger son merely a cat. The younger son bellyached about his miserable inheritance; but the cat told him he did not know his good fortune: 'I can make you rich, if I put my mind to it'. Thereafter every morning, in Basile's tale, the cat went off to catch fish, which it carried to the king, announcing, 'My Lord Gagliuso, your

Puss Presents the Game to the King

Threatening the Reapers

Puss Conduct

Majesty's most humble slave, craves your indulgence, and with all due respects sends you this fish'. At another time the cat went where the fowlers were at work, and gathered up the tasty small birds they had caught. These it took to the king with the same obsequious message. Eventually, of course, the king wished to thank Lord Gagliuso in person. On the morning of the appointment the cat arrived at the palace in a state of distress. He offered Lord Gagliuso's apologies explaining that his lordship's servants had made off during the night with his personal possessions, leaving him without even a shirt to his back. Hearing this the king sent clothes from his own wardrobe; and the beggar's son, dressed in the king's garments, was cordially received and banqueted. After the entertainment the cat remained behind and suggested to the king that as his master was a man whose wealth had no equal, an alliance might be to their advantage.

The king then agreed to send trusted servants to report on the extent of Lord Gagliuso's estates; but when they set out the cat, on a pretext, went ahead. Wherever the cat met a flock of sheep, a herd of cows, a drove of pigs, or a troop of horses, it warned those who were looking after them to beware of brigands who were pillaging the countryside. If they wished to be unharmed, advised the cat, they should say everything belonged to Lord Gagliuso. At length the king's servants became weary asking the same question and receiving the same answer. Everything that could be seen, it appeared, every animal, every field, and every farm, belonged to Lord Gagliuso. They returned with a wondrous tale of his lordship's riches; and the king promised to reward the cat if a marriage could be arranged between

Folding hand-coloured frontispiece to Orlando Hodgson's edition of *Puss in Boots*, 1832

Pug's begging the King to save his Master

he Ogres Castle

The Ogre taking the form of a Lion

his daughter and Gagliuso. The cat, as can be imagined, had little difficulty in persuading the beggar boy to agree to marry the king's daughter, and negotiated in addition a large dowry, which Gagliuso used, on the cat's advice, to buy a fine estate. But the tale does not end here, as it does in Perrault's story. Gagliuso, in his gratitude to the cat, promised that when it died he would have its body preserved in a gold coffin. Three days later, to try him, the cat pretended to be dead; and it suffered the humiliation of hearing Gagliuso tell his wife to take the corpse by the paws and chuck it out of the window. The cat was furious. It jumped to its feet demanding whether this was to be its reward for exerting itself on the beggar boy's behalf; and it rushed out of the building never to be seen again, leaving Gagliuso to look after himself in future.

The resemblance of this tale to Perrault's could scarcely be closer, it might seem, other than that the cat was bootless, and the estate was purchased; but there is no evidence that Perrault knew the *Pentamerone*, which had not, as yet, been translated into French. However the story of a trickster cat had already appeared in Italy at a much earlier date, in Straparola's popular *Piacevole notti* (Night 11, fable 1), 1553, and an edition of Straparola had been published in France in 1560. In some respects Straparola's story is even closer to Perrault's tale than Basile's. Thus a poor woman in Bohemia is said to have had three sons, and to have died leaving them nothing but a kneading trough for the eldest, a pastry board for the second, and a cat for the youngest son, a youth named Costantino Fortunato. Costantino, like Gagliuso, was unimpressed by his inheritance until one day the cat, who we are informed was a fairy in disguise, announced it would provide for Costantino's well-being. It caught a leveret, took it to the palace, and presented it to the king with the now familiar feline servility, telling the king that the young hare was the gift of its master Costantino. This performance the cat repeated a number of times—always managing to purloin something eatable at the palace to bring back to Costantino—until it considered the time was ripe to put the stratagem into practice which now, 400 years

later, is notorious. It told Costantino to strip and throw himself into the river that ran close to the palace. Thereupon the cat set up a cry of 'Help, help, run, run, Master Costantino is drowning!' The trick, of course, succeeded brilliantly. The king himself heard the cry, and sent members of his household to the rescue; and when the cat explained how his master had been on the way to the king with a rich gift of jewels, and had been attacked by robbers who had stolen the jewels and attempted to murder him, the king felt yet more warmly towards the young man, and determined he should have his daughter Elisetta for wife.

When the nuptials were over, and the king had presented Costantino with ten mule-loads of gold, and five mule-loads of rich raiment (clothing is much featured in fairy tales), the bride and groom were sent off with a great troop of retainers to Costantino's home. Costantino, needless to say, was perplexed where to go; but the cat told him not to trouble himself, and rode on ahead of the cavalcade. Wherever the cat met travellers on the road, or shepherds with their sheep, it warned them, in terrifying terms, of the great body of armed men who were approaching. He said if they were asked whose men they were, and wished to be safe, they should answer boldly they were Costantino's men. Thus, as the cavalcade advanced and the king's men inquired of herdsmen the name of their lord, they imagined they were entering Costantino's domains, since every herdsman replied he was Costantino's servant. In the meantime the cat had come to a stately castle which, the owner being absent, was guarded by but a few men. The cat easily frightened these guards into submission, and the cavalcade, being informed the castle was Costantino's, made themselves welcome. Furthermore—and this is the weakest part of Straparola's tale—a fatal accident is said to have befallen the lord of the castle while he was away, so that, conveniently, Costantino was able to remain at the castle. And, when the King of Bohemia died, the people chose Costantino to be their king in his place.

The translation of Perrault's story which follows was made by Robert Samber, and is given as published in *Histories, or Tales of past Times*, 1729.

THE MASTER CAT: or
PUSS IN BOOTS

There was once upon a time a Miller, who left no more estate to the three children that he had, who were all boys, but his mill, his ass, and his Cat. The partition was soon made. Neither the scrivener nor attorney were sent for; they would soon have eaten up all the poor patrimony. The eldest had the mill, the second the ass, and the youngest nothing but the Cat.

The poor young fellow was quite comfortless at having so poor a lot. My brothers, said he, may get their living very handsomly, by joyning their stocks together; but for my part, when I have eaten up my Cat, and made me a muff of his skin, I must die with hunger. The Cat, who heard all this, but made as if he did not, said to him with a grave and serious air, Do not thus afflict your self, my good master, you have nothing else to do, but to give me a bag, and get a pair of boots made for me, that I may scamper through the dirt and the brambles, and you shall see that you have not so bad a portion of me as you imagine.

Though the Cat's master did not build very much upon what he said, he had often however seen him play a great many cunning tricks to catch rats and mice; as when he used to hang by his feet, or hide himself in the meal, and make as if he was dead; so that he did not altogether despair of his affording him some help in his miserable condition. When the Cat had what he asked for, he booted himself very gallantly; and putting his bag about his neck, he held the two strings of it in his two fore-paws, and went into a warren where there was a great number of rabbits. He put bran and sow-thistle into his bag, and stretching himself out at length, as if he had been dead, he waited for some young rabbits, not yet acquainted with the deceits of the world, to come and rummage his bag for what he had put into it.

Scarce was he lain down, but he had what he wanted; a silly rash young rabbit jumped into his bag, and Mr. Puss drawing immediately the strings, took him and killed him without mercy. Proud of his prey, he went with it to the palace, and asked to speak with the King. He was shewed up stairs into his Majesty's apartment, and said to him, I have brought you, Sir, a rabbit of the warren which my master, my lord marquis of *Carabas* (for that was the title he was pleased to give his master) has commanded me to make your Honour a Present of from him. Tell thy master, said the King, that I thank him, and he does me a great deal of pleasure.

Another time he went and hid himself amongst the corn, holding still his bag open; and when he saw a brace of partridges run into it, he drew the strings, and took them. He went and made a present of these to the King, as he had done before of the rabbit.

The King in like manner received the partridges with a great deal of pleasure, and ordered him some money to drink. The Cat continued after this manner for two or three months, to carry, from time to time, game of his master's taking to the King. One day above the rest, when he knew for certain that he was to take the air along the river side with his daughter, the most beautiful Princess in the world, he said to his master, if you will follow my advice, your fortune is made: you have nothing else to do, but go and wash yourself in the river, in that part I shall shew you, and leave the rest to me. The marquis of *Carabas* did what the Cat advised him to, without knowing why or wherefore.

While he was washing, the King passed by, and the Cat began to cry out as loud as he could, Help, help, my Lord Marquis of *Carabas* is going to be drown'd. At this noise the King put his head out of the window of his coach, and finding it was the Cat who had brought him so often so much good game, he commanded his guards to run immediately to the assistance of the Marquis of *Carabas*.

While they were drawing the poor Marquis out of the river, the Cat came up to the coach, and told the King, that while his master was washing, there came by some robbers, who went off with his clothes, though he had cried out thieves several times, as loud as he could: this cunning rogue of a Cat had hidden them under a great stone. The King immediately commanded the officers of his wardrobe to go and fetch one of his best suits of clothes for the Lord Marquis of *Carabas*. The King caressed him after a very extraordinary manner; and as the fine clothes he had given him set off his good mien (for he was well made, and very handsome in his person) the King's daughter took a secret inclination to him, and the Marquis of *Carabas* had no sooner cast two or three respectful and somewhat tender glances, but she fell in love with him to distraction. The King made him to come into the coach, and take part of the airing. The Cat, quite ravished to see his design succeed, marched on before, and meeting with some countrymen, who were mowing a meadow, he said to them, *Good people, you that mow, if you do not tell the King, that the meadow you mow belongs to my Lord Marquis of* Carabas, *you shall be chopped as small as herbs for the pot.*

The King did not fail asking of the mowers, whom the meadow they were mowing belong'd to; to my Lord Marquis of *Carabas*, said they all together; for the Cat's threats had made them terribly afraid. You see, Sir, said the Marquis, this is a meadow which never fails to yield a plentiful harvest every year. The Master-Cat, who went still on before, met with some reapers, and said to them, *Good people, you that reap, if you do not tell the King, that all this corn belongs to the Lord Marquis of* Carabas, *you shall be chopped as small as herbs for the pot.*

The King, who passed by a moment after, would know whom all that corn which he then saw belong'd to; to my Lord Marquis of *Carabas*, said the reapers, and the King was very well pleased with it, as well as the Marquis, whom he congratulated

'Help, help, my Lord Marquis of Carabas is going to be drown'd.' Illustration by Gustave Doré, 1872

thereupon. The Master-Cat, who went always before, said the same words to all that he met: and the King was astonished at the vast estates of my Lord Marquis of *Carabas*. The Master-Cat came at last to a stately castle, the master of which was an *Ogre*, the richest that ever was known; for all the land that the King had then gone over belong'd to this castle. The Cat, who had taken care to inform himself who this *Ogre* was, and what he could do, asked to speak with him, saying, he would not pass so near his castle, without having the honour of paying his respects to him.

The *Ogre* received him as civilly as an *Ogre* could do, and made him sit down. I have been assured, said the Cat, that you have the power of changing yourself into all sorts of creatures you have a mind to; you can, for example, transform your self into a lion, an elephant, and the like. This is true, said the *Ogre* very briskly, and to convince you, you shall see me now a lion. The Cat was so much frightened to see a lion stand before him, that he immediately got upon the gutters, not without a great deal of trouble and danger, because of his boots, which were of no use to him at all in walking upon the tiles. Some time after, when the Cat saw that he had taken his natural form, he came down, and owned he had been very much frightened. I have been moreover informed, said the Cat, but I knew not how to believe it, that you have also the power to take on you the shape of the smallest animals; for example, to change your self into a rat or a mouse, but I must own to you, I take this to be impossible. Impossible! said the *Ogre*, you shall see that presently, and at the same time changed himself into a mouse that began to run about the floor. The Cat no sooner perceived this, but he fell upon him, and eat him up.

The King in the mean while, who saw, as he passed, this fine castle of the *Ogre's*, had a mind to come into it. The Cat, who heard the noise of the coach running over the draw-bridge, ran out, and said to the King, Your Majesty is welcome to this castle of my Lord Marquis of *Carabas*. What, my Lord Marquis, said the King, and does this castle also belong to you? there can be nothing finer than this court, and all these stately buildings that surround it; let us go into it, if you please. The Marquis gave his hand to the Princess, and followed the King, who went up first; they came into a great hall, where they found a magnificent collation, which the *Ogre* had prepared for his friends, who were that very day to come to see him, but dared not enter, knowing the King was there. The King was quite charmed with the good Qualities of my Lord Marquis of *Carabas*, as was his daughter, who was fallen extremely in love with him; and seeing the vast estate he possessed, said to him, after having drunk five or six glasses, it will be owing to yourself only, my Lord Marquis, if you are not my son-in-law. The Marquis making several low bows, accepted the honour the King conferred upon him, and married the same day the Princess forthwith.

The Cat became a great Lord, and never ran more after mice, but for his diversion.

CINDERELLA

The story of Cinderella is undoubtedly the best-known fairy story in the world, and it is a tale whose strangeness has apparently been a wonder to man for a thousand years. The form of the tale popular today, in which a cinder-girl is able to attend a ball through the benevolence of a fairy godmother on condition that she returns before midnight, is due entirely to the skilled retelling of the tale—whether by Charles Perrault or Pierre Perrault—published in *Histoires ou Contes du temps passé*, Paris, 1697.

Were it not for Perrault (father or son) the tale might now be known in Britain in a form such as Andrew Lang found it being told a century ago in Morayshire, in the north-east of Scotland (*Revue Celtique*, vol. III, 1878). A king who had one lovely daughter, and whose wife had died, married for the second time an ill-natured woman with three ugly girls of her own whose envy of the king's daughter was matched by their treatment of her. They made her sit in the kitchen neuk, gave her a garment of rushes to wear so that everyone called her 'Rashin Coatie', and allowed her nothing to eat but their leavings. Rashin Coatie was however not altogether troubled, because her mother, before she died, had given her a little red calf; and Rashin Coatie had only to ask the red calf for anything she wanted, and she could have it. One day, nevertheless, her stepmother found out about the little red calf, and the good food the calf was bringing her, and ordered that the creature be butchered. Rashin Coatie was grief-stricken. But the dead calf said to her:

> Tak' me up, bane by bane,
> And pit me aneth yon grey stane.

If she did this, it was suggested, she would still be able to obtain whatever she wanted. Thus, when Yuletide came, and everyone put on their best clothes to go to the kirk, Rashin Coatie had no fine clothes to wear, and was told she was too dirty a creature to go to the kirk, and must stay at home to cook the dinner. When the others had set off for the kirk, Rashin Coatie went to the grey stone, and told the calf she wanted to go to the kirk too. The calf promptly provided her with 'braw claes'; and she was 'the grandest and brawest lady' at the kirk. A young prince was there, and fell in love with her; but Rashin Coatie left before the blessing so as to be home before the others returned, and the prince was unable to speak to her. The next day, when they again went to the kirk, the same thing happened, and the prince was in love with her more than ever. But Rashin Coatie again slipped away before the blessing. On the third day the prince kept guard at the kirk door. Rashin Coatie had to jump to get past him, and in doing so lost one of her beautiful satin slippers. The young prince proclaimed he would marry whoever the satin slipper fitted. All the ladies in the land tried on the slipper, but not one could fit her foot into it. The 'hen-wife' (the stepmother?) then took her daughter, and forced the slipper on her foot by cutting off her heels and toes, so the prince had to accept her. On the way to the kirk, however, a bird began to sing, and ever it sang:

> Minched fit, and pinched fit,
> Beside the king she rides,
> But braw fit, and bonny fit,
> In the kitchen neuk she hides.

The prince now realized somebody had not yet tried on the shoe. Eventually Rashin Coatie came to him, and when she was near 'the slipper jumped out of his pocket and on to her foot'. The prince married her, and 'they lived happily all their days'.

Several tales such as this, apparently a part of Scandinavian tradition, have been collected in Scotland; and John Leyden (born 1775) seems to have known the story, for he suggested that one of the tales in *The Complaynt of Scotland*, 1540, was 'probably the groundwork of the Fairy tale of "the pure tint Rashy-coat" a common nursery tale'.

In Germany, too, the Grimm brothers found a similar group of tales. Their story 'Aschenputtel' (translated into English in 1826) was formed from three complementary tales current in Hesse. Aschenputtel was a girl in much the position of Rashin Coatie. Her widowed father, a man of substance, had married again, and her stepmother and two stepsisters gave her an old grey bedgown to wear. They put her in the kitchen where she had to work from morn till night, and tormented her by emptying peas and lentils into the ashes for her to pick out. Aschenputtel (Cinder-fool) remained faithful to the memory of her mother, however, on whose grave she had planted a hazel twig, the gift of her father, which had grown to be a great tree. On this tree perched a little white bird which would bring her anything she wished. The king of that land decreed there should be a three-day festival to which every beautiful girl should come, so that his son might choose a bride. The stepsisters, of course, went to the feast, leaving dowdy Aschenputtel behind. Aschenputtel would not stand for this (the heroines in these folk tales were not as passive as Perrault's Cinderella), and begged at her mother's grave for a gold and silver dress. In no time she, too, was off to the feast. The prince, inevitably, was charmed by her, and each day wished to see her home, but each day she escaped him. On the third day, however, the prince ordered the staircase to be smeared with pitch, a dirty trick for a prince, but it was partially successful, for one of Aschenputtel's golden slippers stuck in the pitch and was recovered. Thereupon the king's son announced he would marry no one but her whom the slipper fitted. The elder stepsister had a pretty foot, but when she tried on the slipper she found her big toe would not fit into it. Secretly she obtained a knife and cut off her toe to make the shoe fit. The prince believing he had found his bride rode off with her, but as they were passing the grave, two pigeons in the hazel tree cried out:

> Turn and peep, turn and peep,
> There's blood within the shoe,
> The shoe it is too small for her,
> The true bride waits for you.

The second stepsister then tried on the shoe but found her heel too large. Secretly she sliced off her heel so the shoe would fit. Again the pigeons exposed the deceit. Eventually Aschenputtel tried on the shoe. To the mortification of her stepsisters the shoe fitted like a glove, and the prince rode away with her. At the wedding the pigeons sat on Aschenputtel's shoulders and, as if the stepsisters had not suffered enough already, the pigeons pecked out the sisters' eyes while they were acting as bridesmaids—but this is a Grimm story.

Cinderella's coach, her changes of costume and transferable head, from a paper doll book, 1814

As it happens one version of the Cinderella story had already appeared in English when Perrault's tale was translated. This was Madame d'Aulnoy's tale of 'Finetta the Cinder-girl', published in volume I of her *Collection of Novels and Tales*, 1721. The opening of that story much resembles Hansel and Gretel (see p. 236) in that the parents attempt to do away with their children—at first unsuccessfully—by abandoning them in a forest. But after the three daughters have become lost, have sought refuge in an ogre's home, and have outwitted the ogre, the two elder sisters, enriched by the ogre's treasure, begin to live the grand life, leaving the youngest, Finetta, to do the housework. One night, however, Finetta discovers a little gold key among the ashes, which opens a chest packed with beautiful party dresses. She puts on one of the dresses and takes herself to a ball, where she dances to the admiration of all, but unrecognized by her sisters. This happens on several occasions, until one night she stays longer than ordinary, and in her hurry to be home before her sisters she loses a slipper, one which was 'of Red velvet braided with Pearls'. The next day the king's eldest son comes upon it when out hunting, and thinks the slipper so exquisite he resolves to marry no one but her who can wear it. 'Upon this all the fine Ladies of the Court wash'd and pared their Feet, and made choice of the thinnest Stockings, that they might put on the Slipper; but all to no purpose, since none of them could get it on.' Amongst the would-be brides are the two elder sisters, who set off to court to try on the shoe; but on the way they are overtaken by Finetta, mounted on a fine Spanish horse provided by her fairy godmother, that in passing 'dash'd them all over with Dirt'. However, when Finetta has shown that the shoe is hers, and the prince has proposed to her, she good-naturedly introduces her sisters to the court (this is a tale of the beau-monde) and desires that they, too, shall be well received.

The earliest Cinderella-type tale that has been found in Europe was published in Italy. This is the story of 'La Gatta Cenerentola' (The Hearth-Cat), which Basile included in the *Pentamerone* (Day I, tale 6), 1634. In this tale a girl named Zezolla is the only daughter of a Prince who marries for the second time a woman of some unpleasantness. In this tale, however, the heroine's conduct is by no means exemplary. She plots with her governess to murder her stepmother (this is a feature of middle-eastern variants of the tale), and successfully breaks her stepmother's neck by letting the lid of a great chest fall on her while she is looking at some old dresses. Thereafter she persuades her father to marry her governess, unaware that the woman has six daughters of her own. Zezolla soon learns her mistake. The six stepdaughters are placed above her. Her milieu becomes the kitchen, and her name 'La Gatta Cenerentola'. However when her father returns from a journey abroad, he brings her, on the instructions of a fairy, a seedling date tree which she plants, and which in four days grows to the size

of a woman. In this tree is a fairy who tells Zezolla that whenever she wants to go out without being recognized she has only to ask. Soon afterwards comes the day of the festa, for which everyone but Zezolla prepares. Zezolla runs to the tree and asks if she too can go. Instantly she finds herself attired like a queen, with a white horse to ride on and twelve pages to attend her. Now it happens that the King comes to the festa, and needless to say he is bewitched by Zezolla's loveliness, and instructs a servant to find out where she lives. But Zezolla notices she is being followed, and scatters gold coins in the road, which the servant stops to pick up. On the next feast day Zezolla is again left by the hearthside; and this time the date tree provides her with a coach and six horses. The King is yet more anxious to learn her identity, but the servant who follows her is unable to resist picking up the jewels she lets fall. On the third feast day Zezolla is provided with a coach of gold. The King's servant is instructed on no account to let her out of his sight, and Zezolla, in her anxiety to escape, drops a beautiful stilted shoe she has been wearing, which the servant picks up. The King orders every woman in his realm to attend a banquet to find out whose foot the shoe fits, but no one can get it on. He then orders a second banquet which must be attended even by the kitchen maid Zezolla. When the shoe is near Zezolla's foot it darts forward of its own accord, as iron to a magnet. The King takes Zezolla in his arms, places a crown upon her head, and commands everyone to make obeisance to her as their queen.

Where the story of Cinderella originated is unknown. But Arthur Waley has pointed out that 'the earliest datable version of the Cinderella story anywhere in the world occurs in a Chinese book written about 850-860 A.D.'; and the resemblance of this tale to the stories recorded in Europe so many centuries later will be seen to be remarkable.

Before the Ch'in and Han dynasties—goes the story, which appears in *Folk-Lore*, March, 1947— there was a cave-master called Wu, who was twice married, and by each of his wives had a daughter. One daughter, named Yeh-hsien, was unusually clever; but her mother died, and when her father died too she was sorely ill-treated by her stepmother, who kept her in tattered clothing, and

Cinderella in Georgian, Regency, and early Victorian times. Woodcuts of *c.* 1744, 1817, and *c.* 1840

made her collect firewood in dangerous places and draw water from deep pools. Yeh-hsien possessed a tame fish which she had caught when it was two inches long and which had grown to enormous size, more than ten feet long. Yeh-hsien kept the fish in a pool, and when she came to the water's edge it used to pillow its head on the bank beside her. One day her stepmother put on

Yeh-hsien's tattered dress, and tricked the fish into putting its head down beside her, whereupon she killed it and ate it. Yeh-hsien was grief-stricken; but a man with long hair and coarse clothes came out of the sky and consoled her. He told her the bones of the fish had been buried under the dung hill, and if she collected them and kept them in her room, she had only to pray to them to obtain whatever she wished.

When festival time came the stepmother and her daughter left Yeh-hsien behind to look after the fruit trees. Yeh-hsien put on a cloak of kingfisher feathers and shoes of gold and followed them to the festival. However the stepmother suspected who she was, and Yeh-hsien rushed home. She left in such haste that one of her gold shoes fell off; and it was picked up by one of the cave men. This man sold the shoe; and eventually it was acquired by the ruler of an island kingdom called T'o-han. He ordered that every woman in his kingdom should try the shoe on; but the shoe, which was 'light as down and made no noise even when treading on stone', seems to have been an inch too small even for the smallest foot. The story becomes confused at this point, and the order of events is uncertain. But after a considerable search Yeh-hsien is found, she puts on the shoe, is seen to be as beautiful 'as a heavenly being', and marries the king. In the meantime her stepmother and stepsister have been killed by flying stones.

This story was collected by a man named Tuan Ch'êng-shih, who must surely be one of the earliest of folktale collectors. He recorded he had learnt the story from one, Li Shih-yüan, who had long been in the service of his family, and who was himself originally a man from the caves in South China.

It will be appreciated that none of these tales is likely to be of independent composition. Not only do they have details in common, but their structure and message is similar. In the Chinese tale the long haired man who comes from the sky to give Yeh-hsien magic advice can be compared with the fairy of the Italian story, and the white bird of the German, while the fish of wonderful growth, like the date tree and the willow tree of wonderful growth in Italy and Germany, and the red calf in Scotland, whose bones had to be preserved in the same manner as the bones of the great fish, is the real source of the heroine's fortune. This is, indeed, in keeping with many other of the 700 tales of Cinderella that have been collected. A friendly animal or a bird, rather than a fairy, is the creature who succours the orphan; and it becomes clear that this creature is the spirit or reincarnation of her mother. Thereafter it appears that however much kings or princes are enamoured of Cinderella while she is in her beauteous enchanted state, she cannot be won until—as in many another fairy tale—she has been recognized by her suitor in her mundane, degraded state. In none of these tales, it will be noted, may Cinderella herself reveal her identity; nor may any human being be a party to her secret. She must invariably return home from an outing before the rest of the family, and must resume her workaday appearance so that they do not know she has been out. She seems to be innately aware—if she has not received actual instruction—that if she is recognized in her beauteous state she will never escape from her servitude. Thus however much the prince or king may have the recollection of a vision of loveliness it is essential (in all but Madame d'Aulnoy's literary rendering of the tale) that the royal suitor accepts her as his bride while she is in her humble state. (Compare 'The Frog Prince', together with the Forenote, p. 183). The only clue the Prince is allowed to her identity is her lost shoe or, in some variants of the tale, a finger-ring that fits her. The nature of the shoe itself seems to be of little significance. Very often it is made of silk or other material; and when Perrault heard the story the shoe may well have been made of a variegated fur (*vair*) as has been suggested, rather than of glass (*verre*). It was his genius, nevertheless, to see how much more effective in the story would be a shoe of glass, a shoe which could not be stretched, and a shoe in which the foot could be seen to fit. There is no doubt he himself intended the shoe should be of glass. The tale in *Contes du temps passé*, 1697, is actually entitled 'Cendrillon, ou la petite pantoufle de verre'.

The text that follows is Robert Samber's translation of Perrault's tale, which appeared in *Histories or Tales of past Times*, published in London in 1729.

CINDERILLA:
or, THE LITTLE GLASS SLIPPER

There was once upon a time, a gentleman who married for his second wife the proudest and most haughty woman that ever was known. She had been a widow, and had by her former husband two daughters of her own humour, who were exactly like her in all things. He had also by a former wife a young daughter, but of an unparallelled goodness and sweetness of temper, which she took from her mother, who was the best creature in the world.

No sooner were the ceremonies of the wedding over, but the mother-in-law began to display her ill humour; she could not bear the good qualities of this pretty girl; and the less, because they made her own daughters so much the more hated and despised. She employed her in the meanest work of the house, she cleaned the dishes and stands, and rubbed Madam's chamber, and those of the young Madams her daughters: she lay on the top of the house in a garret, upon a wretched straw bed, while her sisters lay in fine rooms, with floors all inlaid, upon beds of the newest fashion, and where they had looking-glasses so large, that they might see themselves at their full length, from head to foot. The poor girl bore all patiently, and dared not tell her father, who would have rattled her off;[1] for his wife governed him intirely. When she had done her work, she used to go into the chimney corner, and sit down upon the cinders, which made her commonly be called in the house *Cinderbreech:* but the youngest, who was not so rude and uncivil as the eldest, called her *Cinderilla.* However, *Cinderilla*, notwithstanding her poor clothes, was a hundred times handsomer than her sisters, though they wore the most magnificent apparel.

Now, it happened that the King's son gave a ball, and invited all persons of quality to it: our young ladies were also invited; for they made a very great figure. They were very well pleased thereat, and were very busy in choosing out such gowns, petticoats, and head-clothes as might become them best. This was a new trouble to *Cinderilla;* for it was she that ironed her sisters linnen, and plaited their ruffles; they talked all day long of nothing but how they should be dress'd. For my part, said the eldest, I'll wear my red velvet suit, with French trimming. And I, said the youngest, will have my common petticoat; but then, to make amends for that, I'll put on my gold flowered manteau, and my diamond stomacher, which is not the most indifferent in the world. They sent for the best tirewoman they could get, to dress their heads,

[1]Scolded her.

An air-borne (or cloud-borne) fairy godmother touches Cinderella with her wand. Colour wood-engraving by Kronheim & Co. after the design by W. Gunston, from Aunt Louisa's London Toy Book, *Cinderella*, *c.* 1876

and adjust their double pinners, and they had their red brushes and patches from Mrs. *De la poche.*

Cinderilla advised them the best in the world, and offered herself to dress their heads; which they were very willing she should do. As she was doing this, they said to her, *Cinderilla*, would you not be glad to go to the ball? Ah! said she, you only banter me; it is not for such as I am to go thither. You are in the right of it, said they, it would make the people laugh to see a *Cinderbreech* at a ball. Any one but *Cinderilla* would have dressed their heads awry; but she was very good, and dress'd them perfectly well. They were almost two days without eating, so much were they transported with joy: they broke above a dozen of laces in trying to be laced up close, that they might have a fine slender shape, and they were continually at their looking-glass. At last the happy day came; they went to court, and *Cinderilla* followed them with her eyes as long as she could, and when she had lost sight of them, she fell a crying.

Her godmother, who saw her all in tears, asked her what was the matter? I wish I could ——, I wish I could ——; she could not speak the rest, her tears interrupting her. Her godmother, who was a Fairy, said to her, Thou wishest thou could'st go to the ball, is it not so? Y——es, said *Cinderilla*, with a great Sob. Well, said her godmother, be but a good girl, and I'll contrive thou shalt go. Then she took her into her chamber, and said to her, go into the garden, and bring me a pompion;[1] *Cinderilla* went immediately to gather the finest she could get, and brought it to her Godmother, not being able to imagine how this pompion could make her go to the ball: her godmother scooped out all the inside of it, having left nothing but the rind; she struck it with her wand, and the pompion immediately was turned into a fine coach, gilt all over with gold. After that, she went to look into her mouse-trap, where she found six mice all alive; she ordered *Cinderilla* to lift up a little the trap door, and she gave every mouse that went out a stroke with her wand, and the mouse was that moment turned into a fine horse, which all together made a very fine set of six horses, of a beautiful mouse-coloured dapple grey. As she was at a loss for a coach-man, I'll go and see, says *Cinderilla*, if there be never a rat in the rat-trap, we'll make a coach-man of him. You are in the right, said her godmother, go and see. *Cinderilla* brought the trap to her, and in it there were three huge rats: the Fairy made choice of one of the three, which had the largest beard, and having touched him with her wand, he was turned into a fat jolly coach-man, that had the finest whiskers as ever were seen.

After that, she said to her, Go into the garden, and you will find six Lizards behind the watering-pot, bring them to me; she had no sooner done so, but her godmother turned them into six footmen, who skipped up immediately behind the coach, with their liveries all bedaubed with gold and silver, and clung so close behind one another, as if they had done nothing else all their lives. The Fairy then said to *Cinderilla*, Well, you see here an equipage fit to go to the Ball with; are you not pleased with it? O yes, said she, but must I go thither as I am, with these ugly nasty clothes? Her godmother

[1]Pumpkin.

Cinderella in her humble state. Etching by George Cruikshank from his *Fairy Library*, 1854

only just touched her with her wand, and at the same instant her clothes were turned into cloth of gold and silver, all beset with jewels: after this, she gave her a pair of Glass Slippers, the finest in the world. Being thus dress'd out she got into her coach; but her godmother, above all things, commanded her not to stay beyond twelve a clock at night; telling her at the same time, that if she stay'd at the ball one moment longer, her coach would be a pompion again, her horses mice, her footmen lizards, and her clothes resume their old form.

She promised her godmother she would not fail of leaving the ball before midnight, and then departed not a little joyful at her good fortune. The King's son, who was informed that a great Princess, whom they did not know, was come, ran out to receive her; he gave her his hand as she alighted out of the coach, and led her into the hall where the company was: there was a great silence; they left off dancing, and the violins ceased to play, so attentive was every body to contemplate the extraordinary beauties of this unknown person: there was heard nothing but a confused noise of ha! how handsome she is, ha! how handsome she is. The King himself, as old as he was, could not help looking at her, and telling the Queen in a low voice, that it was a long time since that he had seen so beautiful and lovely a creature. All the ladies were busied in considering her clothes and head-dress, that they might have some made the next day after the same pattern, supposing they might get such fine materials, and as able hands to make them.

The King's son shewed her to the most honourable place, and afterwards took her out to dance with him: she danced with so much gracefulness, that they more and more admired her. A fine collation was served up, of which the young Prince eat nothing, so much was he taken up in looking upon her. She went and set herself down by her sisters, and shewed them a thousand civilities: she gave them some of the oranges and lemons that the Prince had presented her with; which very much surprised them; for they did not know her. While the company was thus employed, *Cinderilla* heard the clock go eleven and three quarters; upon which she immediately made a courtesy to the company, and went away as fast as she could.

As soon as she came home, she went to find out her godmother, and after having thanked her, she told her, she could not but heartily wish to go the next day to the ball, because the King's son had desired her. As she was busie in telling her godmother every thing that had passed at the ball, her two sisters knock'd at the door, *Cinderilla* went and opened it. You have stay'd a long while, said she, gaping, rubbing her eyes, and stretching herself as if she had been just awaked out of her sleep; she had however no manner of inclination to sleep since they went from home. If thou hadst been at the ball, said one of her sisters, thou would'st not have been tired with it: there came thither the most beautiful Princess, the most beautiful that ever was seen; she shewed us a thousand civilities, and gave us oranges and lemons. *Cinderilla* seem'd indifferent; she asked them the name of that Princess; but they told her they did not know it, and that the King's son was very uneasy on her account, and would give all the world to know where she was. At this *Cinderilla* smiled, and said, she must then be very handsome indeed; Lord how happy have you been, could not I see her? Ah! good Madam *Charlotte*, lend me your yellow suit of clothes that you wear every day. Undoubtedly, said Madam *Charlotte*, lend my clothes to such a Cinderbreech as you are, who is fool then? *Cinderilla* was very glad of the refusal, for she would have been sadly put to it, if her sister had lent her her clothes.

The next day the two sisters were at the ball, and so was *Cinderilla*, but dressed more richly than she was at first. The King's son was always by her, and saying abundance of tender things to her; the young lady was no ways tired, and forgot what her godmother had recommended to her, so that she heard the clock begin to strike twelve, when she thought it was only eleven, she then rose up and fled as nimble as a deer: the Prince followed her, but could not catch hold of her; she dropt one of her Glass Slippers, which the Prince took up very carefully; *Cinderilla* came home quite out of breath, without coach or footmen, and in her old ugly clothes; she had nothing left her of all her finery, but one of the little Slippers, fellow to that she drop'd. The guards at the palace-gate were asked if they had not seen a Princess go out, who said, they had seen no body go out, but a young woman very badly dress'd, and who had more the air of a poor country wench than a lady.

When the two sisters returned from the ball, *Cinderilla* asked them, if they had been well diverted, and if the fine lady had been there; they told her, Yes, but that she flew away as soon as it had struck twelve a clock, and with so much haste, that she drop'd one of her little Glass Slippers, the prettiest in the world, and which the King's son had taken up, that he did nothing but look at her all the time of the ball, and that certainly he was very much in love with the beautiful person who owned the little Slipper. What they said was very true; for a few days after, the King's son caused it to be proclaimed by sound of trumpet, that he would marry her whose foot this Slipper would just fit. They began to try it on upon the princesses, then the dutchesses, and all the court, but in vain; it was brought to the two sisters, who did all they possibly could to thrust their foot into the Slipper, but they could not effect it. *Cinderilla*, who saw all this, and knew the Slipper, said to them laughing, Let me see if it will not fit me; her sisters burst out a laughing, and began to banter her. The gentleman who was sent to try the Slipper, looked earnestly at *Cinderilla*, and finding her very handsome, said, it was but just that she should try, and that he had orders to let every body do so. He made *Cinderilla* sit down, and putting the Slipper to her foot, he found it went in very easily, and fitted her, as if it had been made of wax. The astonishment her two sisters were in, were very great; but much greater, when *Cinderilla* pulled out of her pocket the other Slipper, and put it upon her foot. Upon this her godmother came in, who having touch'd with her wand *Cinderilla's* clothes, made them more rich and magnificent than ever they were before.

And now, her two sisters found her to be that fine beautiful lady that they had seen at the ball. They threw themselves at her feet, to beg pardon for all the ill treatment they had made her undergo. *Cinderilla* took them up, and told them, as she embraced them, that she forgave them with all her heart, and desired them always to love her. She was conducted to the young Prince dress'd as she was: he thought her more beautiful than ever, and a few days after married her. *Cinderilla*, who was as good as handsome, gave her two sisters lodgings in the palace, and married them the same day to two great lords of the court.

The story of 'Le petit Poucet', which in English has become the story of 'Hop o' my Thumb,' was the last of the tales Perrault included in *Histoires ou contes du temps passé*, 1697. Although *le petit Poucet* was no bigger than a man's thumb when he was born, and the term *le petit poucelot* dates back to the sixteenth century, his story is not really analogous to that of the British Tom Thumb. It is, for instance, not apparent that Little Poucet was still of diminutive size when he was seven years old, his age when the story opens; and except for hiding himself under a stool, as any small child might do, his actions are indistinguishable from those of fairy-tale heroes of reputedly normal size. In fact almost all the incidents in this tale also occur in other stories, the first half of the tale being closely paralleled by the first part of 'Hansel and Gretel' (p. 236). The deliberate abandonment of children whom the parents are no longer able to support is, of course, an old theme and, unhappily, not only in fiction. The secret laying of a trail in dangerous territory so that the hero can find his way back is at least as old as the clew or ball of thread which Theseus took into the labyrinth at Knossos—from which comes our word 'clue'; and in the *Pentamerone* (Day 5, tale 8), 1636, such a trail is featured in

Below: The small engraving that headed the first English translation, 1729

similar circumstances to Little Poucet's. Here a father, who marries again, is forced by his new wife to get rid of his two children ('If you don't take them away you can pick your teeth, I'll never sleep with you again'), and himself leaves a trail of ash so that the children will be able to return to him. When compelled a second time to take them away, however, he is as unfortunate as was Little Poucet with his breadcrumbs. He lays a trail of bran, which an ass eats up, and the children fail to find their way home.

Yet earlier, in 'Ein shône history von einer frawen mitt zweyen kindlin' in Martin Montanus's *Schwankbücher*, 1557-66, another man who has two children and marries again is also beset with domestic troubles. The stepmother conceives an intense dislike for the younger daughter, Margretlin, and wishes to see her dead. She plots with the elder child, Annelin, to take her into the forest and lose her. Margretlin, overhearing the plot, consults her godmother, who advises her to lay a trail of sawdust so she can find her way home. She does this successfully, and is taken out a second time, when she leaves a trail of chaff with equal success. But when she is taken out a third time the trail she leaves is of hempseed, which the birds instantly eat up.

The trick Little Poucet plays on the ogre, to good effect, swopping the crowns of gold worn by the ogre's children while they sleep for the common bonnets worn by his brothers, so that the ogre in his drunken stupor slaughters his own seven children, also has counterparts. In the Hessian story of 'Sweetheart Roland', collected by the Grimm brothers, a witch executes her own daughter instead of her stepdaughter, due to the heroine changing her place in the bed while the other girl sleeps; and in the Swedish story of Roll, in Richard Dybeck's *Runa, en Skrift för Fäderneslandets Fornvänner*, 1843, a giant kills his own eight daughters because Roll, in the night, has switched their caps for his brothers' headcloths. Indeed such a happening was described in antiquity. The second-century mythographer Hyginus tells the story (*Fabulae*, 4) of Themisto, wife of Athamas, whose hatred of her rival Ino was such that she determined to destroy her children. She instructed the nurse to dress Ino's children in black night-gowns, and her own children in white, so that she might differentiate between them in the night. But she was unaware the nurse was Ino in disguise, and Ino put the white nightgowns on her own children and the black on Themisto's. In the dusk the children Themisto murders are her own.

In the tale of 'Sweetheart Roland' a further parallel occurs, for after the witch has beheaded her own daughter, she finds the heroine has fled, and she puts on her many-leagued boots, which go 'an hour's walk every step'. In like manner the ogre who chases Little Poucet donned 'Seven-league boots' (*les bottes de sept lieuës*), articles of wonderful performance which, through this tale, have been added to the imagery of the English language. Likewise in a fairy tale commonly told in Japan, and apparently indigenous, a mother, or more often a stepmother (for cruel stepmothers are stock characters in the East as in the West), abandons her children on the side of a mountain. The children find their way to the home of an *oni* or ogre, who possesses, incidentally, the ability of his kind to smell fresh blood; and he, too, draws on boots of swiftness, capable of covering in one step a thousand *ri* (2,440 miles), footwear that must surely have been styled by the same craftsman who made the winged sandals of Hermes.

The text that follows is the first English transla-tion of 'Le petit Poucet', which was published in *Histories, or Tales of past Times*, 1729. Here, it will be seen, the hero is called 'Little Poucet'. By the sixth edition of these stories, published 1764, the name had been changed to 'Little Thumb'. The name 'Hop o' my Thumb' (Hop on my Thumb), a term for a tiny person which was in common use four hundred years ago, does not seem to have been adopted for this story until the nineteenth century. The first editor to give this name to the hero seems to have been William Godwin in *Tabart's Collection of Popular Stories for the Nursery*, 1804.

Above: The ogre catches Little Thumb. Copperplate from *Little Thumb, And the Ogre*, 1808, which, though by an accomplished hand, is not likely to be by Blake as has been suggested.

Below: Etching by George Cruikshank from *Hop o' my Thumb, and the Seven-League Boots*, 1853

The Giant Ogre in his Seven League Boots, pursuing Hop o' my Thumb & his Brothers, who hide in a Cave

LITTLE POUCET

There was once upon a time a man and his wife, who made faggots for their livelihood, they had seven children all boys. The eldest was but ten years old, and the youngest but seven. People were amazed, that the faggot-maker had so many children in so small a time; but it was because his wife went quick about her business, and brought never less than two at a time. They were very poor, and their seven children incommoded them very much, because not one of them was able to get his bread. That which gave them yet more uneasiness, was, that the youngest was of a very tender constitution, and scarce ever spoke a word, which made them take that for stupidity, which was a sign of good sense; he was very little, and was no bigger when he was born than one's thumb, which made him be called *Little Poucet*, which signifies little Thumb.

The poor child bore the blame of every thing that was done amiss in the house, and he was always in the wrong: he was, notwithstanding all this, more cunning, and had a far greater share of wisdom than all his brothers put together; and if he spoke little, he heard and thought the more.

There happen'd now to come a very bad year, and the famine was so great, that these poor people resolved to rid themselves of their children. One evening, when they were all in bed, and the faggot-maker was sitting with his wife at the fire, he said to her, with his heart ready to break with grief, Thou seest, *Mary*, that we cannot keep our children, and I cannot see them die before my face; I am resolved to lose them in the wood to morrow, which may very easily be done; for while they are busy in tying up the faggots, we may run away, and leave them, without their taking the least notice. Ah! cried out his wife, and canst thou thy self, *Nicholas*, have the heart to take the children out along with thee, on purpose to lose them? In vain did her husband represent to her their extreme poverty, she would not consent to it; she was poor it was true, but she was their mother. However, having considered what a grief it would be to her to see them die with hunger, she at last consented, and went to bed all in tears.

Little Poucet heard every thing that was said; for having understood, as he lay in his bed, by some certain words, what they were talking of, he got up very softly, and slid himself under his father's stool, that he might hear what they said, without being seen himself. He went to bed again, but did not sleep a wink all the rest of the night, thinking on what he had to do. He got up early in the morning, and went to the river's side, where he filled his pockets full of small white pebbles, and then returned home. They all went abroad, but *Little Poucet* never told his brothers one syllable of what he knew. They went into a very thick forrest, where they could not see one another at ten feet distance. The Faggot-maker began to cut wood, and the children to gather up the branches to make faggots. Their father and mother seeing them busy at their work, got from them insensibly, and then ran away from them all at once, through the winding bushes. When the children saw they were left alone, they began to cry as loud as they could. *Little Poucet* let them cry on, knowing very well how to get home again; for as he came out, he dropt all along the way the little white pebbles he had in his pockets. Then he said to them, don't be afraid, Brothers, Father and Mother have left us here, but I'll bring you home again, only follow me; they did so, and he brought them home by the very same way that they came into the forrest: they dared not go in, but sat themselves down at the door, to hear what their Father and Mother said.

The very moment that the Faggot-maker and his Wife came home, the lord of the manour sent them ten crowns which he had owed them a long while, and which they never expected to see. This gave them new life; for the poor people were dying for hunger. The Faggot-maker sent his Wife immediately to the butchers. As it was a long while since they had eaten any thing, they bought three times as much meat as would sup two people: when they had eaten their fill, his wife said, Alas! where are now our poor children? they would make a good feast of what we have left; but as it was you, *Nicholas*, who had a mind to lose them, I told you we should repent of it, what are they now doing in the forrest? Alas! dear God, the wolves have eaten them up: thou hast been very inhumane thus to have lost thy children.

The Faggot-maker grew at last extremely angry, for she repeated it above twenty times, that they should repent of it, and that she was in the right of it for so saying. He threatened to beat her, if she did not hold her tongue. It was not that the Faggot-maker was not perhaps more sorry than his Wife, but that she continually teized him, and that he was of the humour of a great many others, who love those wives who speak well, but think those very importunate that have always done so. She was all in tears: Alas! where are now my children, my poor children? She spoke this once, so very loud, that the children who were at the door, began to cry out altogether, Here we are, here we are: she ran immediately to open the door, and said to them as she kissed them, I am glad to see you, my dear children, you are very hungry and weary; and *Billy*, you are very dirty, come in and let me clean you. Now, you must know, that *Billy* was her eldest son, which she loved above all the rest, because he was somewhat red-hair'd, as she herself was. They sat down to supper, and eat with such an appetite as pleased both father and mother, to whom they told how much afraid they were in the forrest, speaking almost always all together. This good couple were extremely glad to see their children once more at home; and this joy continued as long as the ten crowns lasted; but when the money was all gone, they fell again into their former uneasiness, and resolved to lose them once more; and that they might be the more certain of it, to carry them at a much greater distance than they had done before. They could not talk of this so secretly, but *Little Poucet* heard it, who made account to get out of this difficulty as well as the former; but though he got up very betimes in the morning, to go and pick up some little pebbles, he was disappointed; for the door of the house was double-locked. He was at a stand what to do; when their Father had given each of them a piece of bread for their breakfast, he fancied he might make use of his piece in stead of the pebbles, by throwing it in little bits all along the way they should pass; he put it up therefore very close into his pocket. Their Father and Mother brought them into the thickest and most obscure part of the forrest, and when they were there, they got to a by-path, and left them there. *Little Poucet* was not uneasy at it; for he thought he could very easily find the way again, by means of his bread which he had scattered all the way he went; but he was very much surprized, when he could not find so much as one crumb; the birds came and had eaten it up every bit. They were now in a great deal of trouble; for they wandered still more and more out of their way, and were more and more bewildered in the forrest.

Night now came on, and there arose a very great wind, which made them dreadfully afraid; they fancied they heard on every side of them the howling of wolves that were coming to eat them up; they scarce dared to speak or turn their heads. After this, it rained very hard, which wetted them to the skin; their feet slipped at every step they took, and they fell into the mire, whence they got up in a very dirty condition, and were forced to go upon all four. *Little Poucet* climbed up to the top of a tree, to see if he could discover any thing; having turned his head about on every side, he saw at last a glimmering light, as it were of a candle, but a long way from the forrest: he came down, and then he could see nothing of it; which made him very comfortless. However, having walked for some time with his brothers towards that side on which he had seen the light; he perceived it again when they came out of the wood.

They came at last to a house where this candle was, not without abundance of fear; for very often they lost sight of it, which happened every time they came into a bottom. They knocked at the door, and a good woman came and opened it; she asked them what they would have; *Little Poucet* told her, they were poor children, that had been lost in the forrest, and desired to lodge there for God's sake. The woman seeing them so very pretty, began to weep, and said to them, Alas! poor children, whence came ye; do you know that this house belongs to an *Ogre*, that eats up little children? Ah! dear Madam, answered *Little Poucet*, who trembled every joint of him, as well as his brothers, what shall we do? it is most certain, that the wolves of the forrest will not fail to eat us to night, if you refuse us to lie here; and this being so, we would rather the gentleman your husband should eat us, and perhaps he may take pity upon us, especially if you intercede with him. The *Ogre's* wife, who believed she could conceal them from her husband till the morning, let them come in, and brought them into the kitchen, that they might warm themselves at a very good fire; for there was a whole sheep upon the spit roasting for the *Ogre's* supper. As they began to warm themselves, they heard three or four great raps at the door; this was the *Ogre* that was come home. Upon this she hid them under the bed, and went to open the door. The *Ogre* then asked if supper was ready, and the wine drawn, and then sat himself down to table. The sheep was as yet all raw and bloody; but he liked it the better for that. He sniffed upon the right hand and upon the left, saying, he smelt fresh meat; what you smell so, said his wife, must be the calf which I have just now killed and flead.[1] I smell fresh meat, I tell thee once more, replied the *Ogre*, looking crossly at his wife, and there is something here that I don't understand; as he spoke these words, he got up from the table, and went directly to the bed. Ah, ha! said he, I see then how thou would'st cheat me, thou cursed woman, I don't know why I don't eat up thee too, but thou art an old beast. Here is good game that comes very luckily to entertain three *Ogres* of my acquaintance, who are to come to see me in a day or two. The poor children fell upon their knees, and begged his pardon, but they had to do with one of the most cruel *Ogres* in the world, who, far from having any pity on them, had already devoured them with his eyes, and told his wife, they would be delicate eating, when tossed up with an anchovie, and caper sauce. He then took a great knife, and coming up to these poor children, whetted it upon a great whet-stone that he had in his left hand. He had already taken hold of one of them, when his wife said to him, what need you do it now? is it not time enough to morrow? Hold your prating, said the *Ogre*, they will eat the tenderer. But you have so much victuals already, replied his wife, you have no occasion; here is a calf, two sheep, and half a hog. That is true, said the *Ogre*, give them their belly full, that they may not fall away, and put them to bed.

The good woman was overjoy'd at this, and gave them a good supper, but they were so much afraid, they could not eat a bit. As for the *Ogre*, he sat down again to drink, being highly pleased that he had gotten wherewithal to treat his friends. He drank a dozen glasses more than ordinary, which got up into his head, and obliged him to go to bed.

The *Ogre* had seven daughters, all little children, and these little *Ogresses* had all of them very fine complexions, because they used to eat fresh meat like their father; but they had little grey eyes and intirely round, hooked noses, very large mouths, and very long sharp teeth, standing at a pretty distance from each other. They were not yet very wicked, but they promised it very much, for they had already bitten several little children, that they might suck their blood. They were put to bed very early, and they lay all seven in a great bed, with every one a crown of gold upon her head. There was in the same chamber another bed of the same bigness, and it was into this bed the *Ogre's* wife put the seven little boys, after which she went to bed to her husband. *Little Poucet*, who had observed that the *Ogre's* Daughters had crowns of gold upon their heads, and was afraid lest the *Ogre* should repent his not killing of them, got up about midnight; and taking his brothers bonnets and his own, went very softly, and put them upon the heads of the seven little *Ogresses*, after having taken off their crowns of gold, which he put upon his own head and his brothers, that the *Ogre* might take them for his daughters, and his daughters for the little boys that he had a mind to kill. All this succeeded according to his desire; for the *Ogre* waking a little after, and sorry he

[1]Skinned.

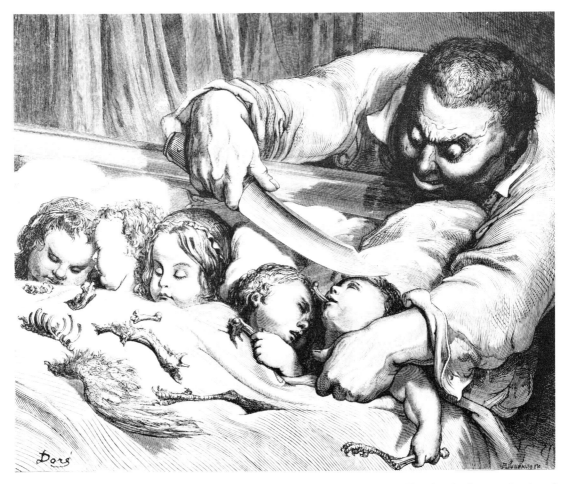

The ogre about to cut the throats of his seven daughters. The masterly but horrific plate by Gustave Doré in *Les Contes de Perrault*, 1862, which was suppressed in the English edition

deferred to do that till the morning, which he might have done over night, he threw himself hastily out of bed, and taking his great knife, Let us see, said he, how our little rogues do, and not make two jobs of the matter. He then went up, groping all the way into his daughters chamber; and coming up to the bed where the little boys lay, and who were every soul of them fast asleep, except *Little Poucet*, who was terribly afraid when he found the *Ogre* feeling about his head, as he had done about his brothers. The *Ogre*, who felt the crowns of gold, said, I should have made a fine piece of work of it truly, I find I have taken too much of the bottle last night, that is certain. Then he went to the bed where the girls lay; and having felt the boys little Bonnets. Hah! said he, my merry little lads, are you there? let us work hard; and saying these words, he cut, without more ado, the throats of all his seven little daughters. Well pleased with what he had done, he went to bed again to his wife. As soon as Little Poucet heard the *Ogre* snore, he waked his brothers, and bad them put on their clothes presently and follow him: they stole down softly into the garden, and got over the wall. They kept running almost all night, and continually trembled, without knowing which way they went.

The *Ogre*, when he awoke, said to his wife, Go up stairs, and dress the little rogues that came here last night: the *Ogress* was very much surprized at this goodness of her husband, not dreaming after what manner he intended she should dress them; but thinking that he had ordered her to go and put on their clothes, went up, and was very much surprized, when she perceived her seven daughters killed, and weltering in their own blood. She fainted away; for this is the first expedient almost all women find in the like misfortunes. The *Ogre* fearing his wife would be too long in doing what he had commanded her, went up himself to help her. He was no less astonished than his wife, at this frightful spectacle. Ah! what have I done? cried he, the cursed rogues shall pay for it, and that presently too. He threw then a pitcher of water upon his wife's face; and having brought her to herself, give me quickly, said he, my boots of seven leagues, that I may go and catch them. He went out into the high way; and having run over a great deal of ground both on this side and that; he came at last into the very road where the poor children were, who were not above an hundred paces from their father's house. They spied the *Ogre*, who went at one step from mountain to mountain, and over rivers as easily as the narrowest gutters. *Little Poucet* seeing a hollow rock near the place where they were, made his brothers hide themselves in it, and crept into it himself, minding always what would become of the *Ogre*.

The *Ogre*, who found himself very weary, after so long a journey, to no manner of purpose (for these same boots of seven leagues, fatigue their man very much) had a great mind to rest himself, and by chance went to sit down upon the rock where these little boys had hidden themselves. As it was impossible he could be more weary than he was, he fell asleep; and after reposing himself some time, began to snore so frightfully, that the poor children were no less afraid of him, than when he held up his great knife, and was going to cut their throats. *Little Poucet* was not so much frightened as his brothers, and told them, that they should run away immediately towards home, while the *Ogre* slept so soundly, and that they should not be in any pain about him. They took his advice, and got home presently. *Little Poucet* came up to the *Ogre*, pulled off his boots, and put them on upon his own legs; the boots were very long and large; but as they were Fairies, they were capable of growing big and little, according to the legs of those that wore them; so that they fitted his feet and legs as well as if they had been made on purpose for him. He went immediately to the *Ogre's* house, where he saw his wife crying bitterly for the loss of her children that were murdered.

Your husband, said *Little Poucet*, is in very great danger, being taken by a gang of thieves, who have sworn to kill him, if he does not give them all his gold and silver. The very moment they held their daggers at his throat, he perceived me, and desired me to come and tell you the condition he is in, and that you should give me every thing he has that is valuable, without exception; for otherwise they will kill him without mercy: and as his case is very pressing, he desires me to make use (you see

I have them on) of his boots of seven leagues, that I might make the more haste, and to shew you that I do not impose upon you.

The good woman being very much affrighted, gave him all she had: for this *Ogre* was a very good husband, though he used to eat up little children. *Little Poucet* having thus gotten all the *Ogre's* money, came home to his father's house, where he was received with a great deal of Joy.

There are a great many Authors, who do not agree in this last circumstance, and pretend, that *Little Poucet* never robbed the *Ogre* of his cash, and that he only thought he might very equitably, and according to good conscience, take off his boots of seven leagues, because he made use of them for no other end, but to run after little children. These Gentlemen say, that they are very well assured of this, and the more, as having drank and eaten often at the Faggot-maker's house. They say further, that when *Little Poucet* had taken off the *Ogre's* boots, he went to Court, where he was informed that they were very much in pain about an army that was two hundred leagues off, and the Success of a battle. He went, say they, to the King, and told him, that if he desired it, he would bring him News from the army before night. The King promised him a great sum of money upon that condition. *Little Poucet* was as good as his word, and returned that same very night with the news; and this first expedition causing him to be known, he got whatever he pleas'd; for the King paid him very well for carrying his orders to the army, and abundance of ladies gave him what he would to bring them news from their lovers; and that this was his greatest gain. There were some married women too, who sent Letters by him to their husbands, but they paid him so ill, that it was not worth his while, and turned to no manner of account. After having for some time carried on the business of a messenger, and gained thereby a great deal of money, he went home to his father, where it was impossible to express the joy they were all in at his return. He made the whole family very easy, bought places for his father and brothers; and by that means settled them very handsomely in the world, and in the mean time made his own court to perfection.

BEAUTY AND THE BEAST

The most symbolic of the fairy tales after Cinderella, and the most intellectually satisfying, 'Beauty and the Beast' is the prime example of the world-wide beast-marriage story, of which the classic text is that of Madame Leprince de Beaumont. This appeared in her *Magasin des enfans, ou dialogues entre une sage Gouvernante et plusieurs de ses Élèves*, published in London in 1756, of which the English translation, *The Young Misses Magazine*, came out in 1761.

Madame de Beaumont undoubtedly had the story from Madame Gabrielle Susanne Barbot de Gallon de Villeneuve, a lady not renowned for conciseness, her long-winded narrative occupying 362 pages of *Les Contes Marins*, 1740. Madame de Villeneuve, in her turn, may have found the theme almost anywhere. Several of the salient points are present in Madame d'Aulnoy's 'Mouton' (translated into English as 'The Royal Ram' in 1721). A similar tale, of a monster that insists on becoming the bridegroom of a beautiful princess, occurs in the *Pentamerone* (Day 2, tale 5), 1634; and a horrifying tale of a Pig Prince, a king's eldest son, born not only in the shape of a pig, but with a pig's inclinations, who must be wedded to no less than three women to be freed of his brutal enchantment, is recounted in Straparola's *Piacevoli notti* (Night 2, story 1), 1550.

In *The Nineteenth Century*, December 1878, W. R. S. Ralston made a collection of stories in which girls are wedded to a goat, a monkey, a wolf, a bear, and even a stove, which eventually become human, the tale being known to him in Norse, German, Sicilian, Cretan, Indian, Russian, and Mongolian variants. In a tale popular among the Kaffirs a crocodile changes into a fine man when his bride consents to lick his face. Further, it is impossible to read the story of Cupid and Psyche in *The Golden Ass* of Apuleius (2nd century A.D.) without feeling one is reading a version of Beauty and the Beast. There is the threatened union of an almost supernaturally beautiful girl with a hideous monster; and the deserted palace where disembodied voices bid the bride welcome and where invisible musicians play while a delicious meal is served by unseen hands. Psyche, like Beauty, is reluctantly allowed to go home to reassure her family, although her contact with them puts the course of true love in jeopardy. Psyche's two elder sisters are as jealous and malicious as are Beauty's, their affection for her is

Woodcuts from *Popular Tales of the Olden Time*, *c.* 1840, showing Beauty being reassured in a dream; and the Beast entreating Beauty to become his wife

as feigned, and in both stories they meet the fate they deserve.

'Beauty and the Beast' varies from the first part of 'Cupid and Psyche' in one important particular. Beauty's wooer has the appearance of a monster, and only after Beauty has overcome her aversion for his vile ·shape can the monster be seen to be a handsome prince. In 'Cupid and Psyche' the marriage takes place without impediment, but the identity of the bridegroom is unknown, since he is unseen; and Psyche loses him as soon as he is released from the spell and materializes as Cupid. There is thus no certainty in the story that Psyche's bridegroom was of loathsome shape, only the omnipresent fear of it, the oracle's awful pronouncement that it would be so:

Nec speres generum mortali stirpe creatum,
Sed saevum atque ferum vipereumque malum;

and the jealous assertions of her sisters that did she but realize it she was spending her nights with a great serpent.

In *The Golden Ass*, it will be recollected, the story of Cupid and Psyche is told by an old woman in the robbers' cave. The tale is 'an old wives' tale'. However much Apuleius improved the story, the tale he told in Latin was almost certainly the retelling of an older Greek story; and when looked at folkloristically the suspicion becomes a near-certainty that in the original tale the girl did marry a snake-shaped monster. Apuleius civilized the tale, making the bridegroom invisible; and 'taking hints,' says Robert Graves, 'from passages in Plato's *Phaedo* and *Republic* he turned it into a neat philosophical allegory of the progress of the rational soul towards intellectual love'.

Madame de Beaumont's text of 'Beauty and the Beast', which follows, is the one regularly used— even if at second and third hand—by the editors of modern fairy-tale collections. It was her telling of the tale which was followed for Tabart's *Popular Stories* in 1804, and which was the basis, whether or not Charles Lamb was the author, of the poetical *Beauty and the Beast: or, A Rough Outside with a Gentle Heart*, published on William Godwin's behalf in 1811. It has been the inspiration of numerous pantomimes and melodramas, such as *Beauty and the Beast; or, The Magic Rose*, produced at the Royal Coburg Theatre in 1819, and Planché's *Beauty and the Beast* at the Theatre Royal, Covent Garden, 1841.

The Beast as visualized by W. Heath Robinson, 1921

BEAUTY AND THE BEAST

There was once a very rich merchant, who had six children, three sons, and three daughters; being a man of sense, he spared no cost for their education, but gave them all kinds of masters. His daughters were extremely handsome, especially the youngest; when she was little every body admired her, and called her '*The little Beauty;*' so that, as she grew up, she still went by the name of *Beauty*, which made her sisters very jealous. The youngest, as she was handsomer, was also better than her sisters. The two eldest had a great deal of pride, because they were rich. They gave themselves ridiculous airs, and would not visit other merchants daughters, nor keep company with any but persons of quality. They went out every day upon parties of pleasure, balls, plays, concerts, &c. and laughed at their youngest sister, because she spent the greatest part of her time in reading good books. As it was known that they were great fortunes, several eminent merchants made their addresses to them; but the two eldest said, they would never marry, unless they could meet with a duke, or an earl at least. Beauty very civilly thanked them that courted her, and told them she was too young yet to marry, but chose to stay with her father a few years longer.

All at once the merchant lost his whole fortune, excepting a small country house at a great distance from town, and told his children with tears in his eyes, they must go there and work for their living. The two eldest answered, that they would not leave the town, for they had several lovers, who they were sure would be glad to have them, tho' they had no fortune; but the good ladies were mistaken, for their lovers slighted and forsook them in their poverty. As they were not beloved on account of their pride, every body said; they do not deserve to be pitied, we are very glad to see their pride humbled, let them go and give themselves quality airs in milking the cows and minding their dairy. But, added they, we are extremely concerned for Beauty, she was such a charming, sweet-tempered creature, spoke so kindly to poor people, and was of such an affable, obliging behaviour. Nay, several gentlemen would have married her, tho' they knew she had not a penny; but she told them she could not think of leaving her poor father in his misfortunes, but was determined to go along with him into the country to comfort and attend him. Poor Beauty at first was sadly grieved at the loss of her fortune; but, said she to herself, were I to cry ever so much, that would not make things better, I must try to make myself happy without a fortune. When they came to their country-house, the merchant and his three sons applied themselves to husbandry and tillage; and Beauty rose at four in the morning, and made haste to have the house clean, and dinner ready for the family. In the beginning she found it very difficult, for she had not been used to work as a servant, but in less than two months she grew stronger and healthier than ever. After she had done her work, she read, played on the harpsichord, or else sung whilst she spun. On the contrary, her two sisters did not know how to spend their time; they got up at ten, and did nothing but saunter about the whole day, lamenting the loss of their fine clothes and acquaintance. Do but see our youngest sister, said they, one to the other, what a poor, stupid, mean-spirited creature she is, to be contented with such an unhappy dismal situation. The good merchant was of quite a different opinion, he knew very well that Beauty outshone her sisters, in her person as well as her mind, and admired her humility and industry, but above all her humility and patience; for her sisters not only left her all the work of the house to do, but insulted her every moment.

The family had lived about a year in this retirement, when the merchant received a letter with an account that a vessel, on board of which he had effects, was safely arrived. This news had liked to have turned the heads of the two eldest daughters, who immediately flattered themselves with the hopes of returning to town, for they were quite weary of a country life; and when they saw their father ready to set out, they begged of him to buy them new gowns, head-dresses, ribbans, and all manner of trifles; but Beauty asked for nothing for she thought to herself, that all the money her father was going to receive, would scarce be sufficient to purchase every thing her sisters wanted. What will you have, Beauty? said her father. Since you have the goodness to think of me, answered she, be so kind to bring me a rose, for as none grows hereabouts, they are a kind of rarity. Not that Beauty cared for a rose, but she asked for something, lest she should seem by her example to condemn her sisters conduct, who would have said she did it only to look particular. The good man went on his journey, but when he came there, they went to law with him about the merchandize, and after a great deal of trouble and pains to no purpose, he came back as poor as before.

He was within thirty miles of his own house, thinking on the pleasure he should have in seeing his children again, when going through a large forest he lost himself. It rained and snowed terribly; besides, the wind was so high, that it threw him twice off his horse, and night coming on, he began to apprehend being either starved to death with cold and hunger, or else devoured by the wolves, whom he heard howling all round him, when, on a sudden, looking through a long walk of trees, he saw a light at some distance, and going on a little farther perceived it came from a place illuminated from top to bottom. The merchant returned God thanks for this happy discovery, and hasted to the place, but was greatly surprized at not meeting with any one in the out-courts. His horse followed him, and seeing a large stable open, went in, and finding both hay and oats, the poor beast, who was almost famished, fell to eating very heartily; the merchant tied him up to the manger, and walking towards the house, where he saw no one, but entering into a large hall, he found a good fire, and a table plentifully set out with but one cover laid. As he was wet quite through with the rain and snow, he drew near the fire to dry himself. I hope, said he, the master of the house, or his servants will excuse the liberty I take; I suppose it will not be long before some of them appear.

He waited a considerable time, till it struck eleven, and still no body came, at last he was so hungry that he could stay no longer, but took a chicken, and eat it in two mouthfuls, trembling all the while. After this he drank a few glasses of wine, and growing more courageous he went out of the hall, and crossed through several grand appartments with magnificent furniture, till he came into a chamber, which had an exceeding good bed in it, and as he was very much fatigued, and it was past midnight, he concluded it was best to shut the door, and go to bed.

It was ten the next morning before the merchant waked, and as he was going to rise he was astonished to see a good suit of clothes in the room of his own, which were quite spoiled; certainly, said he, this palace belongs to some kind fairy, who has seen and pitied my distress. He looked through a window, but instead of snow saw the most delightful arbours, interwoven with the beautifullest flowers that were ever beheld. He then returned to the great hall, where he had supped the night before, and found some chocolate ready made on a little table. Thank you, good Madam Fairy, said he aloud, for being so careful, as to provide me a breakfast, I am extremely obliged to you for all your favours.

The good man drank his chocolate, and then went to look for his horse, but passing thro' an arbour of roses he remembered Beauty's request to him, and gathered a branch on which were several; immediately he heard a great noise, and saw such a frightful Beast coming towards him, that he was ready to faint away. You are very ungrateful, said the Beast to him, in a terrible voice; I have saved your life by receiving you into my castle, and, in return, you steal my roses, which I value beyond any thing in the universe, but you shall die for it; I give you but a quarter of an hour to prepare yourself, and say your prayers. The merchant fell on his knees, and lifted up both his hands: My lord, said he, I beseech you to forgive me, indeed I had no intention to offend in gathering a rose for one of my daughters, who desired me to bring her one. My name is not, My Lord, replied the monster, but Beast; I don't love compliments, not I; I like people should speak as they think; and so do not imagine, I am to be moved by any of your flattering speeches: but you say you have got daughters, I will forgive you, on condition that one of them come willingly, and suffer for you. Let me have no words, but go about your business, and swear that if your daughter refuse to die in your stead, you will return within three months. The merchant had no mind to sacrifice his daughters to the ugly monster, but he thought, in obtaining this respite, he should have the satisfaction of seeing them once more, so he promised, upon oath, he would return, and the Beast told him he might set out when he pleased, but, added he, you shall not depart empty handed, go back to the room where you lay, and you will see a great empty chest, fill it with whatever you like best, and I will send it to your home, and at the same time Beast withdrew. Well, said the good man to himself, if I must die, I shall have the comfort, at least, of leaving something to my poor children.

The merchant begging forgiveness for taking a rose. Illustration by Gordon Browne for
Laura E. Richards's retelling of the story, 1886

He returned to the bed-chamber, and finding a great quantity of broad pieces of
gold, he filled the great chest the Beast had mentioned, locked it, and afterwards took
his horse out of the stable, leaving the palace with as much grief as he had entered it

with joy. The horse, of his own accord, took one of the roads of the forest, and in a few hours the good man was at home. His children came round him, but instead of receiving their embraces with pleasure, he looked on them, and holding up the branch he had in his hands, he burst into tears. Here, Beauty, said he, take these roses, but little do you think how dear they are like to cost your unhappy father, and then related his fatal adventure: immediately the two eldest set up lamentable outcries, and said all manner of ill-natured things to Beauty, who did not cry at all. Do but see the pride of that little wretch, said they; she would not ask for fine clothes, as we did; but no truly, Miss wanted to distinguish herself, so now she will be the death of our poor father, and yet she does not so much as shed a tear. Why should I, answered Beauty, it would be very needless, for my father shall not suffer upon my account, since the monster will accept of one of his daughters, I will deliver myself up to all his fury, and I am very happy in thinking that my death will save my father's life, and be a proof of my tender love for him. No sister, said her three brothers, that shall not be, we will go find the monster, and either kill him, or perish in the attempt. Do not imagine any such thing, my sons, said the merchant, Beast's power is so great, that I have no hopes of your overcoming him: I am charmed with Beauty's kind and generous offer, but I cannot yield to it; I am old, and have not long to live, so can only loose a few years, which I regret for your sakes alone, my dear children. Indeed father, said Beauty, you shall not go to the palace without me, you cannot hinder me from following you. It was to no purpose all they could say, Beauty still insisted on setting out for the fine palace, and her sisters were delighted at it, for her virtue and amiable qualities made them envious and jealous.

The merchant was so afflicted at the thoughts of losing his daughter, that he had quite forgot the chest full of gold, but at night when he retired to rest, no sooner had he shut his chamber-door, than, to his great astonishment, he found it by his bedside; he was determined, however, not to tell his children, that he was grown rich, because they would have wanted to return to town, and he was resolved not to leave the country; but he trusted Beauty with the secret, who informed him, that two gentlemen came in his absence, and courted her sisters; she begged her father to consent to their marriage, and give them fortunes, for she was so good, that she loved them and forgave heartily all their ill usage. These wicked creatures rubbed their eyes with an onion to force some tears when they parted with their sister, but her brothers were really concerned: Beauty was the only one who did not shed tears at parting, because she would not increase their uneasiness.

The horse took the direct road to the palace, and towards evening they perceived it illuminated as at first: the horse went of himself into the stable, and the good man and his daughter came into the great hall, where they found a table splendidly served up, and two covers. The merchant had no heart to eat, but Beauty, endeavouring to appear chearful, sat down to table, and helped him. Afterwards, thought she to herself, Beast surely has a mind to fatten me before he eats me, since he provides such plentiful

Hand-coloured copperplates from the 1813 edition of
Beauty and the Beast: or, A Rough Outside with a Gentle Heart,
a booklet giving a poetical version of the tale,
believed to be by Charles Lamb

entertainment. When they had supped they heard a great noise, and the merchant, all in tears, bid his poor child, farewell, for he thought Beast was coming. Beauty was sadly terrified at his horrid form, but she took courage as well as she could, and the monster having asked her if she came willingly; ye—e—es, said she, trembling: you are very good, and I am greatly obliged to you; honest man, go your ways tomorrow morning, but never think of coming here again. Farewel Beauty, farewel Beast, answered she, and immediately the monster withdrew. Oh, daughter, said the merchant, embracing Beauty, I am almost frightened to death, believe me, you had better go back, and let me stay here; no, father, said Beauty, in a resolute tone, you shall set out to-morrow morning, and leave me to the care and protection of providence. They went to bed, and thought they should not close their eyes all night; but scarce were they laid down, than they fell fast asleep, and Beauty dreamed, a fine lady came, and said to her, I am content, Beauty, with your good will, this good action of yours in giving up your own life to save your fathers shall not go unrewarded. Beauty waked, and told her father her dream, and though it helped to comfort him a little, yet he could not help crying bitterly, when he took leave of his dear child.

As soon as he was gone, Beauty sat down in the great hall, and fell a crying likewise; but as she was mistress of a great deal of resolution, she recommended herself to God, and resolved not to be uneasy the little time she had to live; for she firmly believed Beast would eat her up that night.

However, she thought she might as well walk about till then, and view this fine castle, which she could not help admiring; it was a delightful pleasant place, and she was extremely surprised at seeing a door, over which was wrote, 'BEAUTY'S APARTMENT.' She opened it hastily, and was quite dazzled with the magnificence that reigned throughout; but what chiefly took up her attention, was a large library, a harpsicord, and several music books. Well, said she to herself, I see they will not let my time hang heavy upon my hands for want of amusement. Then she reflected, 'Were I but to stay here a day, there would not have been all these preparations.' This consideration inspired her with fresh courage; and opening the library she took a book, and read these words, in letters of gold:

'Welcome Beauty, banish fear,
You are queen and mistress here:
Speak your wishes, speak your will,
Swift obedience meets them still.'

Alas, said she, with a sigh, there is nothing I desire so much as to see my poor father, and know what he is doing; she had no sooner said this, when casting her eyes on a great looking-glass, to her great amazement, she saw her own home, where her father arrived with a very dejected countenance; her sisters went to meet him, and notwith-standing their endeavours to appear sorrowful, their joy, felt for having got rid of their sister, was visible in every feature: a moment after, every thing disappeared, and Beauty's apprehensions at this proof of Beast's complaisance.

At noon she found dinner ready, and while at table, was entertained with an excellent concert of music, though without seeing any body: but at night, as she was going to sit down to supper, she heard the noise Beast made, and could not help being sadly terrified. Beauty, said the monster, will you give me leave to see you sup? That is as you please, answered Beauty trembling. No, replied the Beast, you alone are mistress here; you need only bid me be gone, if my presence is troublesome, and I will immedi-ately withdraw: but, tell me, do not you think me very ugly? That is true, said Beauty,

'There she found poor Beast stretched out, quite senseless.' Colour wood-engraving by Edmund Evans, after the watercolour drawing by Walter Crane, 1874

for I cannot tell a lie, but I believe you are very good-natured. So I am, said the monster, but then, besides my ugliness, I have no sense; I know very well, that I am a poor, silly, stupid creature. 'Tis no sign of folly to think so, replied Beauty, for never did fool know this, or had so humble a conceit of his own understanding. Eat then, Beauty, said the monster, and endeavour to amuse yourself in your palace, for every thing here is yours, and I should be very uneasy, if you were not happy. You are very obliging, answered Beauty, I own I am pleased with your kindness, and when I consider that, your deformity scarce appears. Yes, yes, said the Beast, my heart is good, but still I am a monster. Among mankind, says Beauty, there are many that deserve that name more than you, and I prefer you, just as you are, to those, who, under a human form, hide a treacherous, corrupt, and ungrateful heart. If I had sense enough, replied the Beast, I would make a fine compliment to thank you, but I am so dull, that I can only say, I am greatly obliged to you. Beauty eat a hearty supper, and had almost conquered her dread of the monster; but she had like to have fainted away, when he said to her, Beauty, will you be my wife? She was some time before she durst answer, for she was afraid of making him angry, if she refused. At last, however, she said, trembling, no Beast. Immediately the poor monster went to sigh, and hissed so frightfully, that the whole palace echoed. But Beauty soon recovered her fright, for Beast having said, in a mournful voice, 'then farewel, Beauty,' left the room; and only turned back, now and then, to look at her as he went out.

When Beauty was alone, she felt a great deal of compassion for poor Beast. Alas, said she, 'tis thousand pities, any thing so good-natured should be so ugly.

Beauty spent three months very contentedly in the palace: every evening Beast paid her a visit, and talked to her, during supper, very rationally, with plain good common sense, but never with what the world calls wit; and Beauty daily discovered some valuable qualifications in the monster, and seeing him often had so accustomed her to his deformity, that, far from dreading the time of his visit, she would often look on her watch to see when it would be nine, for the Beast never missed coming at that hour. There was but one thing that gave Beauty any concern, which was, that every night, before she went to bed, the monster always asked her, if she would be his wife. One day she said to him, Beast, you make me very uneasy, I wish I could consent to marry you, but I am too sincere to make you believe that will ever happen; I shall always esteem you as a friend, endeavour to be satisfied with this. I must, said the Beast, for, alas! I know too well my own misfortune, but then I love you with the tenderest affection: however, I ought to think myself happy, that you will stay here; promise me never to leave me. Beauty blushed at these words; she had seen in her glass, that her father had pined himself sick for the loss of her, and she longed to see him again. I could, answered she, indeed, promise never to leave you entirely, but I have so great a desire to see my father, that I shall fret to death, if you refuse me that satisfaction. I had rather die myself, said the monster, than give you the least uneasiness: I will send you to your father, you shall remain with him, and poor Beast will die with grief. No, said Beauty, weeping, I love you too well to be the cause of your death: I give you my promise to return in a week: you have shewn me, that my sisters are married, and my brothers gone to the army; only let me stay a week with my father, as he is alone. You shall be there to morrow morning, said the Beast, but remember your promise: you need only lay your ring on a table before you go to bed, when you have a mind to come back: farewel Beauty. Beast sighed, as usual, bidding her good night, and Beauty went to bed very sad at seeing him so afflicted. When she waked the next morning, she found herself at her father's, and having rang a little bell, that was by her bedside, she saw the maid come, who, the moment she saw her, gave a loud shriek, at which the good man ran up stairs, and thought he should have died with joy to see his dear daughter again. He held her fast locked in his arms above a quarter of an hour. As soon as the first transports were over, Beauty began to think of rising, and was afraid she had no clothes to put on; but the maid told her, that she had just found, in the next room, a large trunk full of gowns, covered with gold and diamonds. Beauty thanked good Beast for his kind care, and taking one of the plainest of them, she intended to make a present of the others to her sisters. She scarce had said so when the trunk disappeared. Her father told her, that Beast insisted on her keeping them herself, and immediately both gowns and trunk came back again.

Beauty dressed herself, and in the mean time they sent to her sisters, who hasted thither with their husbands. They were both of them very unhappy. The eldest had married a gentleman, extremely handsome indeed, but so fond of his own person, that he was full of nothing but his own dear self, and neglected his wife. The second had married a man of wit, but he only made use of it to plague and torment every body, and his wife most of all. Beauty's sisters sickened with envy, when they saw her dressed like a princess, and more beautiful than ever, nor could all her obliging affectionate behaviour stifle their jealousy, which was ready to burst when she told them how happy she was. They went down into the garden to vent it in tears; and said one to the other, in what is this little creature better than us, that she should be so much happier? Sister, said the oldest, a thought just strikes my mind; let us endeavour to detain her above a week, and perhaps the silly monster will be so enraged at her for breaking her word, that he will devour her. Right, sister, answered the other, therefore we must shew her as much kindness as possible. After they had taken this resolution, they went up, and behaved so affectionately to their sister, that poor Beauty wept for joy. When the week was expired, they cried and tore their hair, and seemed so sorry to part with her, that she promised to stay a week longer.

In the mean time, Beauty could not help reflecting on herself, for the uneasiness she was likely to cause poor Beast, whom she sincerely loved, and really longed to see again. The tenth night she spent at her father's, she dreamed she was in the palace garden, and that she saw Beast extended on the grass-plat, who seemed just expiring, and, in a dying voice, reproached her with her ingratitude. Beauty started out of her sleep, and bursting into tears; am I not very wicked, said she, to act so unkindly to Beast, that has studied so much, to please me in every thing? Is it his fault if he is so ugly, and has so little sense? He is kind and good, and that is sufficient. Why did I refuse to marry him? I should be happier with the monster than my sisters are with their

'She had like to have fainted away, when
he said to her, Beauty, will you be my wife?'
Illustration by Eleanor Vere Boyle, 1875

husbands; it is neither wit, nor a fine person, in a husband, that makes a woman happy, but virtue, sweetness of temper, and complaisance, and Beast has all these valuable qualifications. It is true, I do not feel the tenderness of affection for him, but I find I have the highest gratitude, esteem, and friendship; I will not make him miserable, were I to be so ungrateful I should never forgive myself. Beauty having said this, rose, put her ring on the table, and then laid down again; scarce was she in bed before she fell asleep, and when she waked the next morning, she was overjoyed to find herself in the Beast's palace. She put on one of her richest suits to please him, and waited for evening with the utmost impatience, at last the wished-for hour came, the clock struck nine, yet no Beast appeared. Beauty then feared she had been the cause of his death; she ran crying and wringing her hands all about the palace, like one in despair; after having sought for him every where, she recollected her dream, and flew to the canal in the garden, where she dreamed she saw him. There she found poor Beast stretched out, quite senseless, and, as she imagined, dead. She threw herself upon him without any dread, and finding his heart beat still, she fetched some water from the canal, and poured it on his head. Beast opened his eyes, and said to Beauty, you forgot your promise, and I was so afflicted for having lost you, that I resolved to starve myself, but since I have the happiness of seeing you once more, I die satisfied. No dear Beast, said Beauty, you must not die; live to be my husband; from this moment I give you my hand, and swear to be none but yours. Alas! I thought I had only a friendship for you, but the grief I now feel convinces me, that I cannot live without you. Beauty scarce had pronounced these words, when she saw the palace sparkle with light; and fireworks, instruments of music, every thing seemed to give notice of some great event: but nothing could fix her attention; she turned to her dear Beast, for whom she trembled with fear; but how great was her surprize! Beast was disappeared, and she saw, at her feet, one of the loveliest princes that eye ever beheld; who returned her thanks for having put an end to the charm, under which he had so long resembled a Beast. Though this prince was worthy of all her attention, she could not forbear asking where Beast was. You see him at your feet, said the prince: a wicked fairy had condemned me to remain under that shape till a beautiful virgin should consent to marry me: the fairy likewise enjoined me to conceal my understanding; there was only you in the world generous enough to be won by the goodness of my temper, and in offering you my crown I can't discharge the obligations I have to you. Beauty, agreeably surprized, gave the charming prince her hand to rise; they went together into the castle, and Beauty was overjoyed to find, in the great hall, her father and his whole family, whom the beautiful lady, that appeared to her in her dream, had conveyed thither.

Beauty, said this lady, come and receive the reward of your judicious choice; you have preferred virtue before either wit or beauty, and deserve to find a person in whom all these qualifications are united: you are going to be a great queen, I hope the throne will not lessen your virtue, or make you forget yourself. As to you, ladies, said the fairy to Beauty's two sisters, I know your hearts, and all the malice they contain: become two statues, but, under this transformation, still retain your reason. You shall stand before your sister's palace gate, and be it your punishment to behold her happiness; and it will not be in your power to return to your former state, till you own your faults, but I am very much afraid that you will always remain statues. Pride, anger, gluttony, and idleness are sometimes conquered, but the conversion of a malicious and envious mind is a kind of miracle. Immediately the fairy gave a stroke with her wand, and in a moment all that were in the hall were transported into the prince's dominions: his subjects received him with joy; he married Beauty, and lived with her many years and their happiness as it was founded on virtue was compleat.

Beauty and her father riding to the Beast's palace.
Illustration by A. J. Gaskin from
Baring-Gould's *Book of Fairy Tales*, 1894

Despite a wonderfully long history, this tale does not seem to have been printed in English until the second volume of Madame de Beaumont's *Magasin des Enfans* was translated as *The Young Misses Magazine* in 1761. In the *Magazine* 'Mrs Affable', who tells the story, describes it as a 'pretty tale, which I have read somewhere'. Probably Madame de Beaumont had it from Perrault. It was one of three tales in verse he published prior to his *Histoires ou Contes du temps passé*, appearing (as 'Les Souhaits Ridicules') first in the fashionable paper *Le Mercure Galant*, November 1693, and subsequently in Moetjens' *Recueil de pièces curieuses et nouvelles*, 1694.

Madame de Beaumont's version differs from Perrault's only in detail. She makes the husband a 'not very rich man' instead of a woodcutter; the granter of the wishes a fairy, not Jupiter; and the wife the wisher for the pudding (because the fire is good) not the husband. And in her version the husband hopes that he may still be rich with the last wish, suggesting his wife be compensated by having a case of gold in which to hide her nose.

Possibly, however, the tale had already long been known in Britain. Amongst the fables of Marie de France, a poetess of the twelfth century, is one called 'Dou Vilain qui prist un Folet' or 'Des Troiz Oremens'. In this a rogue catches a goblin who grants him three wishes, two of which the man gives to his wife. But while they are eating a marrow bone for dinner, and having difficulty extracting the marrow, the wife unthinkingly wishes her husband had the beak of a woodcock. The husband, infuriated at finding himself with a long beak on the front of his face, wishes his wife may have one too. They sit there both with their long beaks; with two of their three wishes already used; and with 'no good gained thereby'. It is obvious to both of them what their last wish will have to be. The evidence is that this fable was translated by Marie de France from an English

text; and the source she used is believed to have been a lost collection of fables that has been attributed to King Alfred.

In the *Book of Sindibâd*, a book probably of Persian origin dating from the ninth century, and known in Western Europe as *The Book of the Seven Sages*, a similar tale is given, told by the seventh Sage, as an instance of the deceitfulness of women. A friendly spirit gives a man the formula to make three wishes come true. The man consults his wife about what he should wish for and she, conscious of what she herself appreciates, suggests that since man's greatest comfort is in woman he should be numerously endowed with the means of satisfaction. He makes the wish, but is immediately horrified by the result, for his body is now overburdened. He therefore asks, as his second wish, to have all that embarrasses him removed. However the fulfilment of this new wish leaves him, as Andrew Lang once put it, with 'a frightful *minus* quantity'; and the third wish has to be expended in getting himself restored to his original condition.

A more edifying version of the tale was collected by the Grimm brothers in the Schwalm district of Hesse. In the days when the Lord himself still walked the earth, the Lord begged admittance to a rich man's house, and being refused admittance, tried at a poor man's house opposite, where he was made welcome over night. The next morning the Lord offered three wishes, and the poor man said he would be content if he could have but good health and daily bread. The Lord then suggested that for his third wish he might like a new house, and he agreed. When the rich man saw the new house, and heard the story, he saddled his horse and galloped after the Lord, that he too might have three wishes, which eventually were granted, though the Lord warned him they would do him no good. This he soon learned to his cost, for annoyed by the restlessness of his horse he wished it dead; and weighed down by the saddle he had then to carry he wished his wife stuck fast to it. His third wish had to be used to separate his wife from the saddle. Wilhelm Grimm (born 1786) recalled that this was a tale he had heard the spinning-girls relate when he was a child. Subsequently he found a number of parallels, not only in old German (see F. H. von der Hagen's *Gesammtabenteuer*, no. 37) and other European languages, but in both Indian and Chinese.

That Madame de Beaumont's version, which follows, is the one that has fed English tradition seems clear. Catherine Ann Dorset, in her amusing metrical rendering of the tale, *Think Before You Speak: or, The Three Wishes*, published 1809, acknowledges that the tale is taken from Madame de Beaumont's publication, 'which formed almost the whole library and the delight of the children of the last generation'. And Benjamin Tabart, in

his oft-reprinted *Popular Fairy Tales*, collected together in 1818, gives the tale almost word for word as in *The Young Misses Magazine*.

Dr Katharine Briggs, in *A Dictionary of British Folk-Tales*, 1970, found only a relic of the story, known to an eleven-year-old schoolboy in Aberdeenshire, the three wishes that a man and his wife make being 'Soup again! I wish I had a pudding for a change!' 'One wish gone! I wish the pudding was on your head!' and 'I wish the pudding was off my head'. Our own recollection of our schooldays is that the tale had a more ingenious ending. When two wishes had been wasted, the wisher's last wish was that all the wishes he ever wished should come true. We thought this splendidly clever.

Illustration by Harry Clarke, 1922

THE TALE OF
THE THREE WISHES

There was once a man, not very rich, who had a pretty woman to his wife. One winter's evening, as they sat by their fire, they talked of the happiness of their neighbours, who were richer than they. Said the wife, if it were in my power to have what I wish, I should soon be happier than all of them: So should I too, said the husband; I wish we had fairies now, and that one of them was kind enough to grant me what I should ask. At that instant they saw a very beautiful Lady in their room, who told them, I am a fairy; and I promise to grant you the three first things you shall wish; but take care, after having wished for three things, I will not grant any thing farther. The fairy disappeared, and the man and his wife were much perplexed. For my own part, said the wife, if it is left to my choice, I know very well what I shall wish for: I do not wish yet, but I think nothing is so good as to be handsome, rich, and to be of great quality. But the husband answered, with all these things one may be sick, fretful, and one may die young; it would be much wiser to wish for health, chearfulness, and a long life. But to what purpose is a long life with poverty, says the wife? It would only prolong misery. In truth, the fairy should have promised us a dozen of gifts, for there's, at least, a dozen things which I should want. That's true, said the husband, but let us take time, let us consider, from this time till morning, the three things which are most necessary for us, and then wish. I'll think all night, said the wife, mean while let us warm ourselves, for it is very cold. At the same time, the wife took the tongs to mend the fire, and seeing there were a great many coals thoroughly lighted, she said, without thinking on it; here's a nice fire, I wish we had a yard of black pudding for our supper, we could dress it easily. She had hardly said these words, when down came tumbling thro' the chimney a yard of black pudding: Plague on greedy-guts, with her black pudding, said the husband; here's a fine wish indeed, now we have only two left; for my part, I am so vexed, that I wish the black pudding fast to the tip of your nose. The man soon perceived, that he was sillier than his wife; for, at this second wish, up starts the black pudding, and sticks so fast to the tip of the poor wife's nose, there was no means to take it off. Wretch that I am! cried she; you are a wicked man for wishing the pudding fast to my nose. My dear, answered the husband, I vow I did not think of it; but what shall we do? I am about wishing for vast riches, and propose to make a gold case to hide the pudding. Not at all, answered the wife, for I should kill myself, were I to live with this pudding dangling at my nose; be persuaded; we have still a wish to make; leave it to me, or I shall instantly throw myself out of the window; with this she ran, and opened the window, but the husband, who loved his wife, called out, Hold, my dear wife, I will give you leave to wish for whatever you will. Well, said the wife, my wish is, that this pudding may drop off. At that instant, the pudding dropt off, and the wife, who did not want wit, said to her husband, the fairy has imposed upon us; she was in the right, possibly we should have been more unhappy with riches, than we are at present. Believe me, friend, let us wish for nothing, and take things as it shall please God to send them; in the mean time, let us sup upon our pudding, since that's all that remains to us of our wishes. The husband thought his wife judged right, they supped merrily, and never gave themselves farther trouble about the things which they had designed to wish for.

Illustration by an 'eminent artist' for
The Child's Own Book, 1830

Right: Hand-coloured copperplates from Mrs Dorset's *Think Before you Speak: or, The Three Wishes*, 1809. This was a metrical rendering of the tale, based on the text in Madame de Beaumont's *Magasin des Enfans*, 1756, which Mrs Dorset (born *c.* 1750) had known as a child. Old tales re-told in verse, and issued individually in illustrated booklets, were a feature of juvenile publishing in the early years of the nineteenth century. Other examples are *Beauty and the Beast: or, A Rough Outside with a Gentle Heart*, 1811 (page 144), and *The History of Mother Twaddle and the Marvellous Atchievments of Her Son Jack*, 1807 (page 163)

THE THREE HEADS
IN THE WELL

This haunting tale of a princess obliged to leave home because of stepmother trouble, who good-naturedly washes, combs, and lays down softly three golden heads which appear out of a well, is of particular interest as being the English equivalent to Perrault's 'Diamonds and Toads' (p. 98). In this tale the princess is rewarded for her services by being given outstanding beauty, sweet bodily perfume (apparently aphrodisiac), and a king for a husband; while her hump-backed stepsister who seeks to emulate her obtains a disfigured face, foul breath, and a poor cobbler for mate.

The story is found in a chapbook, *The History of Four Kings, Their Queens and Daughters, Kings of Canterbury, Colchester, Cornwall and Cumberland. Being the Merry Tales of Tom Hodge, And his School-Fellows*, of which a number of editions exist printed in the second half of the eighteenth century. It seems likely, however, that the tale was already traditional in Elizabethan times. In George Peele's *The Old Wiues Tale*, 1595, a comedy as crammed with fairy-tale situations as an extravaganza by Planché, a widower named Lampriscus has two daughters, one handsome, but proud as a peacock; the other hard-favoured, foul, and ill-faced. A friend recommends they be sent to a well for the water of life. When the proud daughter arrives with her pitcher, a head appears from the well and says:

> Gently dip, but not too deepe
> For feare you make the golden birde to weepe,
> Faire maiden white and red,
> Stroke me smoothe, and combe my head:
> And thou shalt haue some cockell bread.

She replies, 'Faith, ile giue you cockell bread', and breaks her pitcher on the head. Then the ill-faced daughter goes to the well. A head comes up which has ears of corn for hair, and commands:

> Gently dip: but not too deepe;
> For feare you make the gouldē beard (sic) to
> weepe.

She combs the corn into her lap, and the head continues:

> Faire maiden white and red,
> Combe me smoothe, and stroke my head:
> And thou shalt haue some cockell bread,
> Gently dippe, but not too deepe,
> For feare thou make the gouldē beard to weep.
> Faire maide, white, and redde,
> Combe me smooth, and stroke my head;
> And euery haire, a sheaue shall be,
> And euery sheaue a goulden tree.

Woodcuts by James March from his penny *Fairy Tales*,
1854, illustrating a 'Frau Holle' version of the tale

Hereupon a second head comes up which is full of gold. This she also combs, combing gold into her lap.

Tales have been found in Norway, Sweden, Denmark, and Germany, that are not altogether dissimilar. In a version of 'Frau Holle' collected by the Grimms in Hesse, two girls, one pretty and the other hideous, are spinning beside a well, and agree that if either lets her distaff fall in the water she must go in after it. This happens to the pretty one, who going into the well after her distaff is not drowned, but discovers under the water an enchanted land where lives Frau Holle, who greets her with the cry 'The wind, the heavenly child! come in and comb my hair'. The girl, who is as complaisant as she is pretty, eventually returns home well-rewarded with gold; and when the ugly girl has to go into the well to fetch her distaff, she comes out in a much less satisfactory condition, one that makes the cock crow out 'Our dirty girl is coming'.

Similarly in one of Madame Villeneuve's tales, 'The Young American', written in the eighteenth century, a stepchild (ill-treated, needless to say) accidentally falls into a well, and there meets a water-nymph, whose hair she is asked to comb, receiving in return a fabulous assortment of gifts, and each time she combs her hair bright flowers fall from it. Her proud stepsister, who jumps into the well in the hope of similar benefits, would have been better advised to remain at home. Her gift is that stinking weeds and rushes shall grow out of her head.

James Orchard Halliwell, in *Popular Rhymes and Nursery Tales*, 1849, gives a text of 'The Three Heads of the Well' which has often been re-printed, and which he says is abridged from an old chapbook *Three Kings of Colchester*. This chapbook has not been found. The one significant difference in it to the text that follows is that when the princess sits beside the well the first golden head sings:

> Wash me, and comb me,
> And lay me down softly,
> And lay me on a bank to dry,
> That I may look pretty,
> When somebody comes by.

This is a rhyme that appeared in a collection of traditional verses, *Songs for the Nursery*, published in 1805, a book with which Halliwell is known to have been familiar; and it is to be suspected he succumbed, as have other scholars before and since, to the temptation of making his source contain what he felt it ought to contain rather than what it did contain. It is noticeable that in a catalogue of *Popular Histories* which he compiled only a month later, Halliwell made no mention of a chapbook entitled *Three Kings of Colchester;* but did possess a copy of *The History of the Four Kings*, a late edition printed at Falkirk in 1823.

The Four Kings was advertised by Cluer Dicey and Richard Marshall in 1764 as being for sale 'at the Printing-Office, in Aldermary Church-Yard, London', and it is an Aldermary Church-Yard text which follows. One who clearly was familiar with the tale was the peasant-poet John Clare. In *The Shepherd's Calendar*, 1827, he recalled tales of childhood 'told to delight, and never failed', which now, sadly, no longer seemed so bewitching:

> The Magic Fountain, where the head
> Rose up, just as the startled maid
> Was stooping from the weedy brink
> To dip her pitcher in to drink,
> That did its half-hid mystery tell
> To smooth its hair, and use it well;
> Which, doing as it bade her do,
> Turn'd to a king and lover too.

It may be added that in the Scottish Highlands a widespread tradition associates certain wells with severed heads, sometimes with severed heads that speak; that in Ireland comparable legends exist in which the water in a well reacts strangely after a severed head has been placed in it; and that an amount of evidence exists, assembled in 1962 by Dr Anne Ross, showing that certain wells, notably in Wales, have long been reputed to have com-menced flowing, or to have acquired healing properties, as the result of the severed head of a saint falling at the spot. It seems that when Peele told of a well containing the water of life, in which lived several severed heads, he was echoing or giving form to a Celtic tradition that belongs to antiquity.

THE KING OF
COLCHESTER'S DAUGHTERS

Long before Arthur and the Knights of the Round Table, reigned in the eastern part of this land, a king, who kept his court at Colchester. He was witty strong and valiant: by which means he subdued his enemies abroad, and planted peace among his subjects at home.

Nevertheless, in the midst of all his earthly glory, his queen died, leaving behind her an only daughter, about fifteen years of age, under the care of her royal husband. This lady for her courtly carriage, beauty, and affability, was the wonder of all that knew her; but as covetousness is the root of all evil, so it happened here.

The King hearing of a Lady who had likewise an only daughter, for the sake of her riches had a mind to marry her; tho' she was old, ugly, hook-nos'd and hump-back'd, yet all could not deter him from marrying her. The daughter of the said piece of deformity was a yellow dowdy, full of envy and ill-nature, and in short was much of the same mould as her mother. This signified nothing, for in a few weeks, the king, attended by the nobility and gentry, brought the said piece of deformity to his palace where the marriage rites were performed. Long they had not been in the court before they set the king against his own beautiful daughter, which was done by false reports and accusations. The young princess having lost her father's love, grew weary of the court, and on a certain day meeting with her father in the garden, she desired him with tears in her eyes to give her a small subsistence, and she would go and seek her fortune, to which the king consented, and ordered her mother-in-law to make up a small sum according to her discretion. To her she went, who gave her a canvas bag of brown bread and hard cheese with a bottle of beer; though this was but a very pitiful dowry for a King's daughter. She takes it, returns thanks, and so proceeded, passing through groves, woods, and valleys, till at length she saw an old man sitting on a stone at the mouth of a cave, who said, Good morrow, fair maiden, whither away so fast? Aged father, says she, I am going to seek my fortune. What has thou in thy bag and bottle? In my bag I have got bread and cheese, and in my bottle good small beer; will you please to partake of either? Yes said he, with all my heart.—With that the Lady pulled out her provision, and bid him eat and welcome. He did and gave her many thanks telling her there was a thick thorny hedge before her which will appear to you impassable, but take this wand in your hand, strike three times, and say, pray hedge let me come through, and it will open immediately: then a little further you will find a well, sit down on the brink of it, and there will come up three golden heads, which will speak, and what they require that do. Then promising she

'The Three Heads in the Well' by Arthur Rackham. From *English Fairy Tales*, 1918

would, she took her leave of him.—Coming to the hedge and following the old man's directions, the hedge divided, and gave her a passage; then coming to the well, she had not sooner sat down but a Golden Head came up with a singing note, Wash me, comb me, lay me down softly, Yes, said the young lady, then putting forth her hand with a silver comb, performed the office, placing it upon a primrose bank. Then came up a second and a third, saying as the former, which she complied with; and then pulling out her provision, eat her dinner. Then said the Heads one to another, What shall we do for this lady, who hath used us so very kindly?—The first said, I will cause such addition to her beauty, that shall charm the most powerful prince in the world. The second said, I will endow her with such perfume both in body and breath, as shall far exceed the sweetest flowers. The third said, My gift shall be none of the least, for as she is a King's daughter, I'll make her so fortunate that she shall become queen to the greatest Prince that reigns.—This done, at their request, she let them down into the well again, and so proceeded on her journey.——She had not travelled long before she saw a King hunting in the park with his nobles; she would have shunned him, but the King having a sight of her, made towards her, and between her beauty and perfumed breath, was so powerfully smitten that he was not able to subdue his passion, but proceeded on his courtship; where after some compliments and kind embraces, he gained her love. And bringing her to his palace, he caused her to be cloathed in the most magnificent manner.

This being ended and the king finding that she was the king of Colchester's daughter, ordered some chariots to be got ready, that he might pay him a visit. The chariot in which the king and queen rode was beautified with rich ornimental gems of gold. The king her father was at first astonished that his daughter had been so fortunate as she was, till the young king made him sensible of all that had happened. Great was the joy at court among the nobility, except the queen and her club-footed daughter, who was ready to burst with malice, and envied her happiness; and the greater was their madness because she was now above them all.——Great rejoicings with feasting and dancing continued many days. Then at length, with the dowry her father gave her, they returned home.

Well, said the fifth boy, had she not been kind and beautiful, such good fortune had never come to her lot. And pray what become of her hump-back'd sister-in-law? ——Indeed I do not know.——Why then said the fifth boy, I can tell you something of her.[1]

She perceiving that her sister was so happy in seeking her fortune, would needs do the same; so disclosing her mind to her mother all preparations was made; not only rich apparel but sweetmeats, sugar almonds, &c. in great quantities, and a large bottle of Malaga Sack. Furnished thus she went the same road as her sister, and coming near the cave, there sat the old man, who said, Young woman, whither so fast?——

[1]In the *History of Four Kings* in which this tale appears, each of the stories is told by a different school friend of Tom Hodge. The tale is now taken up by another boy.

160

H. J. Ford's illustration for the 'Bushy Bride',
a parallel Norwegian tale, from Andrew Lang's *The Red Fairy Book*, 1890

What is that to you, said she.——Then said he, What have you in your bag and bottle? She answered, Good things, which you shall not be troubled with. Won't you give me some, said he? No, not a bit nor a drop, unless it would choak you. The old man frowned, saying, Evil fortune attend thee.——Going on she come to the hedge, through which she espied a gap, where she thought to pass but going in, the hedge closed, and the thorns run into her flesh, so that with great difficulty she got out. Being now in a bloody condition, she looks for water to wash herself and looking round she saw a well, and sitting down, one of the Heads came up to her, saying, Wash me, comb me, lay me down softly. But she bang'd it with her bottle, saying, Hang you, take this for your washing. So the second and third Heads came up, and met with no better welcome than the first whereupon the heads consulted among themselves what evils to plague her with for such usage. The first said, Let her be struck with leprosy in her face. The second said, Let an additional stink be added to her breath. The third bestowed on her a husband, though but a poor country cobler.—This done she goes on till she came to a market town, and it being market day, the people smelt a stink, and seeing such a mangy face, all fled; but a poor cobler who not long before had mended the shoes of an old hermit, who having no money, gave him a box of ointment for the cure of the leprosy, and a bottle of spirits for a stinging-breath. Now the cobler having a mind to do an act of charity was minded to try an experiment; so going up to her, asked her who she was?——I am, said she, the King of Colchester's daughter in law.—— Well, said the Cobler, If I restore you to your natural complexion, and make a sound cure both in face and breath, will you in reward take me for a husband?——Yes, friend, replied she, with all my heart.——With this the cobler applied the remedies, and they worked the effect in a few weeks, which being done, they were married. After some few days spent in town, they set forward for the court at Colchester. At length coming there, and the queen understanding she had married nothing but a poor cobler, fell into distraction, and in wrath hanged herself.——The death of the queen pleased the king much, who was glad he had got rid of her soon. Having buried her, he gave the cobler one hundred pounds, on condition that he and his lady would quit the court. The Cobler received it, and promised he would. Then setting up his trade in a remote part of the kingdom, they lived many years, he mended shoes, and she spinning thread.

Quoth the sixth boy, I think for a King's daughter she hath spun a very fine thread.

JACK AND THE BEANSTALK

The literary history of 'Jack and the Beanstalk' begins not with a telling of the tale, but with a skit upon the telling of the tale, which appeared in a facetious tract *Round about our Coal-Fire: or Christmas Entertainments*, first published in London by J. Roberts about 1730, although the chapter entitled 'Enchantment demonstrated in the Story of Jack Spriggins and the Enchanted Bean' does not seem to have been added until the edition of 1734.

The tale is there a fantastical one, even by fairy-tale standards; but it seems clear the author is familiar with the traditional story. He tells of 'a dirty, lazy, tatter-de-mallion' lad named Jack, who lives with his grandmother in an apartment

Woodcut from *Round about our Coal-Fire*, 1734, re-engraved

that is no more than a hovel. Nevertheless, the grandmother possesses an enchanted bean which Jack purloins and plants. Instantly the bean sprouts out of the earth, growing so quickly 'it gave Jack a Fillip on the Nose, and made him bleed furiously'. The grandmother, needless to say, is without sympathy, especially as she will now turn into a toad; and she chases Jack up 'the Bean' which is already a mile high. On the way up Jack goes into a tavern and calls for a pot of ale. The landlord is unable to provide light refreshment, but turns into a beautiful lady, 'and in pops a dozen pretty Youths, drest like Pages in green Satin, laced with Silver and white Feathers in their Caps, each of them mounted upon an Hobby-horse finely bedecked with Ribbons, Tinsel and Feathers'. Not even a Blanchard, a Planché, or a Ziegfeld could have devised a more dream-wishy script. Jack is addressed by the titles 'Sovereign Lord of the Manor' and 'Invincible Champion', and given the power of possessing all the pleasures he desires. He takes the metamorphized inn-keeper for wife by declaration, wishes for a bed which instantly materializes 'embroidered with gold and pearls', and subsequently, almost without rousing himself, destroys the giant Gogmagog, and releases a number of knights and several thousand virgins who were being fattened for the giant's breakfast table.

Nonsense such as this, the author suggests, 'some old women first set on foot to amuse children'; and he had finished the tale to show that 'Enchantment proceeds from nothing but the Chit-Chat of an old Nurse, or the Maggots in a Madman's Brain'. Indeed the pamphlet as a whole is a product of the New Enlightenment: an exposure of the raw manners, credulous beliefs, and lucrative impostures, still obtaining in the first half of the eighteenth century.

It is curious, however, that another seventy years were to pass before the story of Jack and the

Beanstalk was to be printed in full, and that it should then, in 1807, appear twice. It appeared in *The History of Mother Twaddle, and the Marvellous Atchievments of Her Son Jack*, by B. A. T., which was one of John Harris's superior copperplate books; and it appeared in a sixpenny booklet, one of a series which the impecunious philosopher William Godwin had edited for Benjamin Tabart.

Further, it is evident that the stories in the two publications emanated from separate sources. Whereas Tabart's publication *The History of Jack and the Bean-Stalk, Printed from the Original Manuscript, Never Before Published*, 1807, which is here reprinted, is the source of all substantial retellings of the story,[1] the tale by B. A. T. is based on a different narrative, even allowing for the fact that it is a metrical rendering. Thus Mother Twaddle finds a sixpence while sweeping her floor and sends her son Jack to market to buy a goose. Instead Jack buys a magical bean from a pedlar, is attacked by his mother when he gets home for his stupidity, plants the bean, and the next morning it has grown so tall 'the top was not seen'. Jack climbs up, and at the top finds a grand house. When he knocks, a damsel, who is apparently the giant's servant, opens the door. She hides Jack under a bed, and gives the 'fe-fo-fan' giant a draught of strong wine when he returns. When the giant has fallen asleep, Jack decapitates the monster with an expertise worthy of a professional giant-killer, sends for his mother, and marries the damsel.

The belief that there is, could be, or ought to be, a means of ascending to a land in the sky is, of course, as old or older than Jacob's Ladder and the Tower of Babel. It seems unnecessary to stress, as some mythologists have done, that to primitive man the sky appeared to be a dome placed on top of the world, when modern man can see this is so for himself, and has to use the full power of his intellect to disbelieve it. In the *Prose Edda* a description is given of the mighty ash tree Yggdrasill which stretched up to heaven; and in Asiatic fiction we can read of a branch of the

Jack arriving at the top of the beanstalk. *The History of Mother Twaddle*, 1807

Bo-tree of Buddha, which on being planted in the ground, sprang upwards to the sky with extraordinary swiftness. Perhaps however a story collected by the Grimm brothers is more closely related.

A countryman carrying turnip seed on his back for which he was to receive a thaler per seed, lost one of his seeds, and received one thaler less than he would have done; but on his way home he found the seed had grown into a tree that reached up to the sky. He thought, as he had the chance, he would climb the tree to see what the angels were doing. So he climbed the tree, and found the angels were threshing oats. He was watching them when he realized the tree on which he was standing was tottering. He looked beneath him to the earth and saw someone was about to cut the tree down. He felt he would have a nasty fall, and did not know how better to save himself than by taking the chaff of the oats which lay in heaps and twisting a rope. He also snatched a hoe and a flail which were lying about in heaven, and let himself down by the rope; but landed on earth in the middle of an exceedingly deep hole. It was a real piece of luck he had brought the hoe, for he cut a flight of steps with it, and climbed up them, not forgetting to bring the flail with him as a token of veracity, so that no one could doubt his story. Anyone who can tell a tale as tall as this, it is unnecessary to add, deserves the hand of the old king's daughter.

[1]Close examination shows that the version given by Jacobs in *English Fairy Tales*, as collected in Australia about 1860, is no more than a literary retelling of the text that had been in print for more than half a century.

THE HISTORY OF
JACK AND THE BEAN-STALK

In the days of King Alfred, there lived a poor woman, whose cottage was situated in a remote country village, a great many miles from London.

She had been a widow some years, and had an only child, named Jack, whom she indulged to a fault; the consequence of her blind partiality was, that Jack did not pay the least attention to any thing she said, but was indolent, careless, and extravagant. His follies were not owing to a bad disposition, but that his mother had never checked him. By degrees, she disposed of all she possessed—scarcely any thing remained but a cow.

The poor woman one day met Jack with tears in her eyes; her distress was great, and, for the first time in her life, she could not help reproaching him, saying, 'Indeed, dear son, you have at last brought me to beggary and ruin; I have not money enough to purchase food for another day—nothing remains for me but to sell my cow. I am very sorry to part with her; it grieves me sadly, but we must not starve.'

For five minutes Jack felt a degree of remorse, but it was soon over, and he importuned his mother to let him sell the cow at the next village. As he was going along, he met a butcher, who enquired why he was driving the cow from home? Jack replied, it was his intention to sell it. The butcher held some curious beans in his hat; they were of various colours, and attracted Jack's notice: this did not pass unnoticed by the butcher, who, knowing Jack's easy temper, thought now was the time to take advantage of it, and determined not to let slip so good an opportunity, asked what was the price of the cow, offering at the same time all the beans in his hat for her. The silly boy could not express his pleasure at what he supposed so great an offer: the bargain was struck instantly, and the cow exchanged for a few paltry beans. Jack made the best of his way home, calling aloud to his mother before he reached the house, thinking to surprise her.

When she saw the beans, and heard Jack's account, her patience quite forsook her, she kicked the beans away in a passion—they flew in all directions, some were scattered into the garden. The poor woman reflected on her great loss, and was quite in despair. Not having any thing to eat, they both went supperless to bed.

Jack awoke very early in the morning, and, seeing something uncommon from the window of his bedchamber, ran downstairs into the garden, where he soon discovered that some of the beans had taken root, and sprung up surprisingly: the stalks were of an immense thickness, and had so entwined, that they formed a ladder nearly like a chain in appearance.

Looking upwards, he could not discern the top, it appeared to be lost in the clouds: he tried it, found it firm, and not to be shaken. He quickly formed the resolution of endeavouring to climb up to the top, in order to seek his fortune, and ran to communicate his intention to his mother, not doubting but she would be equally pleased with himself. She declared he should not go; said he would break her heart, entreated, and threatened, but all in vain. Jack set out, and, after climbing for some hours, reached the top of the bean-stalk, fatigued and quite exhausted. Looking around, he found himself in a strange country: it appeared to be a desert, quite barren: not a tree, shrub, house, or living creature to be seen; here and there were scattered fragments of unhewn stone, and, at unequal distances, small heaps of earth were loosely thrown together. Jack seated himself pensively upon a block of stone, thought of his mother, and reflected with sorrow on his disobedience in climbing the bean-stalk against her inclination: he concluded that he must now die with hunger.

However he walked on, hoping to see a house where he might beg something to eat and drink: presently an infirm looking woman appeared at a distance; as she approached, he saw that she was old, her skin much wrinkled, and her tattered garments

Illustration by Arthur Rackham from Flora Annie Steel's *English Fairy Tales*, 1918

proved poverty. She accosted Jack, enquiring how he came there; he related the circumstance of the bean-stalk. She then asked if he recollected his father? he replied he did not; and added, that there must be some mystery relating to him, for he had frequently asked his mother who his father was, but that she always burst into tears, and appeared violently agitated, nor did she recover herself for some days after; one thing, however, he could not avoid observing upon those occasions, which was, that she always carefully avoided answering him, and even seemed afraid of speaking, as if there were some secret connected with his father's history which she must not disclose.[1]

The old woman replied, 'I will reveal the whole story, your mother must not; but, before I begin, I require a solemn promise on your part to do what I command: I am a fairy, and if you do not perform exactly what I desire, your mother and yourself shall both be destroyed.' Jack was frightened at the old woman's menaces, and promised to fulfil her injunctions exactly, and the fairy thus addressed him:—'Your father was a rich man, his disposition remarkably benevolent; he was very good to the poor, and constantly relieving them: he made it a rule never to let a day pass without doing a kindness to some person. On one particular day in the week he kept open house, and invited only those who were reduced and had lived well. He always presided himself, and did all in his power to render his guests comfortable; the rich and the great were not invited. The servants were all happy, and greatly attached to their master and mistress. Your father, though only a private gentleman, was as rich as a prince, and he deserved all he possessed, for he only lived to do good. Such a man was soon known and talked of. A Giant lived a great many miles off; this man was altogether as wicked as your father was good: he was in his heart envious, covetous, and cruel; but he had the art of concealing those vices. He was poor, and wished to enrich himself at any rate.

'Hearing your father spoken of, he was determined to become acquainted with him, hoping to ingratiate himself into your father's favour. He removed quickly into your neighbourhood, caused it to be reported that he was a gentleman who had just lost all he possessed by an earthquake, and found it difficult to escape with his life; his wife was with him. Your father gave credit to his story and pitied him; he gave him handsome apartments in his own house, and caused himself and his wife to be treated like visitors of consequence, little imagining that the Giant was meditating a horrid return for all his favours. Things went on in this way some time, the Giant becoming daily more impatient to put his plan into execution; at last a favourable opportunity presented itself. Your father's house was at some distance from the sea-shore, but with a good glass the coast could be seen distinctly. The Giant was one day using the tele-

[1]In *The Child's Own Book*, *c.* 1837, the person Jack meets is 'a handsome young woman', dressed 'in the most elegant manner', and with 'a small white wand in her hand, on the top of which was a peacock of pure gold'. In *Merry Tales for Little Folk*, 1868, she is 'a young and beautiful woman hovering over him'. One reason for such changes was to make the character agree with illustrations which were already to hand.

'The Giant's Fall.' Colour wood-engraving from Gall and Inglis's Nursery Toy Book *Jack and the Bean Stalk*, 1871

scope; the wind was very high; he saw a fleet of ships in distress off the rocks; he hastened to your father, mentioned the circumstance, and eagerly requested he would send all the servants he could spare to relieve the sufferers. Every one was instantly dispatched, except the porter and your nurse; the Giant then joined your father in the study, and appeared to be delighted—he really was so. Your father recommended a favourite book, and was handing it down: the Giant took the opportunity and stabbed him, he instantly fell dead; the Giant left the body, found the porter and nurse, and presently dispatched them. You were then only three months old; your mother had you in her arms in a remote part of the house, and was ignorant of what was going on; she went into the study, but how was she shocked, on discovering your father a corpse, and weltering in his blood! She was stupified with horror and grief, and was motionless. The Giant, who was seeking her, found her in that state, and hastened to serve her and you as he had done her husband, but she fell at his feet, and in a pathetic manner besought him to spare your life and her's.

'The cruel Giant, for a short time, was struck with remorse, and spared your life and her's; but first he made her swear solemnly, that she never would inform you who your father was, or answer any questions concerning him: assuring her, that if she did he would certainly discover her, and put both of you to death in the most cruel manner. Your mother took you in her arms, and fled as quick as possible; she was scarcely gone, when the Giant repented that he had suffered her to escape; he would have pursued her instantly, but he had his own safety to provide for, as it was necessary he should be gone before the servants returned. Having gained your father's confidence, he knew where to find all his treasure: he soon loaded himself and his wife, set the house on fire in several places, and when the servants returned the house was burnt down to the ground.

'Your poor mother, forlorn, abandoned, and forsaken, wandered with you a great many miles from this scene of desolation; fear added to her haste: she settled in the cottage where you were brought up, and it was entirely owing to her fear of the giant that she has never mentioned your father to you.

'I became your father's guardian at his birth; but fairies have laws to which they are subject as well as mortals. A short time before the Giant went to your father's, I transgressed; my punishment was a total suspension of power for a limited time: an unfortunate circumstance, as it prevented my succouring your father. The day on which you met the butcher, as you went to sell your mother's cow, my power was restored. It was I who secretly prompted you to take the beans in exchange for your cow. By my power, the bean-stalk grew to so great a height and formed a ladder. I need not add, that I inspired you with a strong desire to ascend the ladder.

'The Giant lives in this country; you are the person appointed to punish him for all his wickedness. You will have dangers and difficulties to encounter, but you must persevere in avenging the death of your father, or you will not prosper in any of your undertakings, but always be miserable. As to the Giant's possessions, you may seize upon all with impunity; for every thing he has is your's, though now you are unjustly deprived of it. One thing I strictly charge you—never let your mother be made acquainted with your journies beforehand; the thought of it would kill her, for she has not yet thoroughly overcome the fright she encountered at your father's death.* Go along the direct road, you will soon see the house where your cruel enemy lives. Remember the severe punishment that awaits you if you disobey my commands.' So saying the fairy disappeared, leaving Jack to pursue his journey.

He walked until after sun-set, and soon, to his great joy, espied a large mansion. A plain looking woman was standing at the door, he accosted her, begging she would give him a morsel of bread and a night's lodging. She expressed great surprise on seeing him, said it was quite uncommon to see a human being near their house, for it was well known that her husband was a large and powerful Giant, and that he would never eat any thing but human flesh, if he could possibly get it; that he did not think any thing of walking fifty miles to procure it, usually being out all day for that purpose.

This account terrified Jack, but still he hoped to elude the Giant, and therefore again he entreated the woman to take him in for one night only, and hide him in the oven. The good woman at last suffered herself to be persuaded, for she was of a compassionate disposition. She gave him plenty to eat and drink, and took him into the house. First they entered a large hall, magnificently furnished; they then passed through several spacious rooms, all in the same stile of grandeur, though they appeared to be forsaken and desolate.

A long gallery was next; it was very dark, just light enough to shew that instead of a wall on one side, there was a grating of iron which parted off a dismal dungeon, from whence issued the groans of those poor victims whom the Giant reserved in confinement for his own voracious appetite. Poor Jack

*Jack could not bear to deceive his mother, and besides, he knew it would make her more uneasy to set off clandestinely, than to inform her of his journey. The fairy, at first, strongly opposed this; but Jack entreated her so earnestly, that she reluctantly consented: he promised to make it appear as a frolic of his own, and not that he acted by her commands. [Editor's note 1807.]

Wood-engraving by E. Dalziel after C. W. Cope, for *The Lively History of Jack and the Beanstalk*, 1844

The Giant & Jack in the Oven.

Copperplate from Tabart's *History of Jack and the Bean-stalk,* 1807

was half dead with fear, and would have given the world to be with his mother again, but that he feared could never be; for he gave himself up for lost, and now mistrusted the good woman. At the farther end of the gallery there was a winding staircase, which led them into a spacious kitchen; a very good fire was burning in the grate, and Jack, not seeing any thing to make him uncomfortable, soon forgot his fears, and was just beginning to enjoy himself, when he was aroused by a loud knocking at the street-door; the Giant's wife ran to secure him in the oven, and then made what haste she could to let her husband in, and Jack heard him accost her in a voice like thunder, saying, 'Wife, I smell fresh meat.' 'Oh! my dear,' she replied, 'it is nothing but the people in the dungeon.' The Giant appeared to believe her, and walked down stairs into the very kitchen, where poor Jack was, who shook, trembled, and was more terrified than he had yet been.

At last, the monster seated himself quietly by the fire-side, whilst his wife prepared supper. By degrees Jack recovered himself sufficiently to look at the Giant through a crevice; he was astonished to see how much he devoured, and thought he never would have done eating and drinking. When supper was ended, the Giant desired his wife to bring him his hen. A very beautiful hen was brought, and placed upon the table before him. Jack's curiosity was very great to see what would happen; he observed that every time the Giant said 'lay', the hen laid an egg of solid gold. The Giant amused himself a long time with the hen, meanwhile his wife went to bed. At length the Giant fell asleep by the fireside, and snored like the roaring of a cannon. At day-break, Jack finding the Giant not likely to be soon roused, crept softly out of his hiding-place, seized the hen, and ran off with her.

He met with some difficulty in finding his way out the house, but at last he reached the road in safety, without fear of pursuit: he easily found the way to the bean-stalk, and descended it better and quicker than he expected. His mother was overjoyed to see him; he found her crying bitterly, and lamenting his fate, for she concluded he had come to some shocking end through his rashness.

Jack was impatient to shew his hen, and inform his mother how valuable it was. 'And now, mother,' said Jack, 'I have brought home that which will quickly make you rich without any trouble: I hope I have made you some amends for the affliction I have caused you through my idleness, extravagance, and folly.'—The hen produced them as many eggs as they desired; they sold them, and in a little time became very rich. For some months Jack and his mother lived happily together; but he being very desirous of travelling,* longed to climb the bean-stalk and pay the Giant another visit, in order to carry off some more of his treasures; for during the time Jack was in the Giant's mansion, whilst he lay concealed in the oven, he learned from the conversation which took place between the Giant and his wife, that he possessed some great curiosities. Jack thought on his journey again and again; but still he could not determine how to break it to his mother, being well assured that she would be quite resolved to prevent his going. One day, he told her boldly that he must take a journey up the bean-stalk; she begged he would not think of it, and tried all in her power to dissuade him, saying, that the Giant could not fail of knowing him, and would desire no better than to get him into his power, that he might put him to a cruel death, in order to be revenged for the loss of his hen.

Jack, finding that all his arguments were useless, pretended to give up the point, though resolved to go at all events. He had a dress prepared, which would disguise him, and with something to discolour his skin, he thought it impossible for any one to recollect him. In a few mornings after discoursing with his mother, he rose very early, put on his disguise, changed his complexion, and, unperceived by any one, climbed the bean-stalk. He was greatly fatigued when he reached the top, and very hungry. Having rested some time on one of the stones, he pursued his journey to the Giant's mansion. He reached it late in the evening, the woman was standing at the door as usual; Jack accosted her, at the same time telling her a pitiful tale, and requested she would give him some victuals and drink, and a night's lodging. She told him what he knew before full well, concerning her husband, and also that she one night admitted a poor, hungry, distressed boy, who was half dead with travelling; that he stole one of the Giant's treasures, and, ever since that, her husband was worse than before, and used her very cruelly, continually upbraiding her with being the cause of his loss. Jack was at no loss to discover that he was attending to the account of a story in which he was the principal actor: he did his best to persuade the good woman to admit him, but he found it a very hard task.

At last she consented, and as she led the way, Jack observed that every thing was just as he had found it before; she took him into the kitchen, and hid him in an old lumber-closet. The Giant returned at the usual time, and walked in so heavily that the house was shaken to the foundation. He seated himself by a good fire, saying, 'I smell fresh meat;' the wife replied it was the crows, who had brought a piece of carrion, and laid it at the top of the house upon the leads.

Whilst supper was preparing, the Giant was very ill-tempered and impatient, frequently lifting up his hand to strike his wife for not being quick enough; she,

*Recollecting the fairy's commands, and fearing that if he delayed she would put her threats into execution. [Editor's note 1807.]

however, was always so fortunate as to elude the blow: he was also continually upbraiding her with the loss of his hen.

The Giant, at last, having finished his voracious supper, and eaten till he was quite satisfied, said to his wife—'I must have something to amuse me—either my bags of money or my harp.' After a great deal of ill-humour, and having teased his wife some time, he commanded her to bring his bags of gold and silver. Jack, as before, peeped out of his hiding-place, and presently the woman brought two bags into the room; they were of an immense size, one was filled with new guineas, the other with new shillings. They were both placed before the Giant, he reprimanded his wife most severely for staying so long; the poor woman replied, trembling with fear, that they were so heavy she could scarcely lift them, and concluded, at last, that she never could bring them down stairs, adding, that she had nearly fainted owing to their weight. This so exasperated the Giant, that he raised his hand to strike her; she, however, escaped and went to bed, leaving him to count over his treasures by way of amusement.

First, the bag containing the silver was emptied, and the contents placed upon the table. Jack viewed the glittering heaps with delight, and most heartily wished the contents in his own possession. The Giant (little thinking himself so narrowly watched) reckoned the silver over and over again, then put it all carefully into the bag, which he made very secure. The other bag was opened next, and the guineas placed upon the table. If Jack was pleased at sight of the silver, how much more delighted he felt when he saw such a heap of gold: he had the boldness even to think of gaining it; but soon recollecting himself, he feared the Giant would feign sleep, in order the better to entrap any one who might be concealed. The gold was put up as the silver had been before, and, if possible, more securely. The Giant snored aloud; Jack could compare his noise to nothing but the roaring of the sea in a high wind, when the tide is coming in. At last Jack, concluding him to be asleep, and therefore secure, stole out of his hiding place, and approached the Giant, in order to carry off the two bags of money; but, just as he laid his hand upon one of the bags, a little dog, whom he had not perceived before, started out from under the Giant's chair, and barked at Jack most furiously, who gave himself up for lost; fear rivetted him to the spot—instead of running he stood still, though expecting his enemy to awake every minute. Contrary, however, to expectation, the Giant continued in a sound sleep—the dog grew weary of barking; Jack, looking round, saw a large piece of meat, which he threw to the dog, who took it into the lumber-closet which Jack had just left.

He found himself thus delivered from a noisy and troublesome enemy; and, as the Giant did not awake, Jack seized both the bags, and carried them away; he reached the street-door in safety, and found it quite day-light. In his way to the top of the bean-stalk the only difficulty he had to encounter arose from the weight of the bags, and really they were so heavy he could hardly carry them. Jack was overjoyed when he found himself near the bean-stalk; he soon reached the bottom, and immediately ran to seek his mother. To his great surprise, the cottage was deserted, he went from one room to another, without being able to find any one; he then went out into the street, hoping to see some of the neighbours, who could inform him where he might find his mother. An old woman said she was at a neighbour's, ill of a fever, and directed him to the house where she was. He was shocked on finding her apparently dying, and could scarcely bear his own reflections on knowing himself to be the cause. On being told of his return, by degrees she revived, and began to recover gradually. Jack presented her with his two valuable bags; they lived happily and comfortably: the cottage was repaired and well furnished. For three years Jack heard no more of the bean-stalk, but he could not forget it; though he feared making his mother unhappy; she would not mention the bean-stalk, lest it might remind him of taking another journey. Notwithstanding the comforts Jack enjoyed, his mind dwelt upon the bean-stalk;* he could not think of any thing else, it was in vain endeavouring to amuse himself. His mother found that something preyed upon his mind, and endeavoured to discover the cause; but Jack knew too well what the consequence would be to disclose the cause of his melancholy to her. He did his utmost therefore to conquer the great desire he felt for another journey up the bean-stalk; however, finding the inclination grew too powerful for him, he began to make secret preparations for his journey, and, on the longest day, arose as soon as it was light, ascended the bean-stalk, and reached the top with some trouble. He found the road, journey, &c. much as it

*For the fairy's menaces in case of disobedience on his part, were ever present to his imagination. [Editor's note 1807.]

Colour wood-engraving from
Our Nurse's Picture Book, 1869

had been the two former times; he arrived at the Giant's mansion in the evening, and found his wife standing at the door. Jack had disguised himself so completely, that she did not appear to have the least recollection of him; however, when he pleaded hunger and poverty in order to gain admittance, he found it very difficult indeed to persuade her. At last he prevailed, and was concealed in the copper. When the Giant returned in the evening, he said, 'I smell fresh meat,' but Jack felt quite composed, as he had said so before, and was soon satisfied; however, the Giant started up suddenly, and, notwithstanding all his wife could say, he searched all around the room. Whilst this was going on, Jack was terrified exceedingly, and ready to die with fear, wishing himself at home a thousand times; but when the Giant approached the oven, and put his hand upon the lid, Jack thought his death-warrant was signed. The Giant ended his search there, without moving the lid of the copper, and seated himself quietly. This fright nearly overcame poor Jack; he was afraid of moving or even breathing, lest he should be heard. The Giant at last ate a great supper; when he had finished, he commanded his wife to fetch down his harp. Jack peeped under the copper-lid, and soon saw the most beautiful harp that could be imagined; it was placed by the Giant, he said 'play,' and it instantly played of its own accord, without being touched. The music was very fine, Jack was delighted, and felt more anxious to get the harp into his possession, than either of the former treasures. The Giant's soul was not attuned to harmony, and the music lulled him into a sound sleep. Now therefore was the time to carry off the harp, and the Giant appeared to be in a more profound sleep than usual. Jack quickly determined, got out of the oven, and took the harp. The harp was a fairy; it called out loudly 'master! master! master!' The Giant awoke, stood up, and tried to pursue Jack, but he had drank so much that he could not stand. Poor Jack ran as fast as he could; in a little time the Giant was sufficiently recovered to walk slowly, or rather to reel, after him; had he been sober he must have overtaken Jack instantly; but, as he then was, Jack contrived to be first at the top of the bean-stalk, the Giant calling to him all the way he went, and sometimes he was very near him. The moment Jack set his foot on the bean-stalk, he called for a hatchet; one was brought directly; he soon reached the ground, just at that instant the Giant was beginning to come down; but Jack with his hatchet cut the bean-stalk close off to the root, which made the Giant fall into the garden—the fall killed him. Jack's mother was delighted when she saw the bean stalk destroyed;* he heartily begged his mother's pardon for all the sorrow and affliction he had caused her, promising faithfully to be very dutiful and obedient to her for the future. He proved as good as his word, and was a pattern of affectionate behaviour and attention to parents. His mother and he lived together a great many years, and continued to be always very happy.

*At that instant the fairy appeared; she first addressed Jack's mother, and explained every circumstance relating to the journies up the bean-stalk. Jack was now fully cleared in the opinion of his mother. The fairy then charged Jack to be dutiful and affectionate to his mother, and to follow his father's good example, which was the only way to be respectable and happy. She then took her leave of them, and disappeared. [Editor's note 1807.]

The story of Snow White was one of the tales Jacob and Wilhelm Grimm collected in Cassel from two sisters, Jeannette and Amalie Hassenpflug, whose brother Ludwig was to marry their sister Lotte. The story, a morality, perhaps, on the spitefulness of which beauty queens are capable, was in fact well known in Hesse at the beginning of the nineteenth century; and it has subsequently been found with little variation over a wide area from Ireland to Asia Minor, and in several parts of North and West Africa.

The tale contains elements that lie deep in European folk tradition; but it is not necessarily an old story, and has probably come under literary influence. Thus the theme of the glass coffin, in which lay Snow White's body, remaining ever as beautiful as the day it was laid to rest, was a feature of the story of Lisa in the *Pentamerone* (Day 2, tale 8) published 1634. Lisa, like Snow White, was a lovely seven-year-old child, and she died, or appeared to have died, through having a comb stuck in her head. For years her body was kept secretly in a casket of crystal; and it remained lovely, so lovely that when her uncle's wife discovered it in a locked room, it aroused her most intense jealousy. Further, the story in the *Pentamerone*, printed more than three hundred years ago, throws light on an anomaly in the story of Snow White which—to the rational minded, if to no one else—has always seemed to need explanation: the fact that Snow White, who was seven years old when abandoned in the woods, and apparently not much older when murdered, should be thought mature enough for marriage when the Prince discovers her in her coffin. In the *Pentamerone* it is explained that Lisa, after her apparent death and incarceration, continued to grow like any other girl, and the crystal casket lengthened with her, 'keeping pace as she grew'. The tale in the *Pentamerone* is in fact more satisfactory than the present-day tale in that Lisa's casket, unlike Snow White's glass coffin, was kept hidden, so no one would have seen her growing. In addition the aunt's extreme enmity is shown to have been due to her supposing that her husband was having an affair with the beautiful girl. The aunt did not know Lisa was her husband's niece, and does not seem to have been aware that the girl had for years lain in a coma. When the aunt opens the casket she thinks the maiden merely asleep, takes hold of her by the hair and drags her out, fortuitously dislodging the comb in her head and restoring her to life.

The text that follows appeared under the name 'Snow-drop', in *German Popular Stories, Translated from the Kinder und Haus-Märchen, collected by M. M. Grimm, from Oral Tradition*, 1823. It was the Grimms' version of the tale which Walt Disney brought to the screen in 1938, in a cartoon film (the first of feature length) that seemed at the time a work of compelling power and humour, but which, when seen again in later years, has not lived up to the first impression. The film has, in fact, had an unfortunate effect on fairy-tale illustration. It is interesting, however, that in the film story Disney chose to re-establish an incident glossed over by the early translators, that the queen not only ordered Snow White to be killed, but ordered that her heart be brought back as a token that the deed had been accomplished. In fact in the German original the story was even more unpleasant. When the servant, particularized as a huntsman, came back with the heart of a young boar he had killed, the queen is stated to have had it salted, and to have eaten the heart in the belief that it was Sneewitchen's. To match this, the queen's fate, at the end of the story, was more terrible. At the wedding-feast, when the queen's crime was exposed, slippers of iron were heated in a fire until red hot, and the queen was forced to put them on, and to dance until she dropped dead.

Guide drawings by Walt Disney for the cartoon film *Snow White and the Seven Dwarfs*, 1938. An ethereal Snow White, whom seemingly nothing can harm, dances with the dwarf 'Grumpy'. The beautiful queen, who must be seen to be evil as well as beautiful, is to have 'Well curved eyebrows coming low down towards centre of face. Prominent eyelashes. High Cheekbones'.

SNOW-DROP

It was in the middle of winter, when the broad flakes of snow were falling around, that a certain queen sat working at a window, the frame of which was made of fine black ebony; and as she was looking out upon the snow, she pricked her finger, and three drops of blood fell upon it. Then she gazed thoughtfully upon the red drops which sprinkled the white snow, and said, 'Would that my little daughter may be as white as that snow, as red as the blood, and as black as the ebony window-frame!'[1] And so the little girl grew up: her skin was as white as snow, her cheeks as rosy as the blood, and her hair as black as ebony; and she was called Snow-drop.

But this queen died; and the king soon married another wife, who was very beautiful, but so proud that she could not bear to think that any one could surpass her. She had a magical looking-glass, to which she used to go and gaze upon herself in it, and say,

> 'Tell me, glass, tell me true!
> Of all the ladies in the land,
> Who is the fairest? tell me who?'

And the glass answered,

> 'Thou, queen, art fairest in the land.'

But Snow-drop grew more and more beautiful; and when she was seven years old, she was as bright as the day, and fairer than the queen herself. Then the glass one day answered the queen, when she went to consult it as usual,

> 'Thou, queen, may'st fair and beauteous be,
> But Snow-drop is lovelier far than thee!'[2]

When she heard this, she turned pale with rage and envy; and called to one of her servants and said, 'Take Snow-drop away into the wide wood, that I may never see her more.' Then the servant led her away; but his heart melted when she begged him to spare her life, and he said, 'I will not hurt thee, thou pretty child.' So he left her by herself; and though he thought it most likely that the wild beasts would tear her in

[1]Another tale the Grimms collected, 'The Juniper Tree', opens in a comparable manner. A woman is peeling an apple when she cuts herself, and the blood falls on the snow. 'Ah,' she sighs, 'if I had but a child as red as blood and as white as snow.'

[2]An earlier instance, of striking similarity, of a maiden's beauty being magically revealed occurs in the *Pentamerone*, Day IV, tale 7. Some geese, which the unfortunate Ciommo has been forced to look after, and which his beautiful sister Marziella has been secretly feeding, push their way into the King's garden, and sing under his window:

> Pire, pire, pire!
> Fair is the sun and fair is the moon,
> But the maid who feeds us is fairer still.

pieces, he felt as if a great weight were taken off his heart when he had made up his mind not to kill her, but leave her to her fate.[1]

Then poor Snow-drop wandered along through the wood in great fear; and the wild beasts roared about her, but none did her any harm. In the evening she came to a little cottage, and went in there to rest herself, for her little feet would carry her no further. Every thing was spruce and neat in the cottage: on the table was spread a white cloth, and there were seven little plates with seven little loaves, and seven little glasses with wine in them; and knives and forks laid in order; and by the wall stood seven little beds. Then, as she was very hungry, she picked a little piece off each loaf, and drank a very little wine out of each glass; and after that she thought she would lie down and rest. So she tried all the little beds; and one was too long, and another was too short, till at last the seventh suited her; and there she laid herself down, and went to sleep. Presently in came the masters of the cottage, who were seven little dwarfs that lived among the mountains, and dug and searched about for gold.[2] They lighted up their seven lamps, and saw directly that all was not right. The first said, 'Who has been sitting on my stool?' The second, 'Who has been eating off my plate?' The third, 'Who has been picking my bread?' The fourth, 'Who has been meddling with my spoon?' The fifth, 'Who has been handling my fork?' The sixth, 'Who has been cutting with my knife?' The seventh, 'Who has been drinking my wine?' Then the first looked round and said, 'Who has been lying on my bed?' And the rest came running to him, and every one cried out that somebody had been upon his bed. But the seventh saw Snow-drop, and called all his brethren to come and see her; and they cried out with wonder and astonishment, and brought their lamps to look at her, and said, 'Good heavens! what a lovely child she is!' And they were delighted to see her, and took care not to wake her; and the seventh dwarf slept an hour with each of the other dwarfs in turn, till the night was gone.

In the morning, Snow-drop told them all her story; and they pitied her, and said if she would keep all things in order, and cook and wash, and knit and spin for them, she might stay where she was, and they would take good care of her. Then they went out all day long to their work, seeking for gold and silver in the mountains; and Snow-drop remained at home: and they warned her, and said, 'The queen will soon find out where you are, so take care and let no one in.'

But the queen, now that she thought Snow-drop was dead, believed that she was certainly the handsomest lady in the land; and she went to her glass and said,

---

[1] The compassionate executioner is, understandably, not uncommon in popular literature, the renowned example in English balladry being the ruffian in the 'Children in the Wood' who slew his comrade rather than murder the two babes.

[2] The dwarfs portrayed here correspond with the description of dwarfs in the preface to *Das Heldenbuch*, the collection of thirteenth century epic poetry. 'God . . . produced the dwarfs, because the mountains lay waste and useless, and valuable stores of silver and gold, with gems and pearls, were concealed in them. Therefore God made the dwarfs right wise and crafty, that they could distinguish good and bad, and to what use all things should be applied.'

'Tell me, glass, tell me true!
   Of all the ladies in the land,
Who is fairest? tell me who?'

And the glass answered,

'Thou, queen, art the fairest in all this land;
But over the hills, in the greenwood shade,
Where the seven dwarfs their dwelling have made,
There Snow-drop is hiding her head, and she
Is lovelier far, O queen! than thee.'

Then the queen was very much alarmed; for she knew that the glass always spoke
the truth, and was sure that the servant had betrayed her. And she could not bear to
think that any one lived who was more beautiful than she was; so she disguised herself
as an old pedlar, and went her way over the hills to the place where the dwarfs dwelt.
Then she knocked at the door, and cried 'Fine wares to sell!' Snow-drop looked out
at the window, and said, 'Good-day, good-woman; what have you to sell?' 'Good
wares, fine wares,' said she; 'laces and bobbins of all colours.' 'I will let the old lady in;
she seems to be a very good sort of body,' thought Snow-drop; so she ran down,
and unbolted the door. 'Bless me!' said the old woman, 'how badly your stays are
laced! Let me lace them up with one of my nice new laces.' Snow-drop did not dream
of any mischief; so she stood up before the old woman; but she set to work so nimbly,
and pulled the lace so tight, that Snow-drop lost her breath, and fell down as if she
were dead. 'There's an end of all thy beauty,' said the spiteful queen, and went away
home.

In the evening the seven dwarfs returned; and I need not say how grieved they
were to see their faithful Snow-drop stretched upon the ground motionless, as if she
were quite dead. However, they lifted her up, and when they found what was the
matter, they cut the lace; and in a little time she began to breathe, and soon came to
life again. Then they said, 'The old woman was the queen herself; take care another
time, and let no one in when we are away.'

When the queen got home, she went straight to her glass, and spoke to it as usual;
but to her great surprise it still said,

'Thou, queen, art the fairest in all this land;
But over the hills, in the greenwood shade,
Where the seven dwarfs their dwelling have made,
There Snow-drop is hiding her head; and she
Is lovelier far, O queen! than thee.'

Then the blood ran cold in her heart with spite and malice to see that Snow-drop still lived; and she dressed herself up again in a disguise, but very different from the one she wore before, and took with her a poisoned comb. When she reached the dwarfs' cottage, she knocked at the door, and cried, 'Fine wares to sell!' but Snow-drop said, 'I dare not let any one in.' Then the queen said, 'Only look at my beautiful combs;' and gave her the poisoned one. And it looked so pretty that she took it up and put it into her hair to try it; but the moment it touched her head the poison was so powerful that she fell down senseless. 'There you may lie,' said the queen, and went her way. But by good luck the dwarfs returned very early that evening; and when they saw Snow-drop lying on the ground, they thought what had happened, and soon found the poisoned comb. And when they took it away, she recovered, and told them all that had passed; and they warned her once more not to open the door to any one.

Meantime the queen went home to her glass, and trembled with rage when she received exactly the same answer as before; and she said, 'Snow-drop shall die, if it costs me my life.' So she went secretly into a chamber, and prepared a poisoned apple: the outside looked very rosy and tempting, but whoever tasted it was sure to die. Then she dressed herself up as a peasant's wife, and travelled over the hills to the dwarfs' cottage, and knocked at the door; but Snow-drop put her head out of the window and said, 'I dare not let any one in, for the dwarfs have told me not.' 'Do as you please,' said the old woman, 'but at any rate take this pretty apple; I will make you a present of it.' 'No,' said Snow-drop, 'I dare not take it.' 'You silly girl!' answered the other, 'what are you afraid of? do you think it is poisoned? Come! do you eat one part, and I will eat the other.' Now the apple was so prepared that one side was good, though the other side was poisoned. Then Snow-drop was very much tempted to taste, for the apple looked exceedingly nice; and when she saw the old woman eat, she could refrain no longer. But she had scarcely put the piece into her mouth, when she fell down dead upon the ground. 'This time nothing will save thee,' said the queen; and she went home to her glass, and at last it said

'Thou, queen, art the fairest of all the fair.'

And then her envious heart was glad, and as happy as such a heart could be.

When evening came, and the dwarfs returned home, they found Snow-drop lying on the ground: no breath passed her lips, and they were afraid that she was quite dead. They lifted her up, and combed her hair, and washed her face with wine and water; but all was in vain, for the little girl seemed quite dead. So they laid her down upon a bier, and all seven watched and bewailed her three whole days; and then they proposed to bury her: but her cheeks were still rosy, and her face looked just as it did while she was alive; so they said, 'We will never bury her in the cold ground.' And they made a coffin of glass, so that they might still look at her, and wrote her name upon it, in golden letters, and that she was a king's daughter. And the coffin was placed upon the hill, and one of the dwarfs always sat by it and watched. And the birds of the air

The prince finds Snow White in her coffin of glass. Colour wood-engraving from
Routledge's Shilling Toy Book *Little Snow-White, c.* 1870

came too, and bemoaned Snow-drop: first of all came an owl, and then a raven, but
at last came a dove.

And thus Snow-drop lay for a long long time, and still only looked as though
she were asleep; for she was even now as white as snow, and as red as blood, and as
black as ebony. At last a prince came and called at the dwarfs' house; and he saw

Snow-drop, and read what was written in golden letters. Then he offered the dwarfs money, and earnestly prayed them to let him take her away; but they said, 'We will not part with her for all the gold in the world.' At last however they had pity on him, and gave him the coffin: but the moment he lifted it up to carry it home with him, the piece of apple fell from between her lips, and Snow-drop awoke, and said 'Where am I?' And the prince answered, 'Thou art safe with me.' Then he told her all that had happened, and said, 'I love you better than all the world: come with me to my father's palace, and you shall be my wife.' And Snow-drop consented, and went home with the prince; and every thing was prepared with great pomp and splendour for their wedding.

To the feast was invited, among the rest, Snow-drop's old enemy the queen; and as she was dressing herself in fine rich clothes, she looked in the glass, and said,

> 'Tell me, glass, tell me true!
> Of all the ladies in the land,
> Who is fairest? tell me who?'

And the glass answered,

> 'Thou, lady, art loveliest *here*, I ween;
> But lovelier far is the new-made queen.'

When she heard this, she started with rage; but her envy and curiosity were so great, that she could not help setting out to see the bride. And when she arrived, and saw that it was no other than Snow-drop, who, as she thought, had been dead a long while, she choked with passion, and fell ill and died; but Snow-drop and the prince lived and reigned happily over that land many many years.

John Hassall's pre-Disney differentiation of the seven dwarfs by means of inscribed breeches, *c.* 1921

182

THE FROG PRINCE

The Frog Prince is another tale in which a handsome husband is won by a girl's acceptance of a creature that is at first repulsive to her. It is another tale, too, with a textual history that reveals the dilemma editors of English fairy tales sometimes have to face. Almost certainly the story of the Frog Prince has long been known in Britain, yet no satisfactory text has been preserved. When Walter Scott saw the tale in the Grimms' *Kinder- und Haus-Märchen* he readily recalled from his childhood (he was born in 1771) a legend of a 'Prince Paddock' in which a princess was sent to fetch water in a sieve from the Well of the World's End, and that the feat was achieved by following the advice of a frog who obtained, in return, the princess's lightly-given promise to become its bride. John Leyden (born 1775) was another who recalled 'the popular tale': 'A lady,' he wrote in 1801, 'is sent by her stepmother to draw water from the well of the world's end. She arrives at the well, after encountering many dangers; but soon perceives that her adventures have not reached a conclusion. A frog emerges from the well, and, before it suffers her to draw water, obliges her to betrothe herself to the monster, under the penalty of being torn to pieces. The lady returns safely; but at midnight the frog-lover appears at the door, and demands entrance, according to promise, to the great consternation of the lady and her nurse.

"Open the door, my hinny, my hart,
Open the door, my ain wee thing;
And mind the words that you & I spak
Down in the meadow, at the well-spring."

The frog is admitted, and addresses her—

"Take me up on your knee, my dearie,
Take me up on your knee, my dearie;
And mind the words that you and I spak
At the cauld well sae weary."

The frog is finally disenchanted, and appears as a prince, in his original form.'

This tale, often called 'The Well of the World's End', appears to be listed in *The Complaynt of Scotland* (1549), amongst tales which a group of shepherds are said to have told each other, 'The tayl of the volfe of the varldis end'—*volfe*, according to the lexicographer J. A. H. Murray, being a misprint for 'volle' or 'velle', meaning 'well'. Yet the tale was not recorded in narrative form until Queen Victoria was on the throne, when Robert Chambers, in 1842, set down as much of it as he could—or almost as much, for after the Paddo had asked for the door to be opened, and, that granted, to be given supper, and, that granted, to be put to bed, Chambers drew a veil, commenting 'Here let us abridge a little'. But he did record that afterwards the Paddo sang:

'Now fetch me an aix, my hinnie, my heart,
Now fetch me an aix, my ain true love;
Remember the promise that you and I made,
Down i' the meadow where we twa met.'

And that the lassie brought the axe, and chopped off the frog's head as instructed, 'and nae sooner was that done than he startit up the bonniest young prince that ever was seen'. This version Chambers had been given by the antiquary Charles Kirkpatrick Sharpe, who had learned it from his Annandale nurse, Jenny, about the year 1784. But the story, as taken down, was a fragmentary one, so that Halliwell, in *Popular Rhymes and Nursery Tales*, 1849, felt obliged to fill it out, claiming, with doubtful veracity, that he had had the metrical part of the tale 'from the North of England'. These patches of story were next sewed together by Joseph Jacobs for his *English Fairy Tales*, 1890; and more recent editors, not wishing to deny the tale to their collections, have further embroidered it, so that the English version now almost has a convincing life of its own.

The idea that a kiss, or the marriage bed, could release a person from the curse of monstrousness, was one that thrilled readers in the Middle Ages, the bewitched person most often, as in Icelandic saga, being a young girl who had been turned into a terrifying creature or 'loathly lady'. Thus one of the hearsay tales recounted by 'Sir John Mandeville' in the fourteenth century concerned the daughter of Hippocrates, who was said to have been changed into the 'forme and lykenesse of a gret Dragoun, that is an hundred Fadme of lengthe', and who according to Mandeville's report (chapter IV) 'schalle so endure in that forme of a Dragoun, unto the tyme that a Knighte come, that is so hardy, that dar come to hire and kisse hire on the Mouthe'. Frequently, however, the victim had been turned not into a monster but into a loathsome lady, a hag whose appearance was so vile that not even the most chivalrous knight—and, it must be added, not even the most desperate one—was able to look at her with compassion, let alone make overtures to her. Tales of how such creatures were changed back to lovely damsels are told, for instance, in the fourteenth-century ballad 'The Weddynge of Sr Gawen and Dame Ragnell'; in John Gower's 'The Tale of Florent' in Book I of *Confessio Amantis*, *c.* 1390; and, of course, in the magic tale told by the Wife of Bath to her fellow Canterbury pilgrims.

Despite the fact that the story of the Frog Prince had, it seems, been common property in Scotland for three hundred years, and that it was known, also, in Ireland and in Somerset if Keightley is to be credited (1834), the Grimm brothers in Hesse were the first to set down a complete telling of the tale. The text that follows is the translation of 'Der Froschkönig' as it appeared in *German Popular Stories*, 1823. It was not, as it happens, an exact translation of the Grimms' text; but by taking hints from variants it perhaps comes nearer to the spirit of the original tale than does the text from which it is translated. It is 'deserving of notice', as has been remarked of much lesser coincidences, that in the German texts, as in the Scots, the frog speaks in rhyme.

The princess shares her dinner with the frog.
Colour wood-engraving by Edmund Evans, after the design
by Walter Crane, from *The Frog Prince*, 1874

THE FROG-PRINCE

One fine evening a young princess went into a wood, and sat down by the side of a cool spring of water. She had a golden ball in her hand, which was her favourite play-thing, and she amused herself with tossing it into the air and catching it again as it fell. After a time she threw it up so high that when she stretched out her hand to catch it, the ball bounded away and rolled along upon the ground, till at last it fell into the spring. The princess looked into the spring after her ball; but it was very deep, so deep that she could not see the bottom of it. Then she began to lament her loss, and said, 'Alas! if I could only get my ball again, I would give all my fine clothes and jewels, and every thing that I have in the world.' Whilst she was speaking a frog put its head out of the water, and said 'Princess, why do you weep so bitterly?' 'Alas!' said she, 'what can you do for me, you nasty frog? My golden ball has fallen into the spring.' The frog said, 'I want not your pearls and jewels and fine clothes; but if you will love me and let me live with you, and eat from your little golden plate, and sleep upon your little bed, I will bring you your ball again.' 'What nonsense,' thought the princess, 'this silly frog is talking! He can never get out of the well: however, he may be able to get my ball for me; and therefore I will promise him what he asks.' So she said to the frog, 'Well, if you will bring me my ball, I promise to do all you require.' Then the frog put his head down, and dived deep under the water; and after a little while he came up again with the ball in his mouth, and threw it on the ground. As soon as the young princess saw her ball, she ran to pick it up, and was so overjoyed to have it in her hand again, that she never thought of the frog, but ran home with it as fast as she could. The frog called after her, 'Stay, princess, and take me with you as you promised;' but she did not stop to hear a word.

The next day, just as the princess had sat down to dinner, she heard a strange noise, tap-tap, as if somebody was coming up the marble-staircase; and soon afterwards something knocked gently at the door, and said,

> 'Open the door, my princess dear,
> Open the door to thy true love here!
> And mind the words that thou and I said
> By the fountain cool in the greenwood shade.'

Then the princess ran to the door and opened it, and there she saw the frog, whom she had quite forgotten; she was terribly frightened, and shutting the door as fast as she could, came back to her seat. The king her father asked her what had frightened her. 'There is a nasty frog,' said she, 'at the door, who lifted my ball out of the spring this morning: I promised him that he should live with me here, thinking that he could never get out of the spring; but there he is at the door and wants to come in!' While she was speaking the frog knocked again at the door, and said,

'Open the door, my princess dear,
Open the door to thy true love here!
And mind the words that thou and I said
By the fountain cool in the greenwood shade.'

The king said to the young princess, 'As you have made a promise, you must keep it; so go and let him in.' She did so, and the frog hopped into the room, and came up close to the table. 'Pray lift me upon a chair,' said he to the princess, 'and let me sit next to you.' As soon as she had done this, the frog said 'Put your plate closer to me that I may eat out of it.' This she did, and when he had eaten as much as he could, he said 'Now I am tired; carry me up stairs and put me into your little bed.' And the princess took him up in her hand and put him upon the pillow of her own little bed, where he slept all night long. As soon as it was light he jumped up, hopped down stairs, and went out of the house. 'Now,' thought the princess, 'he is gone, and I shall be troubled with him no more.'

But she was mistaken; for when night came again, she heard the same tapping at the door, and when she opened it, the frog came in and slept upon her pillow as before till the morning broke: and the third night he did the same; but when the princess awoke on the following morning, she was astonished to see, instead of the frog, a handsome prince gazing on her with the most beautiful eyes that ever were seen, and standing at the head of her bed.

He told her that he had been enchanted by a malicious fairy, who had changed him into the form of a frog, in which he was fated to remain till some princess should take him out of the spring and let him sleep upon her bed for three nights. 'You,' said the prince, 'have broken this cruel charm, and now I have nothing to wish for but that you should go with me into my father's kingdom, where I will marry you, and love you as long as you live.'

The young princess, you may be sure, was not long in giving her consent; and as they spoke a splendid carriage drove up with eight beautiful horses decked with plumes of feathers and golden harness, and behind rode the prince's servant, the faithful Henry, who had bewailed the misfortune of his dear master so long and bitterly that his heart had well nigh burst. Then all set out full of joy for the Prince's kingdom; where they arrived safely, and lived happily a great many years.

The princess is squeamish where frogs are concerned. Illustration by Arthur Rackham from *Fairy Tales of the Brothers Grimm*, 1900

THE TWELVE
DANCING PRINCESSES

'The Twelve Dancing Princesses', otherwise known as 'The Dancing Shoes', 'The Worn Shoes', or 'The Shoes that were Danced to Pieces', is one of the more romantic of the Grimms' tales—a tale such as Hans Andersen might have written. The Grimms learnt it from their friends the Haxthausens, who had heard 'Die zertanzten Schuhe' in Münster; and further versions of the story were found in Hesse and Paderborn. In the Hesse variant instead of twelve princesses each wearing out one pair of shoes each night, one princess—or so it seemed to the royal household—nightly wore out twelve pairs of shoes, which kept twelve apprentices busy replacing them throughout the day. However, one night the youngest apprentice remained under the princess's bed, and found that at eleven o'clock she was joined by eleven other princesses. This discovery led eventually to her being released from a spell, and to the young apprentice being chosen to be her husband.

In the version from Paderborn, Westphalia, there were three princesses only whose shoes were found every morning to be in holes. It was announced that whoever could discover the cause of this dilapidation should have the youngest princess for wife, but anyone failing in the attempt must forfeit his life. Twelve men had already failed and been hung when a soldier undertook the task, and won himself a bride. It is in this version that the pleasing incident takes place of the soldier making believe he is drinking drugged wine but in fact letting it run down into a sponge tied under his chin.

The do-or-die terms offered to candidates for a princess's hand are not uncommon in popular literature, but Victorian editors found their harshness unacceptable. In the age of self help, it was not thinkable that those who strove and failed should be worse off than those who had never striven; and in his presentation of the tale Andrew Lang disposed of the unsuccessful candidates as unobtrusively as possible, stating that 'when the morning came they had all disappeared, and no one could tell what had become of them'.

It is curious that in the underworld to which the princesses nightly resort the trees are a particular feature: trees with leaves of silver, trees with leaves of gold, and further on, approaching the great lake that has to be crossed if the princesses are to indulge their passion for footwork, trees whose leaves are glittering diamonds. In the four-thousand-year-old Sumerian epic of Gilgamesh, recorded on tablets collected about 650 B.C. by Assur-bani-pal, King of Assyria, for his palace at Nineveh, the hero Gilgamesh has to make his way through the underworld to the garden of the gods, from which he crosses over the waters of death; and he too finds that the vines and bushes bear jewels instead of fruit.

In its present form the tale of the dancing princesses is unlikely to be earlier than the seventeenth century A.D. Stith Thompson points out that, although more than a hundred variants have been recorded, its distribution is not wide. The tale is primarily Central European; its most frequent appearance being in the area from Serbia north to Finland. It is scarcely known in France, and not found east of Russia.

In the British Isles its nearest parallel seems to be the tale known as 'Kate Crackernuts', which was collected in the Orkneys and published by Andrew Lang in 1889 in *Longman's Magazine*. Here a princess named Kate is the night-watcher; a sickly prince the one who is bewitched. At midnight Princess Kate sees the invalid prince rise up, dress himself, and mount his horse. He does so, however, as if sleepwalking; and Kate leaps lightly onto his horse behind him. Three times the vigilant princess follows him in this manner, each time to a magnificent dance held

The princesses being rowed to the castle.
Arthur Rackham, 1900

underground inside a green hill. After the third outing she succeeds in rescuing him, largely through the artful expenditure of nuts collected from the trees as they gallop through the night. Inevitably she obtains the prince for husband, apparently to everyone's satisfaction, for the story ends 'they all lived happy and dee'd happy, and ne'er drank out o' a dry cappy.'

The translation of 'Die zertanzten Schuhe' which follows appeared in *German Popular Stories, Translated from the Kinder und Haus-Märchen, collected by M. M. Grimm, from Oral Tradition*, 1823.

The princesses leaving their room by the secret
staircase. Illustration by H. J. Ford from
Andrew Lang's *The Red Fairy Book*, 1890

THE TWELVE
DANCING PRINCESSES

There was a king who had twelve beautiful daughters. They slept in twelve beds all in one room; and when they went to bed, the doors were shut and locked up; but every morning their shoes were found to be quite worn through, as if they had been danced in all night; and yet nobody could find out how it happened, or where they had been.

Then the king made it known to all the land, that if any person could discover the secret, and find out where it was that the princesses danced in the night, he should have the one he liked best for his wife, and should be king after his death; but whoever tried and did not succeed, after three days and nights, should be put to death.

A king's son soon came. He was well entertained, and in the evening was taken to the chamber next to the one where the princesses lay in their twelve beds. There he was to sit and watch where they went to dance; and, in order that nothing might pass without his hearing it, the door of his chamber was left open. But the king's son soon fell asleep; and when he awoke in the morning he found that the princesses had all been dancing, for the soles of their shoes were full of holes. The same thing happened the second and third night: so the king ordered his head to be cut off. After him came several others; but they all had the same luck, and all lost their lives in the same manner.

Now it chanced that an old soldier, who had been wounded in battle, and could fight no longer, passed through the country where this king reigned: and as he was travelling through a wood, he met an old woman, who asked him where he was going. 'I hardly know where I am going, or what I had better do,' said the soldier; 'but I think I should like very well to find out where it is that the princesses dance, and then in time I might be a king.' 'Well,' said the old dame, 'that is no very hard task: only take care not to drink any of the wine which one of the princesses will bring to you in the evening; as soon as she leaves you pretend to be fast asleep.'

Then she gave him a cloak, and said, 'As soon as you put that on you will become invisible, and you will then be able to follow the princesses wherever they go.' When the soldier heard all this good counsel, he determined to try his luck; so he went to the king, and said he was willing to undertake the task.

He was as well received as the others had been, and the king ordered fine royal robes to be given him; and when the evening came he was led to the outer chamber. Just as he was going to lie down, the eldest of the princesses brought him a cup of wine; but the soldier threw it all away secretly, taking care not to drink a drop. Then he laid himself down on his bed, and in a little while began to snore very loud as if he was fast asleep. When the twelve princesses heard this they laughed heartily; and the eldest said, 'This fellow too might have done a wiser thing than lose his life in this way!' Then they rose up and opened their drawers and boxes, and took out all their fine clothes, and dressed themselves at the glass, and skipped about as if they were eager to begin dancing. But the youngest said, 'I don't know how it is, while you are so happy I feel very uneasy; I am sure some mischance will befall us.' 'You simpleton,' said the eldest, 'you are always afraid; have you forgotten how many kings' sons have already watched us in vain? And as for this soldier, even if I had not given him his sleeping draught, he would have slept soundly enough.'

When they were all ready, they went and looked at the soldier; but he snored on, and did not stir hand or foot: so they thought they were quite safe; and the eldest went up to her own bed and clapped her hands, and the bed sunk into the floor and a trap-door flew open. The soldier saw them going down through the trap-door one after another, the eldest leading the way; and thinking he had no time to lose, he jumped up, put on the cloak which the old woman had given him, and followed them; but in the middle of the stairs he trod on the gown of the youngest princess, and she cried out to her sisters, 'All is not right; some one took hold of my gown.' 'You silly creature!' said the eldest, 'it is nothing but a nail in the wall.' Then down they all went, and at the bottom they found themselves in a most delightful grove of trees; and the leaves were all of silver, and glittered and sparkled beautifully. The soldier wished to take away some token of the place; so he broke off a little branch, and there came a loud noise from the tree. Then the youngest daughter said again, 'I am sure all is not right—did not you hear that noise? That never happened before.' But the eldest said, 'It is only our princes, who are shouting for joy at our approach.'

Then they came to another grove of trees, where all the leaves were of gold; and afterwards to a third, where the leaves were all glittering diamonds. And the soldier broke a branch from each; and every time there was a loud noise, which made the youngest sister tremble with fear; but the eldest still said, It was only the princes, who were crying for joy. So they went on till they came to a great lake; and at the side of the lake there lay twelve little boats with twelve handsome princes in them, who seemed to be waiting there for the princesses.

One of the princesses went into each boat, and the soldier stepped into the same boat with the youngest. As they were rowing over the lake, the prince who was in the boat with the youngest princess and the soldier said, 'I do not know why it is, but though I am rowing with all my might we do not get on so fast as usual, and I am quite tired: the boat seems very heavy to-day.' 'It is only the heat of the weather,' said the princess; 'I feel it very warm too.'

On the other side of the lake stood a fine illuminated castle, from which came the merry music of horns and trumpets. There they all landed, and went into the castle,

'The Dancing Princesses' depicted by Kay Nielsen. From Arthur Quiller-Couch's *In Powder and Crinoline*, 1913

and each prince danced with his princess; and the soldier, who was all the time invisible, danced with them too; and when any of the princesses had a cup of wine set by her, he drank it all up, so that when she put the cup to her mouth it was empty. At this, too, the youngest sister was terribly frightened, but the eldest always silenced her. They danced on till three o'clock in the morning, and then all their shoes were worn out, so that they were obliged to leave off. The princes rowed them back again over the lake; (but this time the soldier placed himself in the boat with the eldest princess;) and on the opposite shore they took leave of each other, the princesses promising to come again the next night.

When they came to the stairs, the soldier ran on before the princesses, and laid himself down; and as the twelve sisters slowly came up very much tired, they heard him snoring in his bed; so they said, 'Now all is quite safe;' then they undressed themselves, put away their fine clothes, pulled off their shoes, and went to bed. In the morning the soldier said nothing about what had happened, but determined to see more of this strange adventure, and went again the second and third night; and every thing happened just as before; the princesses danced each time till their shoes were worn to pieces, and then returned home. However, on the third night the soldier carried away one of the golden cups as a token of where he had been.

As soon as the time came when he was to declare the secret, he was taken before the king with the three branches and the golden cup; and the twelve princesses stood listening behind the door to hear what he would say. And when the king asked him 'Where do my twelve daughters dance at night?' he answered, 'With twelve princes in a castle under ground.' And then he told the king all that had happened, and showed him the three branches and the golden cup which he had brought with him. Then the king called for the princesses, and asked them whether what the soldier said was true: and when they saw that they were discovered, and that it was of no use to deny what had happened, they confessed it all. And the king asked the soldier which of them he would choose for his wife; and he answered, 'I am not very young, so I will have the eldest.'—And they were married that very day, and the soldier was chosen to be the king's heir.

RUMPELSTILTSKIN

This tale, which is of particular interest to folk-lorists, has been the subject of a number of studies, and the inspiration of at least one book: Edward Clodd's *Tom Tit Tot, An Essay on Savage Philosophy in Folk-Tale*, 1898. It is a moral tale in that it shows the perils of boasting, though this aspect is not stressed. It is a fairy tale in that the heroine receives supernatural assistance. It is a properly constructed dramatic tale in that to obtain such assistance the heroine has to make the most terrible of pledges, the life of her first-born child. And it is a primitive tale in that it hinges on the belief of the interdependence of name and identity: the dwarf's power is only to be broken if his name can be discovered. It is also a tale possessing genuine folk appeal in that a supernatural creature is outwitted by human cleverness, when the dwarf is overheard singing:

> Little does my lady dream
> Rumpel-Stilts-Kin is my name.

The tale is a familiar one over most of Europe, from Scandinavia to Spain and Italy, its principal traits being fairly constant. The Grimm brothers collected four versions in Hesse that were complementary to each other, from which comes their story; and when in 1823 Edgar Taylor issued the English translation, he recollected that he himself had heard a story similar to it in Ireland in which the song ran:

> Little does my Lady wot
> That my name is Trit-a-Trot.

Subsequently the tale was found to be well known in Britain, the fairy or other supernatural creature singing in Suffolk:

> Nimmy nimmy not,
> My name's Tom Tit Tot.

In Cornwall:

> Duffy, my lady, you'll never know—what?
> That my name is Terrytop, Terrytop—top.

Rumpelstiltskin pulling his foot out of the floor. Etching by George Cruikshank from *German Popular Stories*, 1823

And in Scotland:

> Little kens our guid dame at hame
> That Whuppity Stoorie is my name!

Edgar Taylor also pointed out that in a work published in Amsterdam in 1708, *Tour tenebreuse et les jours lumineux, Contes Anglois tirez d'une ancienne chronique composée par Richard surnommé Coeur de Lion, Roy d' Angleterre*, the same incident occurs, the song of the dwarf being as follows:

> Si jeune et tendre femelle
> N'aimant qu'enfantins ebats,
> Avoit mis dans sa cervelle
> Que Ricdin-Ricdon, je m'appelle,
> Point ne viendroit dans mes laqs:
> Mais sera pour moi la belle
> Car un tel nom ne sçait pas.

It should be noted, as the Grimm brothers pointed out, that gnomes do not customarily bear names which are in use among men, so a manikin could believe himself safe when he imposed the condition that his name should be discovered. However Rumpelstiltskin's name, and presumably also his story, seems to have been known for some centuries. Amongst the games and pastimes listed in Johann Fischart's adaptation of Book I of Rabelais' *Gargantua, Geschichtklitterung*, published 1575-90, the 363rd amusement is given as 'Rumpele stilt oder der Poppart'.

The text that follows is from *German Popular Stories, Translated from the Kinder und Haus-Märchen, Collected by M. M. Grimm, From Oral Tradition,* 1823. This is the first printing of the story in English, and has remained the version that is best known in the English-speaking world.

RUMPEL-STILTS-KIN

In a certain kingdom once lived a poor miller who had a very beautiful daughter. She was moreover exceedingly shrewd and clever; and the miller was so vain and proud of her, that he one day told the king of the land that his daughter could spin gold out of straw. Now this king was very fond of money; and when he heard the miller's boast, his avarice was excited, and he ordered the girl to be brought before him. Then he led her to a chamber where there was a great quantity of straw, gave her a spinning-wheel, and said, 'All this must be spun into gold before morning, as you value your life.' It was in vain that the poor maiden declared that she could do no such thing, the chamber was locked and she remained alone.

She sat down in one corner of the room and began to lament over her hard fate, when on a sudden the door opened, and a droll-looking little man hobbled in, and said 'Good morrow to you, my good lass, what are you weeping for?' 'Alas!' answered she, 'I must spin this straw into gold, and I know not how.' 'What will you give me,' said the little man, 'to do it for you?' 'My necklace,' replied the maiden. He took her at her word, and set himself down to the wheel; round about it went merrily, and presently the work was done and the gold all spun.

When the king came and saw this, he was greatly astonished and pleased; but his heart grew still more greedy of gain, and he shut up the poor miller's daughter again with a fresh task. Then she knew not what to do, and sat down once more to weep; but the little man presently opened the door, and said 'What will you give me to do your task?' 'The ring on my finger,' replied she. So her little friend took the ring, and began to work at the wheel, till by the morning all was finished again.

The king was vastly delighted to see all this glittering treasure; but still he was not satisfied, and took the miller's daughter into a yet larger room, and said, 'All this must be spun to-night; and if you succeed, you shall be my queen.' As soon as she was alone the dwarf came in, and said 'What will you give me to spin gold for you this third time?' 'I have nothing left,' said she. 'Then promise me,' said the little man, 'your first little child when you are queen.' 'That may never be,' thought the miller's daughter; and as she knew no other way to get her task done, she promised him what he asked, and he spun once more the whole heap of gold. The king came in the morning, and finding all he wanted, married her, and so the miller's daughter really became queen.

At the birth of her first little child the queen rejoiced very much, and forgot the little man and her promise; but one day he came into her chamber and reminded her of it.

The little man spinning straw into gold. Colour wood-engraving from *Routledge's Coloured Picture Book*, 1870

Then she grieved sorely at her misfortune, and offered him all the treasures of the kingdom in exchange; but in vain, till at last her tears softened him, and he said 'I will give you three days' grace, and if during that time you tell me my name, you shall keep your child.'

Now the queen lay awake all night, thinking of all the odd names that she had ever heard, and dispatched messengers all over the land to inquire after new ones. The next day the little man came, and she began with Timothy, Benjamin, Jeremiah, and all the names she could remember; but to all of them he said, 'That's not my name.'

The second day she began with all the comical names she could hear of, Bandy-legs, Hunch-back, Crook-shanks, and so on, but the little gentleman still said to every one of them, 'That's not my name.'

The third day came back one of the messengers, and said 'I can hear of no one other name; but yesterday, as I was climbing a high hill among the trees of the forest where the fox and the hare bid each other good night, I saw a little hut, and before the hut burnt a fire, and round about the fire danced a funny little man upon one leg, and sung

"Merrily the feast I'll make,
To-day I'll brew, to-morrow bake;
Merrily I'll dance and sing,
For next day will a stranger bring:
Little does my lady dream
Rumpel-Stilts-Kin is my name!"'

The queen tells
Rumpelstiltskin his name.
Illustration by Mervyn Peake,
1946

When the queen heard this, she jumped for joy, and as soon as her little visitor came, and said 'Now, lady, what is my name?' 'It is John?' asked she. 'No!' 'Is it Tom?' 'No!' 'Can your name be Rumpel-stilts-kin?'

'Some witch told you that! Some witch told you that!' cried the little man, and dashed his right foot in a rage so deep into the floor, that he was forced to lay hold of it with both hands to pull it out. Then he made the best of his way off, while every body laughed at him for having had all his trouble for nothing.[1]

[1]In the original German the ending is horrific rather than humorous. When the manikin finds his name has been discovered, he stamps his foot not merely into the floor, but so deep his whole leg goes into the ground: and then in his rage he pulls at his leg so fiercely he tears himself in two.

GOLDILOCKS AND
THE THREE BEARS

In the fourth volume, published 1837, of the anonymous miscellany of linked essays entitled *The Doctor*, Robert Southey inserted a story, for the benefit of the nursery, which he said the Doctor had learnt from his uncle, William Dove. It was the 'Story of the Three Bears'.

The tale was instantly recognizable as a masterpiece. It had never appeared in print before, and the reading public naturally assumed it to be an original creation. Before the year was out the story had been retold in verse by 'G. N.', who made plain his indebtedness in his dedication:

> Unknown Author of "The Doctor,"
> Great, original Concoctor
> Of the rare story of the Bears,
> Their porridge-pots, their beds and chairs,
> Which you with condescending pen,
> To please "Good little women and men,"
> Have writ—I pray you to excuse
> The freedom of my rhyming muse,
> For having ventured to rehearse
> This tale of yours in jingling verse;
> But fearing in your book it might
> Escape some little people's sight,
> I did not like that one should lose
> What will them all so much amuse.

During the next seventy-five years, although a metamorphosis was to take place in the chief character, who changes from an ill-tempered crone to a radiant maiden, Southey's text seems to have been the starting point of each new telling. The general belief about the tale was expressed by Joseph Jacobs in his *English Fairy Tales* (1890): '"The Three Bears" is the only example I know of where a tale that can be definitely traced to a specific author has become a folk-tale.'

By 1894, however, Jacobs had to modify his opinion. John D. Batten, his illustrator, had been told a tale by a 'Mrs H', who had heard it from her mother more than forty years earlier. The story, which told of three bears who lived in a castle in a wood, and of an intruder who sat in their chairs, made free with their milk, and rested in their beds, was similar in essentials to Southey's story, although the intruder was not an old woman but a fox named Scrapefoot. The ingenious suggestion was put forward that the tale Southey had heard (probably from his half-witted uncle William Tyler, his mother's half-brother, an exponent of the traditional tale), featured an old vixen; and that Southey mistook the name for a she-fox for the common appellation for a harridan.

Here the matter rested, and might have continued to rest, had not, in 1951, a manuscript tale of the Three Bears been discovered in the Osborne Collection of Early Children's Books at Toronto Public Library. It was a home-made booklet styled: *The Story of The Three Bears metrically related, with illustrations locating it at Cecil Lodge in September 1831*. 'The celebrated nursery tale', as it was here characterized, had been put into verse and embellished with drawings, as a birthday gift for a little boy, Horace Broke, by his 32-year-old maiden aunt Eleanor Mure. This was six years before the tale appeared in *The Doctor*. Further, Miss Mure's version, which does not seem to have been based on a recital such as Southey must have heard, has points in common with 'Mrs H's' story, despite the fact that the story of Scrapefoot had undoubtedly been influenced during transmission by the popularity of Southey's tale.

In Eleanor Mure's version the unwelcome intruder is an 'angry old woman', but the bowls in the parlour contained not porridge but milk, and the milk in two of the bowls apparently tasted as unpleasant as it did to Scrapefoot. In Southey's version the little old woman jumps out of the window when discovered and is seen no more; in 'Mrs H's' version the bears debate what to do with the intruder, suggesting 'Let's hang him', 'Let's drown him', 'Let's throw him out of the window'. In Eleanor Mure's verses the bears are also at a loss what to do:

> On the fire they throw her, but burn her they couldn't,
> In the water they put her, but drown there she wouldn't;

and they 'chuck her aloft on St. Paul's church-yard steeple'—the steeple of St Paul's being at that time a place of high reputation in nursery lore. Southey, clearly, was doing no more than he claimed: retelling—brilliantly—an old tale, probably in the form he himself had told it to his children at Greta Hall.

And the tale had, of course, a partial analogue in Germany. In 'Sneewitchen', the story of 'Snowdrop' or 'Snow White and the Seven Dwarfs' (see p. 178), Sneewitchen comes upon the house where the seven dwarfs live when it is empty, finds a meal ready served, sits down and helps herself, tries each of the beds in turn, and finally falls asleep in the seventh bed. When the dwarfs return they cry out 'Who has been sitting on my stool?', 'Who has been eating off my plate?', 'Who has been drinking my wine?', 'Who has been lying on my bed?', precisely as if they were disgruntled bears; and modify their annoyance (as who would not?) when they find in one of the beds 'the fairest lady in the land'.

Again, in a Norwegian folktale, a princess comes to a cave inhabited by three bears. She finds a meal ready on the table, a meal which includes porridge, and after eating well she chooses a bed, though she lies not on it but under it, which is probably as well, for the bears are really Russian princes who at night are accustomed to cast off their bearskins.

What is indubitable is that it was Southey who immortalized the tale; and the text which follows is Southey's, as it appeared in *The Doctor*. The special large type for the voice of the large-sized bear, over which he took much trouble, is here reproduced in facsimile.

The one feature of Southey's text which has not survived is the venerableness of his intruder. The man who effectively reduced her age seems to have been Joseph Cundall. In a dedicatory letter to his children, dated Nov. 1849, which Cundall inserted at the beginning of his *Treasury of Pleasure Books for Young Children*, he explained:

> 'The· "Story of the Three Bears" is a very old Nursery Tale, but it was never so well told as by the great poet Southey, whose version I have (with permission) given you, only I have made the intruder a little girl instead of an old woman. This I did because I found that the tale is better known with *Silver-Hair*, and because there are so many other stories of old women.'

This adjustment was made only twelve years after the publication of Southey's text; and 'Silver Hair' remained the usual name of the little girl for many years thereafter. But in *Aunt Mavor's Nursery Tales*, 1858, 'the Village people called her Silver-Locks, because her curly hair was shining.' In *Aunt Friendly's Nursery Book*, *c.* 1868, 'there lived in the same forest a sweet little girl who was called Golden Hair'. And in *Old Nursery Stories and Rhymes*, illustrated by John Hassall, *c.* 1904, 'the little girl had long golden hair, so she was called Goldilocks'. Goldilocks she has remained ever since.

THE STORY OF
THE THREE BEARS

Once upon a time there were Three Bears, who lived together in a house of their own, in a wood. One of them was a Little, Small, Wee Bear; and one was a Middle-sized Bear, and the other was a Great, Huge Bear. They had each a pot for their porridge, a little pot for the Little, Small, Wee Bear; and a middle-sized pot for the Middle Bear, and a great pot for the Great, Huge Bear. And they had each a chair to sit in; a little chair for the Little, Small, Wee Bear; and a middle-sized chair for the Middle Bear; and a great chair for the Great, Huge Bear. And they had each a bed to sleep in; a little bed for the Little, Small, Wee Bear; and a middle-sized bed for the Middle Bear; and a great bed for the Great, Huge Bear.

One day, after they had made the porridge for their breakfast, and poured it into their porridge-pots, they walked out into the wood while the porridge was cooling, that they might not burn their mouths, by beginning too soon to eat it. And while they were walking, a little old Woman came to the house. She could not have been a good, honest old Woman; for first she looked in at the window, and then she peeped in at the keyhole; and seeing nobody in the house, she lifted the latch. The door was not fastened, because the Bears were good Bears, who did nobody any harm, and never suspected that any body would harm them. So the little old Woman opened the door, and went in; and well pleased she was when she saw the porridge on the table. If she had been a good little old Woman, she would have waited till the Bears came home, and then, perhaps, they would have asked her to breakfast; for they were good Bears,—a little rough or so, as the manner of Bears is, but for all that very good natured and hospitable. But she was an impudent, bad old Woman, and set about helping herself.

So first she tasted the porridge of the Great, Huge Bear, and that was too hot for her; and she said a bad word about that. And then she tasted the porridge of the Middle Bear, and that was too cold for her; and she said a bad word about that, too. And then she went to the porridge of the Little, Small, Wee bear, and tasted that; and that was neither too hot, nor too cold, but just right; and she liked it so well, that she ate it all up: but the naughty old Woman said a bad word about the little porridge-pot, because it did not hold enough for her.

Then the little old Woman sate down in the chair of the Great Huge Bear, and that was too hard for her. And then she sate down in the chair of the Middle Bear, and that

The little old woman depicted in the year Southey's tale was published, 1837

The three bears by Harrison Weir. From Joseph Cundall's *A Treasury of Pleasure Books for Young Children*, 1850

was too soft for her. And then she sate down in the chair of the Little, Small, Wee Bear, and that was neither too hard, nor too soft, but just right. So she seated herself in it, and there she sate till the bottom of the chair came out, and down came hers, plump upon the ground. And the naughty old Woman said a wicked word about that too.

Then the little old Woman went up stairs into the bed-chamber in which the three Bears slept. And first she lay down upon the bed of the Great, Huge Bear; but that was too high at the head for her. And next she lay down upon the bed of the Middle Bear; and that was too high at the foot for her. And then she lay down upon the bed of the Little, Small, Wee Bear; and that was neither too high at the head, nor at the foot, but just right. So she covered herself up comfortably, and lay there till she fell fast asleep.

By this time the Three Bears thought their porridge would be cool enough; so they came home to breakfast. Now the little old Woman had left the spoon of the Great, Huge Bear, standing in his porridge.

" Somebody has been at my por=ridge!"

said the Great, Huge Bear, in his great, rough, gruff voice. And when the Middle Bear looked at his, he saw that the spoon was standing in it too. They were wooden spoons; if they had been silver ones, the naughty old Woman would have put them in her pocket.

"Somebody has been at my porridge!"

said the Middle Bear, in his middle voice.

Then the Little, Small, Wee Bear, looked at his, and there was the spoon in the porridge-pot, but the porridge was all gone.

"Somebody has been at my porridge, and has eaten it all up!"

said the Little, Small, Wee Bear, in his little, small, wee voice.

Upon this the Three Bears, seeing that some one had entered their house, and eaten up the Little, Small, Wee Bear's breakfast, began to look about them. Now the little old Woman had not put the hard cushion straight when she rose from the chair of the Great, Huge Bear.

" Somebody has been sitting in my chair!"

said the Great, Huge Bear, in his great, rough, gruff voice.

And the little old Woman had squatted down the soft cushion of the Middle Bear.

"Somebody has been sitting in my chair!"

said the Middle Bear, in his middle voice.

And you know what the little old Woman had done to the third chair.

"Somebody has been sitting in my chair, and has sate the bottom of it out!"

said the Little, Small, Wee Bear, in his little, small, wee voice.

Then the Three Bears thought it necessary that they should make farther search; so they went up stairs into their bed-chamber. Now the little old Woman had pulled the pillow of the Great, Huge Bear, out of its place.

" Somebody has been lying in my bed!"

said the Great, Huge Bear, in his great, rough, gruff voice.

And the little old Woman had pulled the bolster of the Middle Bear out of its place.

"Somebody has been lying in my bed!"

said the Middle Bear, in his middle voice.

And when the Little, Small, Wee Bear, came to look at his bed, there was the bolster in its place; and the pillow in its place upon the bolster; and upon the pillow was the little old Woman's ugly, dirty head,—which was not in its place, for she had no business there.

"Somebody has been lying in my bed,—and here she is!"

said the Little, Small, Wee Bear, in his little, small, wee voice.

The little old Woman had heard in her sleep the great, rough, gruff voice, of the Great, Huge Bear; but she was so fast asleep that it was no more to her than the roaring of wind, or the rumbling of thunder. And she had heard the middle voice of the Middle Bear, but it was only as if she had heard some one speaking in a dream. But when she heard the little, small, wee voice, of the Little, Small, Wee Bear, it was so sharp, and so shrill, that it awakened her at once. Up she started; and when she saw the Three Bears on one side of the bed, she tumbled herself out at the other, and ran to the window. Now the window was open, because the Bears, like good, tidy Bears, as they were, always opened their bed-chamber window when they got up in the morning. Out the little old Woman jumped; and whether she broke her neck in the fall; or ran into the wood and was lost there; or found her way out of the wood, and was taken up by the constable and sent to the House of Correction for a vagrant as she was, I cannot tell. But the Three Bears never saw any thing more of her.

Right: Three-dimensional illustration from *The Three Bears* in Raphael Tuck's 'Combined Expanding Toy and Painting Book Series', *c.*1900
Below: Illustration by John Hassall from *Mother Goose's Book of Nursery Stories*, 1928

Finding Goldenlocks in bed.

'Fyrtøiet' (The Tinder Box) was one of the first fairy tales Hans Andersen wrote. It appeared in a cheap sixty-four-page booklet, *Eventyr, fortalte for Børn* (Tales told for Children), published in Copenhagen, 8 May 1835. Andersen was twenty-nine when he wrote the tale and embarrassingly short of money, so it is easy to see why the story appealed to him. It was in fact a retelling of a Scandinavian folktale, known in Denmark as 'Aanden i Lyset' (The Spirit in the Candle), which Andersen had loved in his childhood, but which was not then well known. In the traditional story a soldier obtains riches by fetching a candle from a sleeping troll at the request of an old woman. He refuses to hand over the candle, lights it, and finds that this summons an iron man to his service, who enables him, since this is his desire, to have meetings with a beautiful princess. The soldier is found out in much the same way as Andersen's soldier, is condemned to be burned at the stake; and is saved only at the last moment by his supernatural henchman, whom he manages to summon by obtaining permission to light his pipe.

Comparison with 'Aladdin and his Wonderful Lamp' need not be resisted, particularly when it is remembered that *The Arabian Nights* was the favourite reading of Hans Andersen's childhood. The tale of Aladdin is, like 'The Tinder Box', a tale of a mortal being made use of by a supernatural, on the promise of rich reward; and several of the incidents have much similarity. The magician knows he cannot himself go into the hole wherein lies the lamp, and inveigles Aladdin to enter it for him. Within the cavern Aladdin finds three halls, much as the soldier finds three chambers—which, incidentally, do not feature in the folktale 'Aanden i Lyset'. Aladdin's discovery of the lamp, his enriching himself with the treasure he finds, and his refusal to hand over the lamp to the magician, are all actions parallelled by the soldier. (If indignation was allowed to be expressed on behalf of witches and wicked magicians, here, surely, are deserving cases, for both the old crone and the magician offered their helpers generous rewards.) Finally, each of these slightly disreputable heroes wins himself a beautiful princess with the aid of his stolen luminant.

The text which follows is the first translation of 'Fyrtøiet', which was made by Charles Boner, and included in *A Danish Story-Book*, 1846.

Original drawing for 'The Tinder Box'
by Vilhelm Pedersen, Andersen's
first illustrator in Denmark

THE TINDER BOX

Once upon a time, a soldier came marching along on the highway. He had his knapsack upon his back, and his sword by his side; for he came from the wars, and was going home. Presently an old witch met him; she was a loathsome-looking creature; for her under-lip hung down over her chin.

'Good evening, soldier!' said she. 'What a fine sword you've got, and what a large knapsack! You look truly like a brave soldier; and therefore you shall have as much money as you can wish for!'

'Thank ye, old witch!' replied the soldier.

'D'ye see the great tree yonder?' asked she, pointing to a stout oak that stood by the wayside. 'That tree is quite hollow; and if you climb up to the top, you will see a hole in the trunk, through which you can slide down and get to the very bottom of the tree. I'll tie a rope round your body, that I may be able to pull you up again when you call.'

'And what have I to do down in the tree?' asked the soldier.

'To fetch money, to be sure! What else do you think!' continued the witch. 'But you must know, that when you have got to the bottom of the oak, you'll find yourself in a large hall, lighted by a hundred lamps. There you will see three doors, all of which you can open, for the key is in every one of them. If you enter the first door, you'll come into a chamber, in the middle of which, on the floor, a great money-chest stands, but which is guarded by a dog with eyes as large as tea-cups; but that you need not mind. I'll give you my coloured apron; you must spread it out on the floor, and then you may boldly lay hold of the dog and put him on it; after which you can take out of the chest as many halfpence as you please. But if you want silver, you must go into the second chamber. However, here sits a dog upon the chest, with a pair of eyes as large as mill-wheels; but that you need not mind: put the dog on the apron, and take as much silver as you please. But if you would rather have gold, you must go into the third chamber, and you can take as much as you can carry. But the dog that guards this money-chest has eyes as large as the Round Tower* at Copenhagen. That's a dog for you! But you need not mind him: put him on my apron, and take as many gold pieces out of the chest as you please; the dog won't do you any harm.'

'That wouldn't be amiss!' said the soldier. 'But what am I to give you, old beldame? For 'tis not very likely you would send me down the hollow tree for nothing!'

'No,' said the witch, 'I don't ask a farthing! You must only bring up with you the tinder-box that my grandmother forgot the last time she was down there.'

*The Observatory; so called on account of its round form. [Translator's note.]

'Well, give me the rope,' said the soldier. 'I'll try!'

'Here it is,' said the witch; 'and here too is my coloured apron.'

The soldier now climbed up to the top of the oak, slipped through the hole in the trunk, and stood suddenly in the great hall, which was lighted, exactly as the old witch had told him, by a hundred lamps.

As soon as he had looked round him a little, he found also the three doors, and immediately opened the first. There really sat the dog with eyes as large as tea-cups, and stared at him.

'Ho, ho, my dog!' said the soldier. 'Good fellow!' And he spread the witch's apron on the floor, and set the dog upon it. He now opened the money-chest, filled all his pockets with copper halfpence, shut it again, put the staring dog on the cover, and went, with his apron, into the second chamber. Good heavens! There sat the dog with eyes as big as mill-wheels.

'You should not look at me so fixedly,' said he to the dog that was keeping watch; 'that weakens the eyes!' He then set the animal on the apron; but when he saw the quantity of silver coin, he threw away the coppers and filled all his pockets and his knapsack with the bright silver. Afterwards he went to the third chamber. Well, that was enough to disgust anybody! The dog really had eyes as large as the Round Tower, and they rolled in his head like turning-wheels.

'Good evening,' said the soldier, putting his hand to his cap and saluting in true military style; for such a monster he had never met before. However, after he had looked at him for some moments, he thought it was enough; so he spread out the apron, lifted the enormous dog off the cover, and opened the money-chest.

What heaps of gold he saw! He could have bought all Copenhagen, all the sugar-plums, all the games of soldiers, all the whips and rocking-horses in Europe, with the money! At the first sight of such rich treasure, the soldier threw away all the silver with which he was laden, and stuffed his pockets, knapsack, cap, and boots, so full of gold pieces, that he could but just move with the weight. Now he had money in abundance. The tremendous dog was put on the cover again, the door of the chamber shut, and the soldier called up the tree.

'Hallo, old hag! Now, then, pull me up again!'

'Have you got the tinder-box?' said the witch in reply.

'I'll be hanged, if I hadn't nearly forgotten it!' said the soldier. He then put the tinder-box in his pocket; the witch drew him up out of the tree; and he soon was standing again on the highway with all his treasure.

'What do you want with the tinder-box?' asked the soldier.

'That's nothing to you,' answered the old hag. 'You've got money in plenty; so give me the tinder-box.'

'No!' said the soldier. 'Tell me directly what you'll do with the tinder-box, or I'll cut your head off with my sword!'

''And what have I to do down in the tree?'' asked the soldier.' Illustration by Harry Clarke, 1916

'No,' cried the witch, 'I won't.'

And the soldier instantly drew his sword and chopped her head from her body; so there was an end of her! He then tied up his money in her apron, put the bundle over his shoulder and the tinder-box in his pocket, and trudged off to the next town.

It was a large city; and he went to the first hotel, asked for the best apartments, and ordered the most delicate things for dinner; for he was now a moneyed man.

The waiters, it is true, thought his boots rather strange-looking for so grand a gentleman; but they were of another opinion next morning, after he had been out shopping; for they now had the most elegant boots to clean, and the finest clothing to brush. The soldier had become quite a dandy; he talked of the curiosities of the town, and was told about the King and the beautiful Princess.

'How can I see her?' asked the soldier.

'She is not to be seen,' was the answer; 'for she lives in a large brazen palace surrounded by many towers and high walls. Only the King visits his daughter; because it has been foretold that the Princess will marry a common soldier, and the King won't hear of such a thing.'

'I'd give the world to see the Princess!' thought the soldier to himself; but as to getting a permission, it was of no use thinking of such a thing.

Meanwhile he led a merry life; went often to the play, drove about in the royal park, and gave a good deal to the poor. It was praiseworthy of him to be charitable; but he knew well enough by experience what a poor fellow feels who has not got a penny. He was, moreover, a rich man, had handsome clothes, and many friends, who told him every day that he was an excellent creature, a perfect gentleman; and all this the soldier liked to hear. But as he was always taking from his money and never received any, he had at last but two-pence-halfpenny left. So he was obliged to leave the handsome lodgings he had lived in till now, and to take a small garret, to clean his own boots, and darn and mend his clothes himself when they wanted it. None of his old friends visited him any more; for they could not, of course, go up so many pair of stairs for his sake.

It was quite dark in his room, and he had not even money enough to buy a candle. Suddenly he remembered that, in the tinder-box which he fetched up from the bottom of the hollow oak, there were a few matches. He therefore took it, and began to strike a light; but as soon as the sparks flew about, the door of his room was thrown open, and the dog with eyes as large as tea-cups walked in, and said, 'What do you please to command?'

'Well done!' cried the soldier, astonished; 'that's a capital tinder-box, if I can get all I want with so little trouble! Well, then, my friend,' said he to the dog with the staring eyes, 'I am in want of money; get me some!' Crack! the dog had vanished, and crack! there he was again standing before the soldier, holding a purse filled with copper coin between his teeth.

Now he perfectly understood how to employ the tinder-box: if he struck with the

The soldier fills his knapsack with coins.
Illustration by H. J. Ford from Andrew Lang's
The Yellow Fairy Book, 1894

flint and steel once, then the dog with the copper money appeared; if twice, the one with the silver coin; and if three times, then came the dog that guarded the chest of gold. After this discovery, he returned immediately to his former handsome lodgings; his numerous kind friends came to him again, and testified their sincere affection and attachment.

'Well,' thought the soldier one day to himself, ' 'tis very strange that no one may see the beautiful Princess! They say she is a great beauty; but what good will that do her, if she is always to stay shut up in the brazen castle with the numerous towers! I wonder if it really be impossible to see her! Where's my tinder-box? I should like to know if it's only money that he can procure.' He struck the flint, and the well-known dog with saucer-eyes stood before him.

'It is midnight, it is true,' said he; 'but I should like so much to see the Princess only for a moment!'

In a moment the dog was out of the room, and before the soldier thought it possible, he saw him return with the Princess, who sat asleep on the dog's back, and was so indescribably beautiful that anybody who saw her would know directly she was a Princess. The soldier could not help it; happen what might, he must give the Princess a kiss, and so he did.

Then the dog ran back again to the palace with the lovely Princess. The next morning at breakfast she told her parents of the curious dream she had had; that she had been riding on a dog, and that a soldier had given her a kiss.

'A very pretty affair indeed!' said the Queen. So now it was agreed that, next night, one of the ladies of the court should watch at the bedside of the Princess, to see into the matter of the dream.

That night the soldier felt a strange longing to see the beautiful Princess in the brazen castle. The dog was therefore despatched, who took her again on his back and ran off with her. But the cunning old lady quickly put on a pair of good walking-boots, and ran after the dog so fast, that she caught sight of him just as he was going into the house where the soldier lived. 'Ah, ah!' thought she; 'all's right now! I know where he is gone to;' and she made a cross on the street-door with a piece of chalk. Then she went back to the palace, and lay down to sleep. The dog, too, came back with the Princess; and when he remarked that there was a cross on the house where the soldier lived, he made crosses on all the street-doors in the town; which was very clever of the animal, for now the lady would not be able to find the right door again.

Early next morning came the King and Queen, the old lady, and all the high officers of the crown, to ascertain where the Princess had gone to in the night.

'Here's the house!' exclaimed the King, when he saw the first door that had a cross on it.

'No, it must be here, my dear,' said the Queen, perceiving the next house with a white cross.

'Here, there, and every where are white crosses!' cried all; for, look where they would, the street-doors had white crosses on them; and they now perceived it would be a vain attempt to try to find the right house.

The Queen, however, was an exceedingly clever woman. She knew something more than merely how to sit in a carriage with an air; and therefore she soon found out a way how to come on the traces of the dog. She took a whole piece of silk, cut it in two with a golden pair of scissors, and with the pieces made a bag. This bag she had fillep with the most finely-sifted flour, and tied it with her own hands round the Princess's neck. When this was done, she took her golden scissors and cut a small hole in the bag, just large enough to let the flour run slowly out when the Princess moved.

The dog came again in the night, took the Princess on his back, and ran off with her to the soldier, who wanted so much only to look at her, and who would have given any thing to be a Prince, so that he might marry the Princess.

But the dog did not observe that his track from the palace to the soldier's house was marked with the flour that had run out of the bag. On the following morning, the King and the Queen now saw where their daughter had been; and had the soldier arrested and put into prison.

There sat the poor soldier, and it was so dark too in his cell; besides, the gaoler told him that he was to be hanged on the morrow. That was indeed no very pleasant news for the soldier; and, more unfortunate than all, he had left his tinder-box at the hotel. When day broke he could see out of his little prison-windows how the people were streaming from the town to see the execution; he heard the drums beat, and saw the

'The three dogs rescue the soldier.' Helen Stratton's evocation of the scene, 1905

soldiers marching to the spot where the scaffold was erected. Among the crowd was a little apprentice, who was in such a hurry that he lost one of his shoes just as he was running by the prison.

'Hallo, my little man!' cried the soldier to the boy; 'you need not be in such a hurry; for nothing can be done till I come! If you will run to the inn, at the sign of the Golden Angel, and fetch me a tinder-box that I left behind in my room, I'll give you a groat for your trouble;—but you must make all the haste you can!'

The boy wanted very much to get the groat; so off he ran to the Golden Angel, found the tinder-box as described in the soldier's room, and brought it to him to his grated window. Now let us see what happened.

Outside the town a high gallows had been erected, which was surrounded by a quantity of soldiers, and thousands of people occupied the large field. The King and Queen sat on a splendid throne that had been erected for them, opposite the judges and the councillors.

The soldier was already on the highest step of the ladder, and the executioner was just about to put the rope round his neck, when he implored that they would grant him, poor sinner that he was, one last wish. He had, he said, a great longing to smoke a pipe of tobacco, and as this was the last act of grace he should ask for in this world, he hoped they would not refuse him.

But the King would not accede to it:[1] so the soldier took out his flint and steel, and struck one, two, three times; when presently all three enchanted dogs stood before him; the one with the saucer-eyes, as well as the other two with eyes like a mill-wheel, or the Round Tower at Copenhagen.

'Help me out of my difficulty!' called the soldier to the dogs. 'Don't let them hang me!' Immediately the three frightful dogs fell on the judge and the councillors, seized one by the leg, another by the nose, and tossed them up in the air, so that in tumbling down they were dashed to pieces.

'We are not graciously pleased—' cried the King; but the dogs cared little for that, and took King and Queen, one after the other, and tossed them like the rest in the air. Then the soldiers grew frightened; and the people called out, 'Good soldier, you shall be our King, and you shall have the beautiful Princess for a wife!'

Then the soldier seated himself in the King's carriage, and all three dogs danced in front of it, and shouted 'Hurrah!' The boys in the street whistled, and the soldiers presented arms.

Now the Princess was liberated from the brazen castle, and was made Queen, which she liked very much. The wedding festivities lasted eight days, and the dogs seated themselves at table, and stared with their great eyes.

[1]The text is here incorrectly translated. In the original, the old soldier remarked that before being executed a prisoner always had the right to ask one harmless favour; and the king did not like to say no.

The happiness of possessing a magic tinder box
is almost overwhelming. Illustration by Thomas
Heath Robinson from Andersen's *Fairy Tales,*
1899

THE PRINCESS ON THE PEA

'Prindsessen paa Ærten' was another of the tales Hans Andersen told in the booklet *Eventyr, fortalte for Børn* (Tales told for Children), published in Copenhagen in 1835; and it, too, was a tale he said he had heard in childhood, as undoubtedly he had, although curiously the tale has never, as far as is known, been traditional in Denmark. Similar tales are known in Sweden, some beginning exactly as does 'The Princess on the Pea', although in the Swedish stories the queen may make the bed with only seven mattresses, and place a pea between each, and the princess is subjected to a number of tests, usually three, such trifles as nuts, grain, pinheads, and even straws, being placed between her mattresses on successive nights. Yet the Swedish folktales have not the wonderfulness of Andersen's tale, for they do not enshrine our secret knowledge that princesses are different from the rest of us. Even when the girl being tested is a real princess she sleeps in the bed as soundly as a trooper; and if it was not for the advice of her dog or of her cat she would not know she should complain of having had an uncomfortable night.

But in the East the sensitivity of those of royal or distinguished blood has been appreciated, or at least made the subject of fable, for many centuries. Thus in Book XII of the *Kathā Sarit Sāgara* of Somadeva, the Kashmiri who lived in the third century A.D., the tale is told of three brothers ordered by their father, a wealthy brahmin, to fetch a turtle from the sea. Each young man excused himself from touching the repulsive creature on the grounds of his superior fastidiousness. The first declared that none was more fastidious than he about eating; the second that none was more fastidious than he about the fair sex; the third that none was more fastidious than he about beds. To decide which of the three was the most sensitive, they took their claims to the king to be investigated. After the two elder brothers had been tested, the third brother went to rest on a bed composed of his customary seven mattresses, upon which had been placed smooth white sheets. But before the first watch of the night had passed he rose up pressing his hand to his side in horrible anguish. When the king's investigators looked at his body they found a crooked red mark, as if a hair had been pressed deep into his side. They examined his bed, and beneath the bottommost mattress in the middle of the bedstead they found a single hair.

Andersen's tale was translated into English by Charles Boner in *A Danish Story-Book*, 1846. But the fact of a single pea being discerned beneath twenty mattresses and twenty feather-beds, as Andersen had said, seems to have over-stretched Boner's credulity. To make the tale more believable he altered it, as can be seen, and said that beneath the mountain of bedding the queen placed not just one pea but *three*.

The princess after her uncomfortable night illustrated (*left*) by Rex Whistler, 1935; (*right*) by Edmund Dulac, 1911

THE PRINCESS AND
THE PEAS

There lived, once upon a time, a Prince, and he wished to marry a Princess, but then she must be really and truly a Princess. So he travelled over the whole world to find one; but there was always something or other to prevent his being successful. Princesses he found in plenty, but he never could make out if they were real Princesses; for sometimes one thing and sometimes another appeared to him not quite right about the ladies. So at last he returned home quite cast down; for he wanted so very much to have a real Princess for a wife.

One evening, a dreadful storm was gathering; it thundered and lightened, and the rain poured down from heaven in torrents; it was, too, as dark as pitch. Suddenly a loud knocking was heard at the town-gates; and the old King, the Prince's father, went out himself to see who was there.

It was a Princess that stood at the gate; but, Lord bless me! what a figure she was from the rain! The water ran down from her hair, and her dress was dripping wet and stuck quite close to her body. She said she was a real Princess.

'We'll soon see that,' thought the old Queen Dowager: however, she said not a word, but went into the bed-room, took out all the bedding, and laid three small peas on the bottom of the bedstead. Then she took, first, twenty mattresses, and laid them one upon the other on the three peas, and then she took twenty feather-beds more, and put these again a-top of the mattresses.

This was the bed the Princess was to sleep in.

The next morning she asked her if she had had a good night.

'Oh, no! a horrid night!' said the Princess. 'I was hardly able to close my eyes the whole night! Heaven knows what was in my bed, but there was a something hard under me, and my whole body is black and blue with bruises! I can't tell you what I've suffered!'

Then they knew that the lady they had lodged was a real Princess, since she had felt the three small peas through twenty mattresses and twenty feather-beds; for it was quite impossible for any one but a true Princess to be so tender.

So the Prince married her; for he was now convinced that he had a real Princess for his wife. The three peas were deposited in the Museum, where they are still to be seen; that is to say, if they have not been lost.

Now was not that a lady of exquisite feeling?

Hans Andersen's story 'Tommelise' was written after the success of his first four tales, and published in Copenhagen in 1836. It was a story of his own invention, a distant tribute perhaps to his confidante Henriette Wulff, the little hunchbacked daughter of the translator of Shakespeare, who had cared for him as the tiny fairy girl had cared for the swallow. The tale, with its acceptable moral that people are happy when with their own kind, is an adventure story from the feminine point of view. Tommelise is passive, the victim of circumstances; whereas the traditional Tom Thumb, despite his misadventures, exerts himself, and makes himself felt. Interestingly, in the original Danish, the tale starts as does 'The History of Tom Thumb', with a wife longing to have a child of her own, who seeks out an old witch to give her aid. When Mary Howitt, whose translation follows, introduced the tale to the English language in *Wonderful Stories for Children*, published February 1846, she did not approve of the superstitious consultation with an old crone, and adjusted the opening to her liking.

'Tommelise' was also translated in 1846 by Charles Boner, who gave the heroine the name 'Little Ellie'. When Madame de Chatelain translated the tale in 1852 the heroine became 'Little Totty'; and the editor of *The Child's Own Book*, 1853, styled her throughout 'Little Maja', the name she ordinarily acquires at the end of the tale. The translator responsible for the name 'Thumbelina' seems to have been H. W. Dulcken, whose influential and oft-reprinted collections of Hans Andersen's tales first appeared in 1864 and 1866.

Top: Thumbelina by Vilhelm Pedersen, 1849
Bottom: Thumbelina by an unknown artist, from *Tales for the Young*, 1847

TOMMELISE

Once upon a time, a beggar woman went to the house of a poor peasant, and asked for something to eat. The peasant's wife gave her some bread and milk. When she had eaten it, she took a barley-corn out of her pocket, and said—'This will I give thee; set it in a flower-pot, and see what will come out of it.'

The woman set the barley-corn in an old flower-pot, and the next day the most beautiful plant had shot up, which looked just like a tulip, but the leaves were shut close together, as if it still were in bud.

'What a pretty flower it is!' said the woman, and kissed the small red and yellow leaves; and just as she had kissed them, the flower gave a great crack, and opened itself. It was a real tulip, only one could see that in the middle of the flower there sat upon the pointal a little tiny girl, so delicate and lovely, and not half so big as my thumb, and, therefore, the woman called her Tommelise.

A pretty polished walnut-shell was her cradle, blue violet leaves were her mattress, and a rose leaf was her coverlet; here she slept at night, but in the day she played upon the table, where the woman had set a plate, around which she placed quite a garland of flowers, the stalks of which were put in water. A large tulip-leaf floated on the water. Tommelise seated herself on this, and sailed from one end of the plate to the other; she had two white horse-hairs to row her little boat with. It looked quite lovely; and then she sang—Oh! so beautifully, as nobody ever had heard!

One night, as she lay in her nice little bed, there came a fat, yellow frog hopping in at the window, in which there was a broken pane. The frog was very large and heavy, but it hopped easily on the table where Tommelise lay and slept under the red rose leaf. 'This would be a beautiful wife for my son!' said the frog; and so she took up the walnut-shell in which Tommelise lay, and hopped away with it, through the broken pane, down into the garden.

Here there ran a large, broad river; but just at its banks it was marshy and muddy: the frog lived here, with her son. Uh! he also was all spotted with green and yellow, and was very like his mother. 'Koax, koax, brekke-ke-kex!' that was all he could say when he saw the pretty little maiden in the walnut-shell.

'Don't make such a noise, or else you will waken her,' said the old frog; 'and if you frighten her, she may run away from us, for she is as light as swan's down! We will take her out on the river, and set her on a waterlily leaf; to her who is so light, it will

The lily-leaf raft. Colour wood-engraving, after the drawing by Eleanor Vere Boyle, from *Fairy Tales by Hans Christian Andersen*, 1872. Andersen, himself, was unimpressed by Mrs Boyle's artistry but acknowledged the sumptuousness of the colours: 'No book of mine has ever been as beautifully got up as this'.

be like an island; she cannot get away from us there, and we will then go and get ready the house in the mud, where you two shall live together.'

There grew a great many waterlilies in the river, with their broad green leaves, which seemed to float upon the water. The old frog swam to the leaf which was the furthest out in the river, and which was the largest also, and there she set the walnut shell, with little Tommelise.

The poor little tiny thing awoke quite early in the morning, and when she saw where she was she began to cry bitterly, for there was water on every side of the large green leaf, and she could not get to land.

The old frog sat down in the mud, and decked her house with sedge and yellow water reeds, that it might be regularly beautiful when her new daughter-in-law came. After this was done, she and her fat son swam away to the lily leaf, where Tommelise stood, that they might fetch her pretty little bed, and so have everything ready before she herself came to the house.

The old frog courtesyed to her in the water, and said,—'Allow me to introduce my son to you, who is to be your husband, and you shall live together, so charmingly, down in the mud!'

'Koax, koax, brekke-ke-kex!' that was all that the son could say.

So they took the pretty little bed, and swam away with it; but Tommelise sat, quite alone, and wept, upon the green leaf, for she did not wish to live with the queer-looking, yellow frog, nor to have her ugly son for her husband. The little fishes which swam down in the water had seen the frog, and had heard what she said, they put up, therefore, their heads, to look at the little girl. The moment they saw her they thought her very pretty; and they felt very sorry that she should have to go down into the mud and live with the frog. No, never should it be! They therefore went down into the water in a great shoal, and gathered round the green stalk of the leaf upon which she stood; they gnawed the stalk in two with their teeth, and thus the leaf floated down the river. Slowly and quietly it floated away, a long way off, where the frog could not come to it.

Tommelise sailed past a great many places, and the little birds sat in the bushes, looked at her, and sang,—'What a pretty little maiden!' The leaf on which she stood floated away further and further, and, at last, she came to a foreign land.

A pretty little white butterfly stayed with her, and flew round about her, and, at length, seated itself upon the leaf; for it knew little Tommelise so well: and she was so pleased, for she knew that now the frog could not come near her, and the land to which she had come was very beautiful. The sun shone upon the water, and it was like the most lovely gold. She took off her girdle, therefore, and bound one end of it to the butterfly, and the other end of it to the leaf, and thus she glided on more swiftly than ever, and she stood upon the leaf as it went.

The swallow's homeland. Another illustration by Eleanor Vere Boyle from the volume of 1872

As she was thus sailing on charmingly, a large stag-beetle came flying towards her; it paused for a moment to look at her, then clasped its claws around her slender waist, and flew up into a tree with her, but the green lily leaf floated down the stream, and the white butterfly with it, because it was fastened to it, and could not get loose.

Poor Tommelise! how frightened she was when the stag-beetle flew away with her up into the trees! but she was most of all distressed for the lovely white butterfly which she had fastened to the leaf. But that did not trouble the stag-beetle at all. It seated itself upon one of the largest green leaves of the tree, gave her the honey of the flowers to eat, and said that she was very pretty, although she was not at all like a stag-beetle. Before long, all the other stag-beetles that lived in the tree came to pay her a visit; they looked at Tommelise; and the misses stag-beetle, they examined her with their antennae, and said,—'Why, she has only two legs, that is very extraordinary!' 'She has no antennae!' said the others. 'She has such a thin body! Why she looks just like a human being!' 'How ugly she is!' said all the lady stag-beetles; and yet Tommelise was exceedingly pretty.

The stag-beetle which had carried her away had thought so himself, at first; but now, as all the others said that she was ugly, he fancied, at last, that she was so, and would not have her, and she could now go where she would. They flew down with her out of the tree, and set her upon a daisy. Here she wept, because she was so ugly, and the stag-beetles would have nothing to do with her; and yet she really was so very lovely as nobody could imagine, as delicate and bright as the most beautiful rose leaf!

Poor Tommelise lived all that long summer through quite alone, in the great wood. She wove herself a bed of grass, and hung it under a large plantain leaf, so that the rain could not come to her; she fed from the honey of the flowers, and drank of the dew which stood in glittering drops every morning on the grass. Thus passed the summer and the autumn; but now came winter, the cold, long winter. All the birds which had sung so sweetly to her were flown away; the trees and the flowers withered; the large plantain leaf under which she had dwelt shrunk together, and became nothing but a dry, yellow stalk; and she was so cold, for her clothes were in rags; and she herself was so delicate and small!—poor Tommelise, she was almost frozen to death! It began to snow, and every snow-flake which fell upon her was just as if a whole drawer full had been thrown upon us, for we are strong, and she was so very, very small! She crept, therefore, into a withered leaf, but that could not keep her warm; she shook with the cold.

Close beside the wood in which she now was, lay a large corn-field; but the corn had long been carried; nothing remained but dry stubble, which stood up on the frozen ground. It was, to her, like going into a bare wood—Oh! how she shivered with cold! Before long she came to the fieldmouse's door. The fieldmouse had a little cave down below the roots of the corn-stubble, and here she dwelt warm and comfortable, and had whole rooms full of corn, and a beautiful kitchen and a store-closet. Poor Tommelise stood before the door, like any other little beggar-child, and prayed for a little bit of a barley-corn, for she had now been two whole days without having eaten the least morsel.

'Thou, poor little thing!' said the fieldmouse, for she was, at heart, a good old fieldmouse; 'come into my warm parlour, and have a bit of dinner with me.'

How kind that seemed to Tommelise.

'Thou canst stop with me the whole winter,' said the old fieldmouse; 'but then thou must be my little maid, and keep my parlour neat and clean, and tell me tales to amuse me, for I am very fond of them!' And Tommelise did all that the good old fieldmouse desired of her, and was very comfortable.

'Before long we shall have a visiter,' said the fieldmouse, soon after Tommelise was settled in her place; 'my neighbour is accustomed to visit me once a week. He is much better off in the world than I am; he has a large house, and always wears such a splendid velvet dress! If thou couldst only manage to get him for thy husband, thou wouldst be lucky,—but then he is blind. Thou canst tell him thy very prettiest story thou knowest.'

But Tommelise gave herself no trouble about him; she did not wish to have the neighbour, for he was only a mole. He came and paid his visits in his black velvet dress; he was very rich and learned, the fieldmouse said, and his dwelling house was twenty times larger than hers; and he had such a deal of learning, although he made but little of the sun and the beautiful flowers; he laughed at them; but then he had never seen them!

The fieldmouse insisted on Tommelise singing, so she sang. She sang both 'Fly, stag-beetle, fly!' and 'The green moss grows by the water side;' and the mole fell deeply in love with her, for the sake of her sweet voice, but he did not say anything, for he was a very discreet gentleman.

He had lately dug a long passage through the earth, between his house and theirs; and in this he gave Tommelise and the fieldmouse leave to walk whenever they liked. But he told them not to be afraid of a dead bird which lay in the passage, for it was an entire bird, with feathers and a beak; which certainly was dead just lately, at the beginning of winter, and had been buried exactly where he began his passage.

The mole took a piece of touchwood in his mouth, for it shines just like fire in the dark, and went before them, to light them in the long, dark passage. When they were come where the dead bird lay, the mole set his broad nose to the ground, and ploughed up the earth, so that there was a large hole, through which the daylight could shine. In the middle of the floor lay a dead swallow, with its beautiful wings pressed close to its sides. Its legs and head were drawn up under the feathers; the poor bird had certainly died of cold. Tommelise was very sorry for it, for she was so fond of little birds; they had, through the whole summer, sung and twittered so beautifully to her; but the mole stood beside it, with his short legs, and said,—'Now it will tweedle no more! It must be a shocking thing to be born a little bird; thank goodness that none of my children have been such; for a bird has nothing at all but its singing; and it may be starved to death in winter!'

'Yes, that you, who are a sensible man, may well say,' said the fieldmouse; 'what has the bird, with all its piping and singing, when winter comes? It may be famished or frozen!'

Tommelise said nothing; but when the two others had turned their backs, she bent over it, stroked aside the feathers which lay over its head, and kissed its closed eyes.

'Perhaps it was that same swallow which sang so sweetly to me in summer,' thought she; 'what a deal of pleasure it caused me, the dear, beautiful bird!'

The mole stopped up the opening which it had made for the daylight to come in, and accompanied the ladies home. Tommelise, however, could not sleep in the night; so she got up out of bed, and wove a small, beautiful mat of hay; and that she carried down and spread over the dead bird; laid soft cotton-wool, which she had found in the fieldmouse's parlour, around the bird, that it might lie warm in the cold earth.

'Farewell, thou pretty little bird,' she said; 'farewell, and thanks for thy beautiful song, in summer, when all the trees were green, and the sun shone so warmly upon us!'

With this she laid her head upon the bird's breast, and the same moment was quite amazed, for it seemed to her as if there were a slight movement within it. It was the bird's heart. The bird was not dead; it lay in a swoon, and now being warmed, it was re-animated.

In the autumn all the swallows fly away to the warm countries; but if there be one which tarries behind, it becomes stiff with cold, so that it falls down as if dead, and the winter's snow covers it.

Tommelise was quite terrified, for in comparison with her the bird was a very large creature; but she took courage, however, laid the cotton-wool closer around the poor swallow, and fetched a coverlet of crysanthemum leaves, which she had for her bed, and laid it over its head.

Next night she listened again, and it was quite living, but so weak that it could only open its eyes a very little, and see Tommelise, who stood with a piece of touchwood in her hand, for other light she had none.

'Thanks thou shalt have, thou pretty little child!' said the sick swallow to her; 'I have been beautifully revived! I shall soon recover my strength, and be able to fly again out into the warm sunshine!'

'O,' said she, 'it is so cold out-of-doors! it snows and freezes! stop in thy warm bed, and I will nurse thee.'

She brought the swallow water, in a flower leaf, and it drank it, and related to her how it had torn one of its wings upon a thorn bush, and, therefore, had not been able to fly so well as the other swallows, who had flown far, far away, into the warm countries. It had, at last, fallen down upon the ground; but more than that it knew not, nor how it had come there.

During the whole winter it continued down here, and Tommelise was very kind to it, and became very fond of it; but neither the mole nor the fieldmouse knew anything about it, for they could not endure swallows.

As soon as ever spring came, and the sun shone warm into the earth, the swallow bade farewell to Tommelise, who opened the hole which the mole had covered up. The sun shone so delightfully down into it, and the swallow asked whether she would not go with him; she might sit upon his back, and he would fly out with her far into the green wood. But Tommelise knew that it would distress the old fieldmouse if she thus left her.

'No, I cannot,' said Tommelise.

'Farewell, farewell, thou good, sweet little maiden!' said the swallow, and flew out into the sunshine. Tommelise looked after it, and the tears came into her eyes, for she was very fond of the swallow, and she felt quite forlorn now it was gone.

'Quivit! quivit!' sung the bird, and flew into the green wood.

Tommelise was very sorrowful. She could not obtain leave to go out into the warm sunshine. The corn which had been sown in the field above the mouse's dwelling, had grown so high that it was now like a thick wood, to her.

'Now, during this summer, thou shalt get thy wedding clothes ready,' said the fieldmouse to her; for the old neighbour, the wealthy mole, had presented himself as a wooer.

'Thou shalt have both woollen and linen clothes; thou shalt have both table and body linen, if thou wilt be the mole's wife,' said the old fieldmouse.

Tommelise was obliged to sit down and spin; and the fieldmouse hired six spiders to spin and weave both night and day. Every evening the mole came to pay a visit, and always said that when the summer was ended, and the sun did not shine so hotly as to bake the earth to a stone,—yes, when the summer was over, then he and Tommelise would have a grand wedding; but this never gave her any pleasure, for she did not like the wealthy old gentleman. Every morning, when the sun rose, and every evening, when it set, she stole out to the door; and if the wind blew the ears of corn aside so that she could see the blue sky, she thought how bright and beautiful it was out there, and she wished so much that she could, just once more, see the dear

'This would be a beautiful wife for my son.'
Illustration by E. A. Lemann from Andersen's
Fairy Tales, 1893

swallow. But he never came; he certainly had flown far, far away from the lovely green wood.

It was now autumn, and all Tommelise's wedding things were ready.

'In four weeks thou shalt be married,' said the old fieldmouse to her. But Tommelise cried, and said that she would not have the rich mole.

'Snick, snack!' said the fieldmouse; 'do not go and be obstinate, else I shall bite thee with my white teeth! He is, indeed, a very fine gentleman! The queen herself has not got a dress equal to his black velvet! He has riches both in kitchen and coffer. Be thankful that thou canst get such a one!'

So the wedding was fixed. The bridegroom was already come, in his best black velvet suit, to fetch away Tommelise. She was to live with him deep under ground, never to come out into the warm sunshine, for that he could not bear. The poor child was full of sorrow; she must once more say farewell to the beautiful sun; and she begged so hard, that the fieldmouse gave her leave to go to the door to do so.

'Farewell, thou bright sun!' said she, and stretched forth her arms, and went a few paces from the fieldmouse's door, for the corn was now cut, and again there was nothing but the dry stubble.

'Farewell! farewell!' said she, and threw her small arms around a little red flower which grew there; 'greet the little swallow for me, if thou chance to see him!'

'Quivit! quivit!' said the swallow, that very moment, above her head; she looked up, there was the little swallow which had just come by. As soon as Tommelise saw it she was very glad; she told it how unwilling she was to marry the rich old mole, and live so deep underground, where the sun never shone. She could not help weeping as she told him.

'The cold winter is just at hand,' said the little swallow; 'I am going far away to the warm countries, wilt thou go with me? Thou canst sit upon my back; bind thyself fast with thy girdle, and so we will fly away from the rich mole and his dark parlour, far away over the mountains, to the warm countries, where the sun shines more beautifully than here, and where there always is summer, and where the beautiful flowers are always in bloom. Only fly away with me, thou sweet little Tommelise, who didst save my life when I lay frozen in the dark prison of the earth!'

'Yes, I will go with thee!' said Tommelise, and seated herself upon the bird's back, with her feet upon one of his outspread wings. She bound her girdle to one of the strongest of his feathers, and thus the swallow flew aloft into the air, over wood and over sea, high up above the great mountains, where lies the perpetual snow, and Tommelise shivered with the intensely cold air; but she then crept among the bird's warm feathers, and only put out her little head, that she might look at all the magnificent prospect that lay below her.

Thus they came to the warm countries. There the sun shone much brighter than it does here; the heavens were twice as high, and upon trellis and hedge grew the most splendid purple and green grapes. Oranges and lemons hung golden in the woods, and myrtle and wild thyme sent forth their fragrance; the most beautiful children, on the highways, ran after, and played with large, brilliantly-coloured butterflies. But the swallow still flew onward, and it became more and more beautiful. Among lovely green trees, and beside a beautiful blue lake, stood a palace, built of the shining white marble of antiquity. Vines clambered up the tall pillars; on the topmost of these were many swallow nests, and in one of these dwelt the very swallow which carried Tommelise.

'Here is my home!' said the swallow; 'but wilt thou now seek out for thyself one of the lovely flowers which grow below, and then I will place thee there, and thou shalt make thyself as comfortable as thou pleasest?'

'That is charming!' said she, and clapped her small hands.

Just by there lay a large white marble pillar, which had fallen down, and broken into three pieces, but amongst these grew the most exquisite large white flowers.

The swallow flew down with Tommelise, and seated her upon one of the broad leaves,—but how amazed she was! There sat a little man in the middle of the flower, as white and transparent as if he were of glass; the most lovely crown of gold was upon his head, and the most beautiful bright wings upon his shoulders; and he, too, was no larger than Tommelise. He was the angel of the flower. In every flower lived such a little man or woman, but this was the king of them all.

'Good heavens! how small he is!' whispered Tommelise to the swallow. The little prince was as much frightened at the swallow, for it was, indeed, a great, gigantic bird in comparison of him, who was so very small and delicate; but when he saw Tommelise, he was very glad, for she was the prettiest little maiden that ever he had seen. He took, therefore, the golden crown from off his head, and set it upon hers, and asked her, what was her name, and whether she would be his wife, and be the queen of all the flowers? Yes, he was really and truly a little man, quite different to the frog's son, and to the mole, with his black velvet dress; she therefore said, Yes, to the pretty prince; and so there came out of every flower a lady or a gentleman, so lovely that it was quite a pleasure to see them, and brought, every one of them, a present to Tommelise; but the best of all was a pair of beautiful wings, of fine white pearl, and these were fastened on Tommelise's shoulders, and thus she also could fly from flower to flower,—that was such a delight! And the little swallow sat up in its nest and sang to them as well as it could, but still it was a little bit sad at heart, for it was very fond of Tommelise, and wished never to have parted from her.

'Thou shalt not be called Tommelise!' said the angel of the flowers to her; 'it is an ugly name, and thou art so beautiful. We will call thee Maia!'

'Farewell, farewell!' said the little swallow, and flew again forth from the warm countries, far, far away, to Denmark. There it had a little nest above the window of a room in which dwelt a poet, who can tell beautiful tales; for him it sang,—'Quivit, quivit!' and from the swallow, therefore, have we this history.

This tale by Hans Christian Andersen can be appreciated as an entertainment appealing equally, as Andersen intended, to young and old; or as a morality; or as an expression of Andersen's personality—he, with simply a rose and singing bird to offer, the aspiring prince, and Louise Collin, whom he sought to woo, the proud princess; or as a literary creation, to be compared with tales the folk had preserved, a comparison which seems to show that 'The Swineherd', for all its warmth and seeming perfection, lacks the folktales' deeper significance. In the opening scene Andersen appears to take fairy-tale morality a step further than it had been taken hitherto. The princess, instead of finding nobility behind an unpromising exterior, actually resents reality when she discovers that the rose and nightingale, that have so delighted her, are not artificial. The prince then succeeds in pleasing her (or in seducing her,

had he wished) with magic playthings of merely superficial character.

However the punishing of proud princesses is, as might be expected, a favourite theme in the *Märchen;* and whether Andersen knew it or not a close parallel to his tale had already been in existence for at least two hundred years, being recorded in the *Pentamerone* (Day 4, tale 10), 1634. Here, a proud princess named Cinziella, the lovely daughter of the King of Solcolungo, was wooed with no success by the King of Belpaese. The more he courted her the more bitingly she scorned him, until his love for her was broken; and he determined on revenge. He grew a beard, dyed his face, as did Andersen's prince, and took humble employment in the King of Solcolungo's garden. One day, he laid out under the princess's window a beautiful robe decorated with gold and diamonds. The princess's maids of honour, who feature as

The swineherd and the princess by
Thomas Heath Robinson, 1899

The swineherd exacting his price.
Thomas Heath Robinson, 1899

prominently as in Andersen's tale, told the princess about the robe, and she sent word to inquire its price. The gardener replied he was not an old clothes seller; but she might have it if she would let him sleep one night in her apartments. The maids of honour urged her acceptance, asking what harm could there be, and she agreed. The second day, when a gorgeous dress was temptingly displayed, the gardener requested permission to sleep one night in the princess's antechamber; and this granted, on the third day, when the gardener displayed a wonderful under-vest to match the dress, he demanded one night in her room. Urged on alike by her cupidity and by the court ladies 'who were helping the dog to climb', she agreed to his proposal, drawing a charcoal line on the floor of her room beyond which he must not pass. As soon as she was asleep, however, the gardener-king considered it time to work in the fields of love. The princess soon found such field-work not unpleasant, until, a month or two later, she realized it was to produce an embarrassing harvest, and agreed to run away with him. The king, still pretending to be a penniless ruffian, made her suffer numerous indignities, as, in like circumstances, did King Thrushbeard, in a similar

tale collected by the Grimm brothers, continuously humiliating her before he revealed who he was. In fact in one version of 'König Drosselbart', that the Grimms collected in Paderborn, an additional similarity to Andersen's tale is that the disguised suitor attracts the princess, and obtains his demands, with the aid of a golden wheel which makes beautiful music, a prototype, it would seem, of the rattle the swineherd made which played waltzes.

Andersen's story is less sentimental than the traditional tales. When his prince does obtain the princess's complaisance he seems to signal his impotence by spurning her, declaring his contempt of someone who rejects a prince but would—to obtain a toy—kiss a swineherd. In the traditional tales the message goes beyond *The Taming of the Shrew*. It is concerned with more than the softening of a proud woman. In the traditional tales the proud princess, who has learnt to accept the hard and lowly man with whom she has got herself involved, joyfully continues to love him when he is revealed to be the royal suitor she formerly scorned.

Andersen's tale was first translated into English, as follows, by Charles Boner in *A Danish Story-Book*, 1846.

THE SWINEHERD

Once upon a time there lived a prince and he had a principality: it was very small, but still it was enough to enable him to maintain a wife, and so marry he would.

Now it was certainly rather bold of him to think of saying to the Emperor's daughter, 'Will you have me?' but he did do so nevertheless; for his name was celebrated far and near, and there were hundreds of princesses who would have answered, 'Oh yes, with pleasure!'—but we will see if this one said so.

Now only listen.

On the spot where the Prince's father was buried grew a rose-bush: but, oh! it was such a beautiful rose-bush, and it blossomed only once in five years, and then bore but a single flower. But what a flower! It smelt so sweetly that it made one forget all one's trouble and sorrows; and besides this, the prince had a nightingale, that could sing as if all the most charming songs were in her throat. Both rose and nightingale were to be given to the Princess; so they were packed up in silver cases and sent to her.

The Emperor had them carried before him into the great hall, where the Princess was playing at 'visiting' with her maids of honour. As soon as she saw the large cases with the presents, she clapped her hands for joy.

'Oh, if it were but a little pussy-cat!' said she; but the rose-bush with the beautiful rose appeared.

'How nicely it is made!' said all the ladies.

'It is more than nicely made,' said the Emperor; 'it is charming.'

But the Princess felt it, and almost burst into tears.

'O papa,' said she, 'it is not made at all—it is a real rose!'

'Oh,' said the maids of honour, 'it is a real rose!'

'But let us first see what is in the other case before we get angry,' said the Emperor. And then the nightingale appeared; she sang so sweetly that at first it was impossible to say any thing against her.

'*Superbe! Charmant!*' said the ladies; for every one of them spoke French, one worse than the other.

'How the bird reminds me of the musical-box of her Majesty the late Empress!' said an old courtier. 'Oh, yes, it is the very same tone—the same execution.'

'Ah, yes!' said the Emperor, weeping like a little child.

'I hope it will not turn out to be a real bird after all,' said the Princess.

'Yes, it is a real bird,' said the people who had brought the presents.

'Well, then, let it fly,' said the Princess; and she could not be prevailed upon to give the Prince an audience.

He, however, was not to be frightened; he painted his face brown and black, pulled his cap low down over his ears, and knocked at the door.

'Good day, Sir Emperor!' said he; 'pray, could I get a place here in the palace?'

'Oh yes,' said the Emperor: 'I am just in want of some one to look after the pigs; for we have a good many of those animals here.'

And so the Prince got a place as imperial Swineherd. He had a nasty little room given him close to the pig-sty, where he was obliged to live; but the whole day he sat and worked, and by the evening had made a nice little pipkin. Little bells hung all round it, and as soon as the pipkin boiled, all the little bells began tinkling in the prettiest way imaginable, and played the old air—

'O dear, what can the matter be?
O dear, what shall I do?'

But the cleverest of all was, that if a person held his finger in the steam of the pipkin when it boiled, he could immediately smell what was being dressed on every fire in the whole town;—a very different sort of thing that to the rose!

Now the Princess and her ladies came walking by the place where the Prince was; and when she heard the air, she stopped and looked quite pleased; for she too could play, 'O dear, what can the matter be?' It was the only piece she knew, but she played it with ONE finger.

'Why, that is my piece!' said the Princess; 'that is, no doubt, a very accomplished Swineherd! Here, just go in and ask him what is the price of his instrument.'

And one of the maids of honour was obliged to run in, but she put a pair of goloshes on first.

'How much do you ask for your pipkin?' said the lady.

'Ten kisses from the Princess is the price,' said the Swineherd.

'What are you thinking of?' said the lady.

Illustration by Arthur J. Gaskin, 1893

233

Illustration by Rex Whistler, 1935

'I cannot take less,' said the Swineherd.

'He is an impudent fellow!' said the Princess, and went away; but after she had gone a short distance the bells sounded so prettily:

'O dear, what can the matter be?

O dear, what shall I do?'

'Hark ye,' said the Princess; 'ask him if he will take ten kisses from my maids of honour.'

'Very much obliged to you,' said the Swineherd: 'ten kisses from the Princess, or else I keep my pipkin.'

'It is really unbearable,' said the Princess; 'but then you must all stand round, so that no one sees me.'

And the ladies stood round her; and so the Swineherd got his ten kisses, and the Princess the pipkin.

What fun it was! The whole evening and the whole of the next day the pipkin was kept boiling. Not a single hearth or fire-place in the town but they knew what was being cooked there; whether it was a count's or a cobbler's, it was all the same. The maids of honour danced and clapped their hands for joy.

'Now we know who has fried potatoes and bacon; we know who has turbot and lobster-sauce! Oh, how interesting it is!'

'Yes, but mind you keep my secret; for remember I am the Emperor's daughter.'

'Oh, of course!' said all the ladies.

The Swineherd—that is to say, the Prince, but they did not know that he was any thing but an ugly swineherd—let not a single day pass without having some work in hand; and one day he made a rattle, which, when one turned round, played all the waltzes and Scotch reels that have been heard since the world was created.

'Oh, that is superb!' said the Princess as she passed by. 'I have never heard a more beautiful composition! Do just go in, and ask him what the instrument costs: but, mind, I will not give any kisses for it!'

'He asks a hundred kisses from the Princess,' said the lady who had gone in to make the inquiry.

'I think he is out of his mind,' said the Princess, going away; but after she had walked some distance, she stopped. 'One must encourage art,' said she; 'I am daughter of the Emperor. Tell him he shall have ten kisses from me, the same as yesterday, and my ladies shall give him the rest.'

'Oh—but we should not like that at all!' said the maids of honour.

'Pooh, nonsense!' said the Princess. 'If I can kiss him, you surely can do so too. Remember whose bread you eat,' and so the ladies were obliged to go in again.

'A hundred kisses from the Princess,' said he, 'or each one keeps one's own.'

'Stand round!' said the Princess: and all the maids of honour stood round as before, and she paid the kisses.

'What's the matter down there, near the pig-sty?' said the Emperor, who just stepped out on the balcony. He rubbed his eyes, and put on his spectacles: 'Why, those are the ladies of the court! I must go down to them and see!' So he pulled his slippers up at heel; for they were old shoes that he had trodden down in that manner.

As soon as he had come down in the court, he walked along as quietly as possible; and the ladies had so much to do with counting the kisses that there might be no cheating, that they did not observe the Emperor.

He stood on tiptoe.

'What the deuce is that?' said he, giving each of them a good box on the ear with his slipper, just as the Swineherd had got to the eighty-sixth kiss.

'Be off!' said the Emperor, for he was very angry; and both Princess and Swineherd were banished the kingdom.

There she stood and wept, the Swineherd scolded, and the rain poured down in torrents.

'Oh, unhappy creature that I am!' said the Princess: 'had I but taken the handsome Prince! oh, how unhappy I am!'

And the Swineherd went behind a tree, wiped the brown and black paint from off his face, threw away the miserable clothes, and appeared before the Princess in his own dress, and looking so handsome that she bowed before him.

'I am come to tell you how I despise you,' said he. 'An honourable Prince you would not have; the rose and the nightingale you were unable to appreciate: but for the sake of a toy you could kiss a keeper of swine! You have now your desert!'

So saying he left her, and returned to his principality: now well might she sing—

'O dear, what can the matter be?
O dear, what shall I do?'

The story of 'Hansel and Gretel' is one of a series of tales well known throughout Europe—particularly it appears in the Baltic countries—in which small children outwit an ogre into whose hands they have fallen. Their contact with this ogre is involuntary, unlike the youthful heroes of the 'Jack' tales, whose great object is to make contact with uppish monsters, whether to win glory, obtain loot, or indulge their love of blood sports. 'Hansel and Gretel' was one of the stories which the Grimm brothers were told in Cassel by the young girl Dortchen Wild, who years later was to become Wilhelm Grimm's wife. The fame the tale enjoys today is undoubtedly due to the success of Humperdinck's children's opera, first produced in Munich in 1893. The opera in fact omits the most painful part of the traditional story, the parents' deliberate abandonment of their children to the wild beasts of the forest, although it would seem that this opening, together with the first return home through the secret laying of a trail, has long been a feature of the story. It occurs, for instance, in Perrault's 'Le petit Poucet' (see p. 131), published 1697, the first half of which closely resembles the first part of 'Hansel and Gretel'; and it further occurs in the story of 'Finette Cendron' by Madame d'Aulnoy, published in English as 'Finetta the Cinder-Girl' in 1721. In this tale an impoverished ex-king and queen determine to abandon their three daughters in a deep wood, only to be frustrated at the first and second attempts by Finetta—the Princess Fine-Ear—who on the advice of her fairy godmother leaves a trail of thread on the bushes so that she can find the way home, and the second time a trail of ashes; and fails to find the way home only on the third occasion when, lacking fairy advice, she leaves a trail of peas, which is gobbled up by the pigeons 'with which that country abounded'.

The story of 'Finette Cendron', which had been published in Les Contes nouveaux, ou les fées à la Mode, 1698, bears still further resemblance to 'Hansel and Gretel' in that after the three princesses have become lost, have found their way to a giant's house (which was made not of cake and sugar but—more attractive to princesses—of gold and jewels), and have been taken captive, Finetta successfully pushes the giant into his oven and burns him to cinders, by a ruse similar to Gretel's when she incinerates the witch. The trick Hansel plays, when the witch wishes to know how plump he is becoming, poking a piece of dry bone from his cage instead of his finger, is duplicated, and even improved upon, in a Swedish tale, where a young captive sticks out a peg of elder instead of his finger. When the ogre makes an incision in it, to test the boy's tenderness, he is deceived by the hard peg since red sap drops from the wood. The vision of a house built of delicious foodstuffs, to which any visitor may help himself, is likewise not unique to Hansel and Gretel. In the Utopian Land of Cockayne, far out to sea to the west of Spain, there was, according to an early fourteenth-century manuscript (MS. Harley 913), a 'fair abbey of white monkes and of grey' where

> Ther beeth cloisters, bowres and halles:
> Al of pasteyes beeth the walles,
> Of flesh, of fishe and riche mete,
> The likfullest that man may ete;
> Flouren cakes beeth the shingles alle
> Of cherche, cloister, bowr and halle;
> The pinnes beeth fat pudinges,
> Riche mete to princes and kinges.
> Man may therof ete ynough,
> All with right and nought with wough.

The text which follows was first published in 1853. Although a tale entitled 'Hansel and Grettel' was included in Edgar Taylor's German Popular Stories, 1823, the tale given was in fact a translation of the first part of the Grimms' story 'Brüderchen und Schwesterchen'; while, for no obvious reason, the greater part of their 'Hänsel und

Grethel'—though by no means the whole of it—appeared under the name 'Roland and Maybird' in the second volume, 1826. In a note there Taylor actually apologizes for the way three stories, 'Fundevogel', 'Der Liebste Roland', and 'Hänsel und Grethel', had been combined in one narrative; and since no rendering of the story was included in *The Fairy Ring*, 1846, a further translation of the tales by Edgar Taylor's relative John Edward Taylor, the text which follows is the anonymous translation that appeared in *Household Stories collected by the Brothers Grimm*, published by Addey and Co.

The telling of fairy tales to children, and the telling even of tales of horror, is possible, and mind-stretching, and even in a curious way reassuring, if the tales are told in the right circumstances, that is if the child and the adult are already united by a bond of confidence or affection, if the child sees the teller of the tale as a co-adventurer with him in listening to the exploits, and if the child appreciates that the story is fantasy, or that the action is distant in time, or distant in place. It is sad to report, as Jella Lepman has done in *A Bridge of Children's Books*, 1969, that when the great exhibition of children's books was staged in Munich immediately after the Hitlerian war, an exhibition that was intended to be, and was, an opening of doors to the new generation in Germany, it was found that the story of 'Hansel and Gretel' was not always regarded as preposterous, that the fantasy was too close to reality, that for some the witch's oven too much resembled the gas chamber at Auschwitz.

Hansel and Gretel caught sampling the gingerbread house. Wood-engraving by Edmund Evans, after the design by 'Phiz' (Hablot K. Browne), from *Grimm's Goblins*, 1861

HANSEL AND GRETEL

Once upon a time there dwelt near a large wood a poor woodcutter with his wife and two children by his former marriage, a little boy called Hansel, and a girl named Gretel. He had little enough to break or bite, and once, when there was a great famine in the land, he could not procure even his daily bread; and as he lay thinking in his bed one evening, rolling about for trouble, he sighed, and said to his wife, 'What will become of us? How can we feed our children when we have no more than we can eat ourselves?'

'Know then, my husband,' answered she, 'we will lead them away quite early in the morning into the thickest part of the wood, and there make them a fire, and give them each a little piece of bread; then we will go to our work and leave them alone, so they will not find the way home again, and we shall be freed from them.' 'No, wife,' replied he, 'that I can never do; how can you bring your heart to leave my children all alone in the wood, for the wild beasts will soon come and tear them to pieces?'

'Oh, you simpleton!' said she, 'then we must all four die of hunger; you had better plane the coffins for us.' But she left him no peace till he consented, saying, 'Ah, but I shall regret the poor children.'

The two children, however, had not gone to sleep for very hunger, and so they overheard what the stepmother said to their father. Gretel wept bitterly, and said to Hansel, 'What will become of us?' 'Be quiet, Gretel,' said he; 'do not cry, I will soon help you.' And as soon as their parents had fallen asleep, he got up, put on his coat, and unbarring the back-door, slipped out. The moon shone brightly, and the white pebbles which lay before the door seemed like silver pieces, they glittered so brightly. Hansel stooped down, and put as many into his pocket as it would hold, and then going back he said to Gretel, 'Be comforted, dear sister, and sleep in peace; God will not forsake us;' and so saying he went to bed again.

The next morning, before the sun arose, the wife went and awoke the two children. 'Get up, you lazy things; we are going into the forest to chop wood.' Then she gave them each a piece of bread, saying, 'There is something for your dinner; do not eat it before the time, for you will get nothing else.' Gretel took the bread in her apron, for Hansel's pocket was full of pebbles, and so they all set out upon their way. When they had gone a little distance, Hansel stood still, and peeped back at the house; and this

Illustration by Kay Nielsen from *Hansel and Gretel*, 1925

238

he repeated several times, till his father said, 'Hansel, what are you peeping at, and why do you lag behind? Take care, and remember your legs.'

'Ah! father,' said Hansel, 'I am looking at my white cat sitting upon the roof of the house, and trying to say good-bye.' 'You simpleton!' said the wife, 'that is not a cat; it is only the sun shining on the white chimney.' But in reality Hansel was not looking at a cat; but every time he stopped he dropped a pebble out of his pocket upon the path.

When they came to the middle of the wood the father told the children to collect wood, and he would make them a fire, so that they should not be cold; so Hansel and Gretel gathered together quite a little mountain of twigs. Then they set fire to

Frontispiece by Arthur Rackham
from *Fairy Tales of the Brothers Grimm*, 1900

them, and as the flame burnt up high, the wife said, 'Now, you children, lie down near the fire and rest yourselves, whilst we go into the forest and chop wood; when we are ready I will come and call you.'

Hansel and Gretel sat down by the fire, and when it was noon, each ate the piece of bread, and, because they could hear the blows of an axe, they thought their father was near; but it was not an axe, but a branch which he had bound to a withered tree, so as to be blown to and fro by the wind. They waited so long that at last their eyes closed from weariness, and they fell fast asleep. When they awoke it was quite dark, and Gretel began to cry; 'How shall we get out of the wood?' But Hansel tried to comfort her by saying, 'Wait a little while till the moon rises, and then we will quickly find the way.' The moon soon shone forth, and Hansel, taking his sister's hand, followed the pebbles, which glittered like new-coined silver pieces, and showed them the path. All night long they walked on, and as day broke they came to their father's house. They knocked at the door, and when the wife opened it, and saw Hansel and Gretel, she exclaimed, 'You wicked children! why did you sleep so long in the wood? We thought you were never coming home again.' But their father was very glad, for it had grieved his heart to leave them all alone.

Not long afterwards there was again great scarcity in every corner of the land; and one night the children overheard their mother saying to their father, 'Everything is again consumed; we have only half a loaf left, and then the song is ended: the children must be sent away. We will take them deeper into the wood, so that they may not find the way out again; it is the only means of escape for us.'

But her husband felt heavy at heart, and thought, 'It were better to share the last crust with the children.' His wife, however, would listen to nothing that he said, and scolded and reproached him without end.

He who says A must say B too; and he who consents the first time must also the second.

The children, however, had heard the conversation as they lay awake, and as soon as the old people went to sleep Hansel got up, intending to pick up some pebbles as before; but the wife had locked the door, so that he could not get out. Nevertheless he comforted Gretel, saying, 'Do not cry; sleep in quiet; the good God will not forsake us.'

Early in the morning the stepmother came and pulled them out of bed, and gave them each a slice of bread, which was still smaller than the former piece. On the way, Hansel broke his in his pocket, and, stooping every now and then, dropped a crumb upon the path. 'Hansel, why do you stop and look about?' said the father, 'keep in the path.' 'I am looking at my little dove,' answered Hansel, 'nodding a good-bye to me.' 'Simpleton!' said the wife, 'that is no dove, but only the sun shining on the chimney.' But Hansel kept still dropping crumbs as he went along.

The mother led the children deep into the wood, where they had never been before, and there making an immense fire, she said to them, 'Sit down here and rest, and when you feel tired you can sleep for a little while. We are going into the forest to hew wood, and in the evening, when we are ready, we will come and fetch you.'

When noon came Gretel shared her bread with Hansel, who had strewn his on the path. Then they went to sleep; but the evening arrived and no one came to visit the poor children, and in the dark night they awoke, and Hansel comforted his sister by saying, 'Only wait, Gretel, till the moon comes out, then we shall see the crumbs of bread which I have dropped, and they will show us the way home.' The moon shone and they got up, but they could not see any crumbs, for the thousands of birds which had been flying about in the woods and fields had picked them all up. Hansel kept saying to Gretel, 'We will soon find the way;' but they did not, and they walked the whole night long and the next day, but still they did not come out of the wood; and they got so hungry, for they had nothing to eat but the berries which they found upon the bushes. Soon they got so tired that they could not drag themselves along, so they lay down under a tree and went to sleep.

It was now the third morning since they had left their father's house, and they still walked on; but they only got deeper and deeper into the wood, and Hansel saw that if help did not come very soon they would die of hunger. As soon as it was noon they saw a beautiful snow-white bird sitting upon a bough, which sang so sweetly that they stood still and listened to it. It soon left off, and spreading its wings flew off; and they followed it until it arrived at a cottage, upon the roof of which it perched; and when they went close up to it they saw that the cottage was made of bread and cakes, and the window-panes were of clear sugar.

'We will go in there,' said Hansel, 'and have a glorious feast. I will eat a piece of the roof, and you can eat the window. Will they not be sweet?' So Hansel reached up and broke a piece off the roof, in order to see how it tasted; while Gretel stepped up to the window and began to bite it. Then a sweet voice called out in the room, 'Tip-tap, tip-tap, who raps at my door?' and the children answered, 'The wind, the wind, the child of heaven;' and they went on eating without interruption. Hansel thought the roof tasted very nice, and so he tore off a great piece; while Gretel broke a large round pane out of the window, and sat down quite contentedly. Just then the door opened, and a very old woman, walking upon crutches, came out. Hansel and Gretel were so frightened that they let fall what they had in their hands; but the old woman, nodding her head, said, 'Ah, you dear children, what has brought you here? Come in and stop with me, and no harm shall befall you;' and so saying she took them both by the hand, and led them into her cottage. A good meal of milk and pancakes, with sugar, apples, and nuts, was spread on the table, and in the back room were two nice little beds, covered with white, where Hansel and Gretel laid themselves down, and thought themselves in heaven. The old woman had behaved very kindly to them, but in reality she was a wicked witch who waylaid children, and built the bread-house in order to entice them in; but as soon as they were in her power she killed them, cooked and ate them, and made a great festival of the day. Witches have red eyes, and cannot

'Hansel, stretch out your finger that I
may feel whether you are getting fat.'
Arthur Rackham, *Fairy Tales of the
Brothers Grimm*, 1900

see very far; but they have a fine sense of smelling, like wild beasts, so that they know when children approach them. When Hansel and Gretel came near the witch's house she laughed wickedly, saying, 'Here come two who shall not escape me.' And early in the morning, before they awoke, she went up to them, and saw how lovingly they lay sleeping, with their chubby red cheeks; and she mumbled to herself, 'That will be a good bite.' Then she took up Hansel with her rough hand, and shut him up in a little cage with a lattice-door; and although he screamed loudly it was of no use. Gretel came next, and, shaking her till she awoke, she said, 'Get up, you lazy thing, and fetch some water to cook something good for your brother, who must remain in that stall and get fat; when he is fat enough I shall eat him.' Gretel began to cry, but it was all useless, for the old witch made her do as she wished. So a nice meal was cooked for Hansel, but Gretel got nothing else but a crab's claw.

Every morning the old witch came to the cage and said, 'Hansel, stretch out your finger that I may feel whether you are getting fat.' But Hansel used to stretch out a bone, and the old woman, having very bad sight, thought it was his finger, and wondered very much that he did not get more fat. When four weeks had passed, and Hansel still kept quite lean, she lost all her patience and would not wait any longer. 'Gretel,' she called out in a passion, 'get some water quickly; be Hansel fat or lean, this morning I will kill and cook him.' Oh, how the poor little sister grieved, as she was forced to fetch the water, and fast the tears ran down her cheeks! 'Dear good God, help us now!' she exclaimed. 'Had we only been eaten by the wild beasts in the wood, then we should have died together.' But the old witch called out, 'Leave off that noise; it will not help you a bit.'

So early in the morning Gretel was forced to go out and fill the kettle, and make a fire. 'First we will bake, however,' said the old woman; 'I have already heated the oven and kneaded the dough;' and so saying she pushed poor Gretel up to the oven, out of which the flames were burning fiercely. 'Creep in,' said the witch, 'and see if it is hot enough, and then we will put in the bread;' but she intended when Gretel got in to shut up the oven and let her bake, so that she might eat her as well as Hansel. Gretel perceived what her thoughts were, and said, 'I do not know how to do it; how shall I get in?' 'You stupid goose,' said she, 'the opening is big enough. See, I could even get in myself!' and she got up and put her head into the oven. Then Gretel gave her a push, so that she fell right in, and then shutting the iron door she bolted it. Oh! how horribly she howled; but Gretel ran away, and left the ungodly witch to burn to ashes.

Now she ran to Hansel, and, opening his door, called out, 'Hansel, we are saved; the old witch is dead!' So he sprang out, like a bird out of his cage when the door is opened; and they were so glad that they fell upon each other's neck, and kissed each other over and over again. And now, as there was nothing to fear, they went into the witch's house, where in every corner were caskets full of pearls and precious stones. 'These are better than pebbles,' said Hansel, putting as many into his pocket as it would hold; while Gretel thought, 'I will take some home too,' and filled her apron full. 'We must be off now,' said Hansel, 'and get out of this enchanted forest;' but when they had walked for two hours they came to a large piece of water. 'We cannot get over,' said Hansel; 'I can see no bridge at all.' 'And there is no boat either,' said Gretel, 'but there swims a white duck, I will ask her to help us over;' and she sang,

> 'Little Duck, good little Duck,
> Gretel and Hansel, here we stand;
> There is neither stile nor bridge,
> Take us on your back to land.'

So the Duck came to them, and Hansel sat himself on, and bade his sister sit behind him. 'No,' answered Gretel, 'that will be too much for the Duck, she shall take us over one at a time.' This the good little bird did, and when both were happily arrived on the other side, and had gone a little way, they came to a well-known wood, which they knew the better every step they went, and at last they perceived their father's house. Then they began to run, and, bursting into the house, they fell on their father's neck. He had not had one happy hour since he had left the children in the forest: and his wife was dead. Gretel shook her apron, and the pearls and precious stones rolled out upon the floor, and Hansel threw down one handful after the other out of his pocket. Then all their sorrows were ended, and they lived together in great happiness.

My tale is done. There runs a mouse; whoever catches her may make a great, great cap out of her fur.

CHIEF COMMENTARIES CONSULTED

The following are the chief works which have been consulted for background information.
Source books for the texts are not included.

ANDERSEN, HANS CHRISTIAN. *The True Story of My Life: A Sketch.* Translated by Mary Howitt. London: Longman, Brown, Green, and Longmans, 1847.

ANONYMOUS. 'The Three Bears', *Times Literary Supplement*, 23 November 1951, p. xiii.

ASHTON, JOHN. *Chap-books of the Eighteenth Century.* With Facsimiles, Notes, and Introduction. London: Chatto and Windus, 1882.

BARCHILON, JACQUES. *Perrault's Tales of Mother Goose: The Dedication Manuscript of 1695 reproduced in collotype facsimile with introduction and critical text.* New York: The Pierpont Morgan Library, 2 vols, 1956.

——, and PETTIT, HENRY. *The Authentic Mother Goose Fairy Tales and Nursery Rhymes.* Denver: Alan Swallow, 1960.

BOLTE, JOHANNES. *Martin Montanus Schwankbücher, 1557–1566.* Bibliothek des literarischen Vereins in Stuttgart, no. 217. Tübingen, 1899.

——, and POLÍVKA, GEORG. *Ammerkungen zu den Kinder- und Hausmärchen der Brüder Grimm.* Leipzig: Dieterich-'sche Verlagsbuchhandlung, 5 vols, 1913–1932.

BOSSARD, EUGÈNE. *Gilles de Rais, Maréchal de France, dit Barbe-Bleue.* Paris, 1886.

BREDSDORFF, ELIAS. *Hans Christian Andersen: Catalogue of a Jubilee Exhibition held at the National Book League.* London & Copenhagen, 1955.

BRERETON, GEOFFREY. *The Fairy Tales of Charles Perrault.* Translated with an Introduction. London: Penguin Books, 1957.

BRIGGS, KATHARINE M. *The Anatomy of Puck. An Examination of Fairy Beliefs among Shakespeare's Contemporaries and Successors.* London: Routledge and Kegan Paul, 1959.

——, *A Dictionary of British Folk-Tales in the English Language incorporating the F. J. Norton Collection.* Part A, Folk Narratives. London: Routledge & Kegan Paul, 2 vols, 1970. A review by Peter Opie appeared in *New Society*, 2 April 1970, pp. 568–569.

——, and TONGUE, RUTH L. *Folktales of England.* Foreword by Richard M. Dorson. London: Routledge & Kegan Paul, 1965.

BUHLER, CURT F., editor. *The History of Tom Thumbe, 1621* (published with *Merie Tales of the Mad Men of Gotam*, ed. Stanley Kahrl). Renaissance English Text Society, 1965.

CHAMBERS, ROBERT. *Popular Rhymes, Fireside Stories, and Amusements, of Scotland.* Edinburgh: William and Robert Chambers, 1842. Also enlarged edition 1870.

CHESTERTON, G. K. *All Things Considered.* London: Methuen & Co., 1908. 'Fairy Tales', pp. 253–258.

CLODD, EDWARD. 'The Philosophy of Rumpelstiltskin', *The Folk-Lore Journal*, vol. VII, 1889, pp. 135–168.

——. *Tom Tit Tot: An Essay on Savage Philosophy in Folk-tale.* London: Duckworth and Co., 1898.

CLOUSTON, W. A. *Popular Tales and Fictions, their Migrations and Transformations.* Edinburgh and London: William Blackwood and Sons, 2 vols. 1887.

——. 'The Knight and the Loathly Lady: Variant and Analogues', *Originals and Analogues of some of Chaucer's Canterbury Tales*, edited F. J. Furnivall and others, for the Chaucer Society, 1888, pp. 481–524.

——. 'The Story of "The Frog Prince": Breton Variant, and Some Analogues', *Folk-Lore*, vol. I, 1890, pp. 493–506.

COMPARETTI, DOMENICO. *Researches respecting the Book of Sindibâd.* [Translated by H. C. Coote.] London: Published for the Folk-Lore Society, 1882.

COOK, ELIZABETH. *The Ordinary and the Fabulous: An Introduction to Myths, Legends and Fairy Tales for Teachers and Storytellers.* Cambridge: At the University Press, 1969.

COX, MARIAN ROALFE. *Cinderella: Three hundred and forty-five Variants of Cinderella, Catskin, and Cap o' Rushes, abstracted and tabulated, with a Discussion of Mediaeval Analogues, and Notes.* With an Introduction by Andrew Lang, M.A. London: The Folk-Lore Society, 1893. An important review of this work by W. W. Newell appeared in the *Journal of American Folklore*, vol. VI, 1893, pp. 159–161.

CROKER, T. CROFTON. *Fairy Legends and Traditions of the South of Ireland.* New edition edited by Thomas Wright. With a memoir of the author by his son T. F. Dillon Croker. London: William Tegg, [1862].

CUMINGS, EDGAR C. 'A Chronological List of Grimms' Kinder- und Hausmärchen', *Journal of American Folklore*, vol. 48, 1935, pp. 362–373.

DAL, ERIK. *Hans Christian Andersen's First Three Tales.* With Illustrations from many countries and an Introduction. Translated from the Danish by David Hohnen. Copenhagen: Høst & Søn, 1960.

DAVIDSON, H. R. ELLIS. *Gods and Myths of Northern Europe.* London: Penguin Books, 1964.

DÉGH, LINDA. *Folktales and Society. Story-telling in a Hungarian Peasant Community.* Translated by Emily M. Schossberger. Bloomington/London: Indiana University Press, 1969.

DELARUE, PAUL. 'Les Contes merveilleux de Perrault et la tradition populaire', *Bulletin Folklorique d'Ile de France*, Nouvelle Serie, vols XIII–XV, 1951–1953, *passim*.

——. 'Les Contes merveilleux de Perrault: faits et rapprochements nouveaux', *Arts et traditions populaires*, No. 3, 1954, pp. 1–22, 251–274.

GASTER, MOSES. 'The Modern Origin of Fairy-Tales', *The Folk-Lore Journal*, vol. V, 1887, pp. 339–351.

GOLLANCZ, HERMANN. 'The History of Sindban and the Seven Wise Masters, translated for the first time from the Syriac into English', *Folk-Lore*, vol. VIII, 1897, pp. 99–130.

GRIMM, JACOB and WILHELM. *German Popular Stories*. With Illustrations after the original designs of George Cruikshank. Edited by Edgar Taylor, with Introduction by John Ruskin, M.A. London: J. C. Hotten, [1869]. A reprint of the original translation of 1823–1826, with new introduction.

——. *Grimm's Household Tales with the Author's Notes*. Translated from the German and Edited by Margaret Hunt. With an Introduction by Andrew Lang. London: Henry G. Bohn, 2 vols, 1884.

——. *Grimm's Fairy Tales. Complete edition*. With 212 Illustrations by Josef Scharl. London: Routledge and Kegan Paul, 1948. Margaret Hunt's text edited by James Stern, with 'folkloristic commentary' by Joseph Campbell.

HALLIDAY, W. R. 'Notes upon Indo-European Folktales and the problem of their diffusion', *Folk-Lore*, vol. XXXIV, 1923, pp. 117–140.

HALLIWELL, JAMES ORCHARD. *Descriptive Notices of Popular English Histories*. London: Printed for the Percy Society, 1848.

—— *Popular Rhymes and Nursery Tales*. London: John Russell Smith, 1849.

HARTLAND, EDWIN SIDNEY. 'The Forbidden Chamber', *The Folk-Lore Journal*, vol. III, 1885, pp. 193–242.

—— *The Science of Fairy Tales: An Enquiry into Fairy Mythology*. London: Walter Scott, 1890. Reissued, with Introduction by A. A. Milne, by Methuen & Co. Ltd, 1925.

HAZLITT, W. CAREW. *Remains of the Early Popular Poetry of England; collected and edited with Introductions and Notes*. Vols II and IV. London: John Russell Smith, 1866.

—— *Fairy Tales, Legends and Romances Illustrating Shakespeare and other Early English Writers*. London: Frank & William Kerslake, 1875. An amalgamation of Ritson's *Fairy Tales*, 1831, and Halliwell's *Illustrations of the Fairy Mythology of a Midsummer-Night's Dream*, 1845.

JACKSON, ANTHONY. 'The Science of Fairy Tales?', *Folklore*, vol. 84, Summer 1973, pp. 120–141.

JACOBS, JOSEPH. *English Fairy Tales*. Illustrated by John D. Batten. London: David Nutt, 1890.

—— 'Cinderella in Britain', *Folk-Lore*, vol. IV, 1893, pp. 269–284.

—— *More English Fairy Tales*. Illustrated by John D. Batten. London: David Nutt, 1894.

JAMES, M. R. *Hans Andersen: Forty Stories newly trans-lated from the Danish*. London: Faber & Faber Limited, 1930.

[KEIGHTLEY, THOMAS.] *The Fairy Mythology*. London, 2 vols, 1828. Also revised and enlarged edition, 1860.

—— *Tales and Popular Fictions; Their Resemblance, and Transmission from Country to Country*. London: Whittaker and Co., 1834.

KIRBY, W. F. 'The Forbidden Doors of the Thousand and One Nights', *The Folk-Lore Journal*, vol. V, 1887, pp. 112–124.

KOEHLER, REINHOLD. 'Rashin Coatie: A Scotch Tale', *Revue Celtique*, vol. III, 1876–78, pp. 365–374.

KRAPPE, ALEXANDER HAGGERTY. *The Science of Folk-Lore*. London: Methuen & Co. Ltd., 1930. Chapter I 'The Fairy Tale', pp. 1–44.

LANG, ANDREW. 'At the Sign of the Ship', *Longman's Magazine*, vol. XIII, 1889, pp. 660–663 and vol. XIV, 1889, pp. 330–334.

—— *Perrault's Popular Tales*. Edited from the Original Editions, with Introduction, etc. Oxford: at the Clarendon Press, 1888.

—— 'Cinderella and the Diffusion of Tales', *Folk-Lore*, vol. IV, 1893, pp. 413–433.

LEFÈVRE, ANDRÉ. *Les Contes de Charles Perrault. Avec deux Essais sur la Vie et les Œuvres de Perrault et sur la Mythologie dans ses Contes*. Paris: Alphonse Lemerre, 1875.

LESCURE, MATHURIN DE. *Le Monde enchanté, choix de douze contes de fées de Perrault, Mlle L'Héretier, Mme D'Aulnoy . . . Mme Leprince de Beaumont . . . précédé d'une Histoire des fées et de la littérature féerique en France*. Paris, 1883.

[LEYDEN, JOHN, editor.] *The Complaynt of Scotland, written in 1548, with a Preliminary Dissertation, and Glossary*. Edinburgh: Archibald Constable, 1801.

LODS, JEANNE. *Le Roman de Perceforest: origines—composition—caractères—valeur et influence*. Société de Publications Romanes et Françaises, No. 32. Genève: Librairie Droz; Lille: Librairie Giard, 1951.

MACCULLOCH, J. A. *The Childhood of Fiction: A Study of Folk Tales and Primitive Thought*. London: John Murray, 1905.

MARSHALL, HOWARD WIGHT. '"Tom Tit Tot": A Comparative Essay on Aarne-Thompson Type 500— The Name of the Helper', *Folklore*, vol. 84, 1973, pp. 51–57.

MASSIGNON, GENEVIÈVE. *Folktales of France*. Translated by Jacqueline Hyland. Foreword by Richard M. Dorson. London: Routledge & Kegan Paul, 1968.

MICHAELIS-JENA, RUTH. *The Brothers Grimm*. London: Routledge & Kegan Paul, 1970.

NUTT, ALFRED. 'Cinderella and Britain', *Folk-Lore*, vol. IV, 1893, pp. 133–141.

—— 'Some Recent Utterances of Mr. Newell and Mr. Jacobs', *Folk-Lore*, vol. IV, 1893, pp. 434–450. On 'Cinderella'.

[PALGRAVE, FRANCIS.] 'Antiquities of Nursery Literature', *The Quarterly Review*, vol. XXI, 1819, pp. 91–112.

PARRY, B. E. 'The Origin of the Book of Sindbad', *Fabula*, vol. III, 1960, pp. 1–94.

PENZER, N. M., editor. *The Ocean of Story: Being C. H. Tawney's translation of Somadeva's Kathā Sarit Sāgara.* London: Privately Printed for Subscribers only, 10 vols, 1924–1928.

——, editor. *The Pentamerone of Giambattista Basile. Translated from the Italian of Benedetto Croce.* London: John Lane the Bodley Head Ltd., 2 vols, 1932. A valuable review by Moses Gaster appeared in *Folk-Lore*, vol. XLII, pp. 496–500.

PLANCHÉ, J. R. *Fairy Tales by The Countess d'Aulnoy.* London: Routledge & Co., 1855.

RALSTON, W. R. S. 'Beauty and the Beast', *The Nineteenth Century*, December 1878, pp. 990–1012.

RANKE, KURT. *Folktales of Germany.* Translated by Lotte Baumann. Foreword by Richard M. Dorson. Chicago: University of Chicago Press, 1966.

RITCHIE, ANNE THACKERAY. *The Fairy Tales of Madame d'Aulnoy, Newly done into English.* With an Introduction. London: Lawrence and Bullen, 1892.

ROBERTS, WARREN E. 'The special forms of Aarne-Thompson type 480 and their distribution', *Fabula: Zeitschrift für Erzählforschung. Journal of Folklore Studies.* Berlin, vol. I, 1957, pp. 85–102. On 'Diamonds and Toads' and related tales.

ROOTH, ANNA BIRGITTA. *The Cinderella Cycle.* Lund: C. W. K. Gleerup, 1951.

ROSS, ANNE. 'Severed Heads in Wells: An aspect of the Well Cult', *Scottish Studies*, vol. VI, 1962, pp. 31–48.

ST. JOHN, JUDITH, editor. Eleanor Mure, *The Story of The Three Bears.* London: Oxford University Press, 1967.

SAINTYVES, P. [ÉMILE NOURRY]. *Les Contes de Perrault et les récits parallèles, leur origines (coutumes primitives et liturgies populaires).* Paris: Librairie critique, 1923. A useful review appeared in *Folk-Lore*, vol. XXXV, 1924, pp. 99–104.

SANDERS, N. K. *The Epic of Gilgamesh: An English Version with an Introduction.* Revised edition incorporating new material. London: Penguin Books, 1972.

SEKI, KEIGO. *Folktales of Japan.* Translated by Robert J. Adams. London: Routledge & Kegan Paul, 1963.

SHAMBURGER, M. J. and LACHMANN, V. R. 'Southey and "The Three Bears" ', *Journal of American Folklore*, vol. 59, 1946, pp. 400–403.

SPINK, REGINALD. *Hans Christian Andersen and his World.* London: Thames and Hudson, 1972.

STORER, MARY ELIZABETH. *La Mode des Contes de Fées (1685–1700).* Paris: Librairie Ancienne Honoré Champion, 1928.

—— *Contes de Fées du Grand Siècle.* New York: Publications of the Institute of French Studies, Inc., Columbia University, 1934.

STRAPAROLA, GIOVANNI FRANCESCO. *The Nights of Straparola.* Now first translated into English by W. G. Waters. Illustrated by E. R. Hughes, A.R.W.S. London: Lawrence and Bullen, 2 vols, 1894.

—— *The Most Delectable Nights of Straparola of Caravaggio. The First Complete Translation into English . . . with an Introduction and Notes.* [Anonymous translation.] Paris: Charles Carrington, 2 vols, 1906.

TAYLOR, EDGAR. See GRIMM, JACOB and WILHELM.

TAYLOR, JOHN EDWARD, translator and editor. *The Pentamerone, or The Story of Stories, Fun for the Little Ones.* By Giambattista Basile. With illustrations by George Cruikshank. London: David Bogue and J. Cundall, 1847.

THOMPSON, STITH. *The Folktale.* New York: The Dryden Press, 1946. Important reviews of this work appear in *Folk-Lore*, vol. LVIII, 1947, pp. 339–341, and vol. LIX, 1948, pp. 136–140.

THORPE, BENJAMIN. *Yule-Tide Stories. A Collection of Scandinavian and North German Popular Tales and Traditions, from the Swedish, Danish, and German.* London: Henry G. Bohn, 1853.

TOKSVIG, SIGNE. *The Life of Hans Christian Andersen.* London: Macmillan and Co., 1933.

TOLKIEN, J. R. R. *Tree and Leaf.* London: George Allen & Unwin Ltd, 1964. 'On Fairy-Stories', pp. 11–70. (Originally a lecture delivered in 1938; first published 'with a little enlargement' in *Essays presented to Charles Williams*, Oxford University Press, 1947.)

VIZETELLY, ERNEST ALFRED. *Bluebeard: An Account of Comorre the Cursed and Gilles de Rais, with summaries of various tales and traditions.* London: Chatto & Windus, 1902.

WALEY, ARTHUR. 'The Chinese Cinderella Story', *Folk-Lore*, vol. LVIII, 1947, pp. 226–238.

WEISS, HARRY B. 'The Autochthonal Tale of Jack the Giant Killer', *Scientific Monthly*, vol. 28, February 1929, pp. 126–133.

—— 'Three Hundred Years of Tom Thumb', *Scientific Monthly*, vol. 34, 1932, pp. 157–166.

—— *Little Red Riding Hood: A Terror Tale of the Nursery.* Privately printed. Trenton, 1939.

WILSON, THOMAS. *Blue-Beard: A Contribution to History and Folk-lore, being the history of Gilles de Retz of Brittany, France, who was executed at Nantes in 1440 A.D. and who was the original of Blue-Beard in the tales of Mother Goose.* New York and London: G. P. Putnam's Sons, 1899.

YEARSLEY, MACLEOD. *The Folklore of Fairy-Tale.* London: Watts & Co., 1924.

[YONGE, CHARLOTTE.] *The History of Sir Thomas Thumb.* Illustrated by J. B. [Jane Blackburn]. Edinburgh: Thomas Constable and Co. London: Hamilton, Adams, and Co., 1855. A retelling of the tale; but with fifty-two pages of notes at the end, embodying much poetry about the fairies.

SOURCES OF THE ILLUSTRATIONS

All illustrations are from material in the Westerfield House Collection of Child Life and Literature unless otherwise acknowledged. All photographs not otherwise credited are by Derrick Witty.

Frontispiece: 'Pamela tells a nursery tale'. Painting by Joseph Highmore, *c.* 1744. (Reproduced by permission of the Syndics of the Fitzwilliam Museum, Cambridge)

10 Original sepia ink and watercolour by Rex Whistler, *c.* 1935. (By courtesy of Mrs Herbert Agar. Reproduced by permission of Laurence Whistler Esq., C.B.E.)

19 *Tabart's Collection of Popular Stories for the Nursery: Newly Translated and Revised from the French, Italian, and Old English Writers.* 3 vols. London: Tabart & Co., 1804

22 Charles Perrault (Photo *The Times* Newspapers Limited)

23 *Histories, or Tales of Passed Times With Morals.* Written in French by M. Perrault, and Englished by R. S. Gent. [Robert Samber] The Second Edition, Corrected. London: R. Montagu & J. Pote, 1737. First published 1729, with slightly different title. (By courtesy of the Victoria and Albert Museum, London)

26 Jacob and Wilhelm Grimm. Drawing by Ludwig Emil Grimm. (Photo Staatsbibliothek, Berlin)

27 *Punch, or The London Charivari*, vol. XXXII. London: At the Office, 85, Fleet Street, 1857

28 *German Fairy Tales as told by Gammer Grethel.* London: Henry G. Bohn, 1849

29 *Our Nurse's Picture Book.* London: George Routledge & Sons. [1869] (By courtesy of the Victoria and Albert Museum, London)

30 *The History of Tom Thumbe, the Little, for his small stature surnamed, King Arthvrs Dwarfe.* London: Tho: Langley, 1621. (By courtesy of the Trustees of the Pierpont Morgan Library)

31 *The History of Tom Thumb.* Devonport: S. & J. Keys, *c.* 1835

32 *Tom Thumbe, His Life and Death.* London: Iohn Wright, 1630. (By courtesy of the Curators of the Bodleian Library)

36–37 *The Life and Adventures of Tom Thumb.* Derby: Henry Mozley and Sons, *c.* 1840

38 *Household Stories Collected by the Brothers Grimm.* London: George Routledge & Sons, 1876. Illustration by E. H. Wehnert depicting Germany's Thumbling

40 *Tom Thumb.* By Hal. Wills, Student at Law. Illustrations by Alfred Crowquill [A. H. Forrester]. London: Wm S. Orr & Co. [1844]

41 *The Life and Adventures of Tom Thumb.* Derby: Henry Mozley and Sons, *c.* 1840

42 *The Famous History of Tom Thumb.* Part the Third. London: Printed for the Booksellers, *c.* 1780

45 *The History of Tom Thumb.* London & Edinburgh: T. Nelson & Sons, *c.* 1864

46 *The Famous History of Tom Thumb.* London: Printed and Sold in Aldermary Church-Yard, *c.* 1770. (By courtesy of The British Library; photo John R. Freeman)

48 *Aunt Mavor's Nursery Tales for Good Little People.* London: George Routledge & Co., 1858

49 *Jack the Giant Killer.* London: George Routledge & Sons, *c.* 1872

50 (left) *Jack the Giant-Killer.* London: J. T. Wood, *c.* 1845

50 (centre) *Jack the Giant-Killer.* Devonport: Samuel and John Keys, *c.* 1835

50 (right) *Jack the Giant-Killer and Other Stories.* Edinburgh: Oliver and Boyd, 1862

53 *Jack the Giant Killer.* Hugh Thomson's Illustrated Fairy Books. London: Macmillan & Co. Limited. New York: The Macmillan Company, 1898

56 *Tabart's Collection of Popular Stories for the Nursery.* vol. III. London: Tabart & Co., 1804

59 *Jack the Giant Killer*, A Hero Celebrated by ancient Historians. Banbury: J. G. Rusher, *c.* 1840

60 *Jack the Giant Killer*, by Richard Doyle. London: Eyre and Spottiswoode. [1888] Facsimile of the manuscript of 1842

63 *Tommy Thumb's Song Book, for all little Masters and Misses.* The Second Worcester Edition. Worcester, Massachusetts: Isaiah Thomas, 1794. First issued at Worcester 1788

66 *Fairy Tales by the Countess d'Aulnoy.* Translated by J. R. Planché. London: George Routledge and Sons Ltd., 1888 [1887]. Additional illustrations by Gordon Browne. (Reproduced by permission of Routledge & Kegan Paul Ltd)

67   *The History of the Yellow Dwarf.* Glasgow: Printed for the Booksellers, 1852

69   *Grimm's Goblins.* London: George Vickers, 1861. (Photo John R. Freeman)

70   *The Child's Own Book.* The Sixth Edition. London: Thomas Tegg, 1839. First issued 1830

72   *The Yellow Dwarf.* Walter Crane's Toy Books. London & New York: George Routledge and Sons, 1875

82   *Forget Me Not; A Christmas, New Year's, and Birthday Present, for MDCCCXXXVII.* Edited by Frederic Shoberl. London: Ackermann and Co.

84   *The Sleeping Beauty in the Wood.* George Routledge & Sons, 1872

87   *The Sleeping Beauty.* London: Geographia Ltd., *c.* 1925. Illustrations by E. Dorothy Rees

89   *Four and Twenty Fairy Tales.* Selected from those of Perrault and other popular writers. Translated by J. R. Planché. London: George Routledge & Co., 1858. (By courtesy of The British Library; photo John R. Freeman)

91 (above)   *Histories or Tales of Past Times, told by Mother Goose.* Salisbury: B. Collins, 1777

91 (below)   *The Fairy Book. The Best Popular Fairy Stories selected and rendered anew* [by D. M. Craik]. London and Cambridge: Macmillan and Co., 1863

92   *Bewick's Woodcuts.* With an Introduction by Thomas Hugo. London: L. Reeve & Co., 1870

93   *Theatrical Picture-book* [Printed in Germany?] *c.* 1870

94   Advertisement for Fry's Cocoa, 1891. (From the Robert Opie Collection)

95   *Fairy Tales Told Again.* Illustrated by Gustave Doré. London, Paris, and New York: Cassell, Petter and Galpin, 1872

96   *Favourite Stories for the Nursery.* London, Edinburgh, and New York: Thomas Nelson and Sons, 1900

97   *Little Red Riding-hood.* London: Read, Brooks and Co., *c.* 1880

99   *The Story of Toads & Diamonds.* London: Read, Brooks & Co., *c.* 1865

101   *Diamonds and Toads.* Aunt Louisa's London Toy Books. London: Frederick Warne & Co.

102   *The Fairy Tales of Charles Perrault.* Illustrated by Harry Clarke with an Introduction by Thomas Bodkin. London: George G. Harrap & Co. Ltd [1922]. (Reproduced by permission of the publisher)

104   *Tales of Passed Times.* Written for Children by Mr. Perrault & Newly Decorated by John Austen. London:

Selwyn & Blount Ltd, 1922. (By courtesy of the Victoria and Albert Museum, London)

105   *The Fairy Tales of Charles Perrault.* Illustrated by Harry Clarke with an Introduction by Thomas Bodkin. London: George G. Harrap & Co. Ltd [1922]. (Reproduced by permission of the publisher)

106   *Blue Beard; or, Female Curiosity.* London: Dean & Son, *c.* 1850

108   *History of Blue Beard.* London: J. L. Marks, *c.* 1845

110–111   *Puss in Boots, and Diamonds and Toads.* London: Orlando Hodgson [1832]

115   *Fairy Tales Told Again.* Illustrated by Gustave Doré. London, Paris, and New York: Cassell, Petter and Galpin, 1872

118–119   *Cinderella; or The Little Glass Slipper; versified and beautifully Illustrated with Figures.* London: S. and J. Fuller, 1814

120 (top)   *A Pretty Book for Children: Or, an Easy Guide to the English Tongue.* Twenty-Second Edition. London: T. Carnan, 1789. (First issued *c.* 1744)

120 (centre)   *The Celebrated Tales of Mother Goose.* London: J. Harris, 1817

120 (bottom)   *Popular Tales of the Olden Time.* By a Lady. London: Dean and Munday, *c.* 1840

122   *Cinderella.* From Coloured Designs by W. Gunston. London: Frederick Warne & Co., *c.* 1876

125   *Cinderella and the Glass Slipper.* Edited and illustrated by George Cruikshank. London: David Bogue [1854]

128   *Histories, or Tales of Passed Times. With Morals.* Written in French by M. Perrault, and Englished by R. S. Gent. [Robert Samber] The Second Edition, Corrected. London: R. Montagu & J. Pote, 1737. First published in 1729 with a slightly different title. (By courtesy of the Victoria and Albert Museum, London)

129 (above)   *Little Thumb, And the Ogre. Being a Versification of one of the celebrated Tales of Mother Goose.* London: R. Dutton, 1808

129 (below)   *Hop o' my Thumb and The Seven-League Boots.* Edited and illustrated by George Cruikshank. London: David Bogue [1853]

134   *Les Contes de Perrault.* Dessins par Gustave Doré. Préface par P. -J. Stahl. J. Hetzel, Editeur. Paris: Librarie Firmin Didot Frères et fils, 1862. (By courtesy of The British Library; photo John R. Freeman)

136   *Hop o' My Thumb.* The Drawings by Gordon Browne. The Story Retold by Laura E. Richards. London: Blackie and Son [1886]. (Reproduced by permission of the publisher)

137 *Popular Tales of the Olden Time.* London: Dean and Munday, *c.* 1840

140 *Old Time Stories told by Master Charles Perrault.* Translated from the French by A. E. Johnson. With illustrations by W. Heath Robinson. London: Constable & Co. Ltd, 1921. (By courtesy of The Victoria and Albert Museum, London. Reproduced by permission of the publisher)

142 *Beauty and the Beast.* The Drawings by Gordon Browne. The Story Retold by Laura E. Richards. London: Blackie and Son [1886]. (By courtesy of The British Library; photo John R. Freeman. Reproduced by permission of the publisher)

144 *Beauty and the Beast: or, A Rough Outside with a Gentle Heart.* A Poetical Version of an Ancient Tale [by Charles Lamb?]. London: M. J. Godwin, 1813. (First issued 1811)

146 *Beauty and the Beast.* Walter Crane's Toy Books Shilling Series. London & New York: George Routledge and Sons [1874]

149 *Beauty and the Beast.* An Old Tale New-told, with Pictures by E. V. B. [Eleanor Vere Boyle]. London: Sampson, Low & Co. [1875]. (By courtesy of the Victoria and Albert Museum, London)

150 *A Book of Fairy Tales.* Retold by S. Baring-Gould. With Pictures by A. J. Gaskin. London: Methuen & Co., 1894. (By courtesy of The British Library; photo John R. Freeman)

152 *The Fairy Tales of Charles Perrault.* Illustrated by Harry Clarke with an Introduction by Thomas Bodkin. London: George G. Harrap & Co. Ltd [1922]. (Reproduced by permission of the publisher)

154 *The Child's Own Book.* The Sixth Edition. London: Thomas Tegg, 1839. (First issued 1830)

155 *Think Before You Speak: or, The Three Wishes.* A Tale by the Author of the Peacock at Home [Catherine Ann Dorset]. London: M. J. Godwin, 1809

156 *Fairy Tales.* London: J. March [1854]

158 *English Fairy Tales.* Retold by Flora Annie Steel. Illustrated by Arthur Rackham. London: Macmillan & Co., 1918. (Photo A. C. Cooper Ltd. Reproduced by permission of Mrs Barbara Edwards)

161 *The Red Fairy Book.* Edited by Andrew Lang. London: Longmans, Green & Co., 1890. (Reproduced by permission of the publisher)

162 *Christmas Entertainments.* London: Field & Tuer [1883]

163 *The History of Mother Twaddle and the Marvellous Atchievments of Her Son Jack*, by B. A. T. London: J. Harris, 1807. (By courtesy of The British Library; photo John R. Freeman)

165 *English Fairy Tales.* Retold by Flora Annie Steel. Illustrated by Arthur Rackham. London: Macmillan & Co., 1918. (Photo A. C. Cooper Ltd) Reproduced by permission of Mrs. Barbara Edwards

167 *Jack and the Bean Stalk.* Edinburgh: Gall & Inglis [1871]

169 *The Traditional Fairy Tales of Little Red Riding Hood, Beauty & the Beast, and Jack and the Bean Stalk.* Edited by Felix Summerly [Henry Cole]. London: Chapman and Hall, *c.* 1850. (Contains the plates of 1844)

170 *The History of Jack and the Bean-stalk, Printed from the Original Manuscript, Never before Published.* London: B. Tabart, 1807

173 *Our Nurse's Picture Book.* London: George Routledge & Sons [1869]. (By courtesy of the Victoria and Albert Museum, London)

176 *Walt Disney's Sketch Book of Snow White and the Seven Dwarfs.* London: William Collins, Sons & Co. Ltd [1938]. (Copyright Walt Disney Productions)

179 *Grimm's Household Tales.* Edited and partly translated anew by M. Edwardes. With Illustrations by R. A. Bell. London: J. M. Dent & Co., 1901. (By courtesy of The British Library; photo John R. Freeman)

181 *Little Snow-White.* London: George Routledge & Sons, *c.* 1870

182 *Hansel and Grettel and Snow-drop.* Illustrated by John Hassall. London and Glasgow: Blackie & Son Ltd, *c.* 1921. (Reproduced by permission of the publisher)

184 *The Frog Prince.* Walter Crane's Toy Books Shilling Series. London & New York: George Routledge and Sons [1874]. (By courtesy of the Victoria and Albert Museum, London)

187 and **189** *Fairy Tales of the Brothers Grimm.* A New Translation by Mrs. Edgar Lucas. With Illustrations by Arthur Rackham. London: Freemantle & Co., 1900. (By courtesy of the Victoria and Albert Museum, London. Reproduced by permission of Mrs Barbara Edwards)

190 *The Red Fairy Book.* Edited by Andrew Lang. London: Longmans, Green & Co., 1890. (Reproduced by permission of the publisher)

193 *In Powder & Crinoline: Old Fairy Tales.* Retold by Sir Arthur Quiller-Couch. Illustrated by Kay Nielsen. London: Hodder & Stoughton. [1913]. (Reproduced by permission of The Brockhampton Press Ltd)

194 *Household Stories Collected by the Brothers Grimm.* With Illustrations by E. H. Wehnert. London: George Routledge and Sons, Limited, *c.* 1890. Originally published 1853

195 *German Popular Stories, Translated from the Kinder und Haus-Märchen, collected by M. M. Grimm, from Oral Tradition.* London: C. Baldwyn, 1823

196 *Routledge's Coloured Picture Book.* London: George Routledge and Sons [1870]

198 *Household Tales by the Brothers Grimm.* Illustrated by Mervyn Peake. London: Eyre and Spottiswoode, 1946. (Reproduced by permission of Methuen Children's Books Ltd)

200 *The Story of the Three Bears.* Second Edition. London: Wright, 60, Pall Mall, 1839 (First published 1837)

202 *A Treasury of Pleasure Books for Young Children.* London: Grant and Griffith; and Joseph Cundall, 1850

204 *Mother Goose's Book of Nursery Stories, Rhymes and Fables.* London and Glasgow: Blackie & Son Limited [1928]. (Reproduced by permission of the publisher)

205 *The Three Bears.* London, Paris & New York: Raphael Tuck & Sons, *c.* 1900

206 Original drawing by Vilhelm Pedersen, 1849. (By courtesy of the Hans Christian Andersen Museum, Odense)

209 *Fairy Tales by Hans Christian Andersen.* Illustrated by Harry Clarke. London: George G. Harrap & Co. Ltd [1930]. (Reproduced by permission of the publisher)

211 *The Yellow Fairy Book.* Edited by Andrew Lang. With Numerous Illustrations by H. J. Ford. London: Longmans, Green, and Co., 1894. (Reproduced by permission of the publisher)

213 *Hans Andersen's Fairy Tales selected and edited for Little Folk.* Illustrated by Helen Stratton. London: Blackie & Son [1905]. (By courtesy of the Victoria and Albert Museum, London. Reproduced by permission of the publisher)

215 *Fairy Tales from Hans Christian Andersen.* Translated by Mrs. E. Lucas and Illustrated by Thomas, Chas. and William Robinson. London: J. M. Dent & Co. New York: E. P. Dutton & Co., 1899. (By courtesy of the Victoria and Albert Museum, London)

216 *Fairy Tales and Legends by Hans Andersen.* Illustrated by Rex Whistler. London: Cobden-Sanderson, 1935. (By courtesy of the Victoria and Albert Museum, London. Reproduced by permission of The Bodley Head)

217 *Stories from Hans Andersen.* With Illustrations by Edmund Dulac. London: Hodder & Stoughton, 1911.

(By courtesy of the Victoria and Albert Museum, London. Reproduced by permission of The Brockhampton Press Ltd)

219 (above) Original drawing by Vilhelm Pedersen, 1849. (By courtesy of the Hans Christian Andersen Museum, Odense)

219 (below) *Tales for the Young.* By Hans Christian Andersen. A New Translation. London: James Burns, 1847

220 and **222** *Fairy Tales by Hans Christian Andersen.* Illustrated by E.V.B. [Eleanor Vere Boyle] Newly translated by H. L. D. Ward and Augusta Plesner. London: Sampson Low, Marston, Low and Searle, 1872 [for 1871]. (By courtesy of the Victoria and Albert Museum, London)

227 *Fairy Tales.* By Hans Christian Andersen. Illustrated by E. A. Lemann. London: Edward Arnold [1893]

230 and **231** *Fairy Tales from Hans Christian Andersen.* Translated by Mrs. E. Lucas and Illustrated by Thomas, Chas. and William Robinson. London: J. M. Dent & Co. New York: E. P. Dutton & Co., 1899. (By courtesy of the Victoria and Albert Museum, London)

233 *Stories and Fairy Tales by Hans Christian Andersen.* Translated by H. Oskar Sommer, Ph.D. With Pictures by Arthur J. Gaskin. London & Orpington: George Allen, 1893. (By courtesy of The British Library; photo John R. Freeman)

234 *Fairy Tales and Legends by Hans Andersen.* Illustrated by Rex Whistler. London: Cobden-Sanderson, 1935. (By courtesy of the Victoria and Albert Museum, London. Reproduced by permission of The Bodley Head)

237 *Grimm's Goblins.* London: George Vickers, 1861 (Photo John R. Freeman)

239 *Hansel and Gretel and other stories by the brothers Grimm.* Illustrated by Kay Nielsen. London: Hodder and Stoughton, 1925. (Reproduced by permission of The Brockhampton Press Ltd)

240 and **243** *Fairy Tales of the Brothers Grimm.* A New Translation by Mrs. Edgar Lucas. With Illustrations by Arthur Rackham. London: Freemantle & Co., 1900. (By courtesy of the Victoria and Albert Museum, London. Reproduced by permission of Mrs Barbara Edwards)

The comment on fairy tales by Edmund Gosse (page 9) is quoted from *Father and Son*, 1907, by permission of the publisher William Heinemann Ltd

INDEX

Page numbers in italic type refer to illustrations.